city-pick

DUBLIN

Oxygen Books

Published by Oxygen Books 2010

This selection and commentary copyright © Heather Reyes 2010

Illustrations © Eduardo Reyes 2010

Copyright Acknowledgements at the end of this volume constitute an extension of this copyright page.

A CIP catalogue record for this book is available from the British Library.

ISBN 978–0–9559700–1–6

Typeset in Sabon by
Bookcraft Limited, Stroud, Gloucestershire

Printed and bound in Great Britain by
Henry Ling Ltd, Dorset Press, Dorchester

Praise for the series

'Brilliant ... the best way to get under the skin of a city. The perfect read for travellers and book lovers of all ages'

Kate Mosse, best-selling author of *Labyrinth*

'An inviting new series of travel guides which collects some of the best writing on European cities to give a real flavour of the place ... Such an *idée formidable*, it seems amazing it hasn't been done before'

Editor's Pick, *The Bookseller*

'This impressive little series'

Sunday Telegraph

'An attractive-looking list of destination-based literature anthologies ... a great range of writers'

The Independent

' ... something for everyone – an ideal gift'

Travel Bookseller

'A very clever idea: take the best and most beloved books about a city, sift through them for the pithiest excerpts, and then compile it all into a single volume for the literary-minded tourists'

Jeremy Mercer, author of *Books, Baguettes and Bedbugs*

' ... the excellent series, which uses descriptions of a city penned by writers, both living and dead, to illuminate the metropolis in question'

Giles Foden, *Condé Nast Traveller*

'The perfect books for the armchair traveller as well as those of you visiting cities around the globe'

Lovereading

'A breath of fresh air ... each volume offers what it says on the tin: *perfect gems of city writing*'

Mslexia

Editor's Note

It has been a particular pleasure to edit a collection of writing on Dublin. My first visit to the city felt like a home-coming: since the age of eleven, when I began my education with the Ursuline Sisters in a school near London, I have lived with the voices of Ireland in my head. A non-Catholic 'scholarship girl', this was my first encounter both with nuns and with Irishness: the distinctive lilt and phraseology of Irish English was as fascinating to me as the traditions of St Patrick's Day when the sisters would appear with bright clumps of shamrock fastened to their sober black habits and girls of Irish descent were allowed to flout the strict uniform rules and sport a tin brooch – a golden harp on a piece of folded green ribbon – and even green ribbons in their hair. The nuns – intelligent, loving, dedicated, strict but broad-minded and independent women – instilled, along with the rules of Latin grammar and quadratic equations, a great respect for the country from which most of them had come. When, as a student of literature, I discovered it to be also the country of Swift, Wilde, Shaw, Joyce, Beckett and a host of other great writers, I often wondered how such a small country with a difficult history could have produced so many great people.

This collection aims to be a lyrical but realistic exploration of and tribute to Ireland's capital. If there are fewer foreign voices in *city-pick DUBLIN* than in other volumes in the series so far, it is mainly because a city so rich in writers should be allowed to speak for itself. With so much to choose from, there are inevitable omissions – sometimes the result of hard decisions due to lack of space, sometimes to 'rights' difficulties, sometimes from the wish to give exposure to lesser-known voices rather than the already famous, and sometimes simply from personal taste. In the case of James Joyce, I felt that those who already love his work do not need it repeated here, while those yet to be persuaded of its great riches and pleasures could hardly be converted by a short extract: this is why I have chosen passages that give a way into Joyce, rather than face the hopeless task of choosing a 'representative' passage (which is impossible).

I hope the reader will find here, along with a little of the 'expected', some less familiar voices and surprising gems, and the inspiration to seek out the whole texts from which their favourite extracts are taken – and to look more deeply and widely into the great treasure chest of writing about this great European city which even names bridges after its writers.

Heather Reyes

Contents

Contents

Dubliners – old and new

The Great Escape

Publin

The good, the bad and the (just a little bit) ugly

Contents

All in the past

Reading Dublin
by Orna Ross

Some years ago, I had occasion to bring a visiting creative writing professor from Chicago to visit Dublin's Writers' Museum. I still recall the delight with which he paused on its steps. "How wonderful it must be," he breathed, "to live in a city that so reveres its writers."

Well sometimes, maybe, yes. All Dubliners, from politicians to taxi drivers, are proud of the city's literary reputation. When ranked No 4 in a survey of literary destinations recently – behind London, Stratford-Upon-Avon and Edinburgh but ahead of New York, Paris and St Petersburg – the general feeling in Dublin was: shouldn't we have been No 1?

Okay, London might have its share of good writers and yes, Edinburgh is a UNESCO City of Literature, and all right, I suppose you have to hand it to Shakespeare but in a straight contest – great writers per head of population – isn't Dublin the clear winner?

Haven't we four Nobel prizewinners (Shaw, Yeats, Beckett and Heaney) out of only a million or so inhabitants? As well as the world's best novelist (Joyce) who should have got one too? Isn't our national theatre (the Abbey of Synge, Yeats, Gregory, O'Casey, Behan, Friel, Roche) known the world over and didn't we have enough playwrights left to storm the English stage while we were at it (Congreve, Sheridan, Goldsmith, Shaw, Wilde, McDonagh)?

Haven't we given the English language its best satirist (Swift) and a string of superlative short story writers (O'Flaherty, Lavin, Joyce, O'Connor, O'Faolain, Enright)? And let's not even get started on the novelists (Edgeworth, Stoker, Bowen, Murdoch, Keane, O'Brien, Tóibín, Banville,

O'Connor, Doyle, Enright again. And Joyce of course. Have we mentioned Joyce?)

Thus runs the literary propaganda, and it exerts a hold, even though we know that writing isn't produced by a place called Dublin but by a human imagination in harness to a blank page. Even though we know that some of the writers listed have only tenuous links with the city and others fled the place as fast as they could. Joyce spoke for many when he said: "How sick, sick, sick I am of Dublin! It is the city of failure, of rancour and of unhappiness, I long to be out of it."

"Don't mind him," the city shrugged in reply. "Didn't he spend the whole time he was away writing about us?"

And on it got with setting up The Bloomsday festival and The James Joyce Centre and putting his image on mugs and postcards and T-shirts to sell to all the lovely tourists who were arriving through those writings and who needed something to buy on their tribute trip.

Academics tend to be highly critical of such literary tourism. A recent book deems it an embarrassment, a naïve and "deeply counterintuitive response to the pleasures and possibilities of imaginative reading"[1]. Counterintuitive to that reader, perhaps, but not to the hundreds of thousands of visitors who flock to Dublin each year.

What is being contested here is ownership and of course nobody owns writing. Not the writer, not the reader, not the academic and certainly not the city. Creative writing is free as only an imaginative act can be, coming alive only in the creative act of reading.

When I first came to Dublin at the age of 17, I walked streets that were already familiar to me through my reading – books like Plunkett's *Strumpet City*, O'Brien's *Girl With Green Eyes*, O'Flaherty's *Mr Gilhooley*, Joyce's *Dubliners*, Stephen's *The*

---

1 Watson, N. *The Literary Tourist.*

Charwoman's Daughter and also a dusty box of very old penny- periodicals that had been preserved in date order by some word loving ancestor and passed down to my parents' bookshelf.

How the young me thrilled to these bulletins from Victorian Dublin life, high and low, especially the running stories with their cliffhangers and their summary of the previous episode and, especially, their edict that always sounded inside me like a fanfare heralding a new kingdom: *Now Read On.*

I was a literary cliché, one of those young readers who experiences the fictional as more real, more engaging, more alive than anyone in "real" life. Now I write myself and know that is just the kind of reader every writer wants. One who brings the same honesty, openness and receptivity to consuming a text that the writer tries to bring to creating it.

Other people might label it sad or nerdy but we who conjoin in imaginative intercourse know the truth: that "Now Read On" are, actually, the three most thrilling words in the English language.

* * *

Dublin used to like its writers dead. For the first fifty years of the Irish state, any living author who wrote a worthwhile word was censored and, often, hounded out[2]. Once their reputations were established abroad, and especially if they were safely deceased, the city would grasp them (if not their writing) to its bosom, like a pardoning parent, denying old differences while still excoriating their younger siblings.

This began to change in that time of great global shift: the late 1960s. Paris had the Molotov cocktails of *les événe-*

---

2 Victims of a raft of censorship law and obsessive right wing Roman Catholicism. The laws also denied most of the major writers of the twentieth century – Bellow, Faulkner, Gordimer, Hemingway, Koestler, Moravio, Nabokov, Proust, Sartre, Stead, Zola all had works banned – to Irish readers.

ments; San Francisco its Summer of Love; for Dublin, the old world ended with a whimper: legislation. Specifically, the dismantling of the shameful censorship law and the passing of a statute that enabled free secondary school education for all.

As liberating in their way as the more revolutionary uprisings elsewhere, it took time for the effects of these legislative changes to seep through. Now, forty years on, Dublin has become a city where reading and creative writing groups offer courses and mentoring at every level, from basic literacy to masterclass; where writers benefit from government funding for publishing enterprises, writer bursaries and tax breaks; where vibrant literary events of every size and type abound, from open-mic poetry slams in the local pub to major festivals attracting readers from all over the world.

Through it all, the love-affair with dead writers survives and even living writers can find themselves signed up in service to the economy, used to flog merchandise and pubs and the city itself. They tend to be deeply ambivalent about this, on the one hand, seeing it as a more sophisticated form of censorship, the hoopla drowning out truths emerging from contemporary pens; on the other understanding the impulse to honour writing, not just because it's in their own occupational interest but because writers, it's sometimes forgotten, are the most passionate of readers and as likely as any other reader to take a literary excursion. Some have even – whisper it! – been known to buy a mug.

I know I have continued to enjoy the multi-layered vision I first brought to Dublin and I regularly visit other literary haunts, where my own experience of place is adorned with versions that I-and-a-writer created earlier.

I believe there can be, and often is, magic in such visits. A kind of holiness. A tribute to the pleasure and knowledge gained through reading yes – but more than that too.

In a secular time, artists become very important because they are the only people offering up their lives to the pursuit of what Yeats called "Higher Things". This is why a literary jaunt can feel like a pilgrimage and why the bric-a-brac in the tourist shop so resembles the knick-knacks at Lourdes or Rome. Homage is being paid not just to the text but to the writer for keeping faith with the source of inspiration.

"There is only one perfection and only one search for perfection," Yeats said, and religion and art both originate in that search. In the materialist 21st century, we don't have a shared language with which to acknowledge this but we know it when we touch off it. And if we can't find the words, well, we can walk the streets, visit the birthplace, buy the mug with the quote on it or clink a glass of Guinness in the pub where words that have touched us, pleasured us, perhaps even changed us, were conjured up out of nothing.

It is only if we do all this *instead of* reading, if we substitute a commercial transaction for the writer's gift freely offered to us, that the souvenir mug becomes a muzzle akin to the censorship of old and the literary location a mere greasy till, its writer more read about than read.

We all know this. So we all know what to do.

Now read on.

ORNA ROSS is a novelist and she writes and speaks on the subject of Creative Intelligence. She founded, and for some years ran, Font Writing Centre & Literary Agency, Dublin . Her most recent book is *A Dance in Time* (Penguin 2008) and she is at work on a third novel. www.ornaross.com.

Dublin's fair city ...

Dublin.

Plural proper noun.

There is a Dublin of the rich of course, and a Dublin of the poor. That's standard stuff. But there's more than that. The rich like a little multiplicity after all; the poor are wealthy in variation. And then there's the neither rich nor poor – the getting by, the middle mass, the bulk. Where do they live?

They live in Dublin with the others. A million kittens in a sack, down by the river.

Working Dublin, queer Dublin, junkie Dublin, media Dublin, party Dublin, executive Dublin, homeless Dublin, suburban Dublin, teenage Dublin, gangland Dublin, Dublin with the flags out, mother Dublin, culchie Dublin, Muslim Dublin, the wind ripped rain at eleven o'clock in the morning on Pearse Street in February Dublin, drunken Dublin, hungry Dublin, Dublin of the vice squad and the syphilis outbreak, dancing Dublin, pro-Cathedral Dublin, writer's Dublin, politician's Dublin, Dublin on the telly, Bono's Dublin, Ronnie Drew's Dublin, Bloomsday Dublin, the Dublin of Arbour Hill and Kilmainham Jail, Gandon's Dublin, Durcan's Dublin, Teaching English as a Foreign Language Dublin, Jewish Dublin, the emigrant's Dublin, the immigrant's Dublin, Dublin where they beat you up, railings Dublin, Dublin where they rob you, fanlight Dublin, Dublin where they rape you, golf club Dublin, Dublin where they kill you, the American Dublin, the St Patrick's Day Dublin, the Phoenix Park Dublin, serial killer's Dublin, paradise, scary Dublin, money in brown envelopes Dublin, traffic jam Dublin, property Dublin, inept Dublin, the Dublin you can't afford, the Dublin that needs you, the Dublin that doesn't, Dublin with its view of the hills, Dublin with the sea in the bay and the river stumbling towards it, drunk.

Dublin.

Keith Ridgway, *The Parts* (2003)

✳ ✳ ✳

Welcome to Dublin, a city – like all great cities – full of contradictions and variety, beauty and sadness, vibrant modernity and brooding history, where everything constantly changes ... and yet so much stays the same. We set out for a walk with Honor Tracy, then go a little further with Neil Hegarty.

It was a bright sunny day with small fleecy clouds scudding over the sky. Having left my things at the hotel I went for a walk. The first hours in Dublin are always delightful, for the city throws all it has at the newcomer, discreetly flattering, gently soothing, feeding at once the eye and the imagination. The airs of grace and of leisure have not departed even if the society which gave them birth is past and gone. It is a city of ghosts, but ghosts of the so newly dead that something of their earthly presence still lingers in the wide streets, the pleasant squares, that were their home; as you walk through them, you feel that Dublin still must be a bed of poetry and wit, almost you expect to see Yeats and A.E. passing each other in Merrion Square ...

Honor Tracy, *Mind You, I've said Nothing!* (1953)

❊ ❊ ❊

One of my favourite walks in Dublin is from the docks out to the Poolbeg Lighthouse. Surely, few capital cities can boast such an exhilarating walk: along the long, low South Wall breakwater, across which waves can pitch and wash in windy weather, from the mouth of the Liffey to a red-painted lighthouse which seems to stand suspended on the sea. The city vanishes behind me and all I can see is the lighthouse ahead, Howth stretched to the left, and an immensity of sky. There are great signs at the entrance to the walk warning against 'Danger', and warning me that I pass 'At My Own Risk'. But it's a risk worth taking, I think: as I walk into the horizon, the water laps and breaks on either side, and the air is full of a tang of salt. It is like being on a boat.

I reach the lighthouse and turn to go back: Dublin suddenly, startlingly opens up in the distance. The bend of the bay is even more pronounced from this angle and the land seems suddenly to envelop me. The view now is uncompromisingly industrial, but stark and beautiful still. Straight ahead, the red-and-white stripes of the Pigeonhouse power station chimneys loom up into the still, expansive sky. The Pigeonhouse stands in the estuary of the River Liffey and has become a de facto emblem of the city. Beyond it the dockyards and depots tread across the landscape for what seems like miles. From here, it seems as though the only way into Dublin is by water – up the Liffey to the quays of the city. [...]

A little further up the Liffey, pushing against the river's flow as it empties into the Irish Sea, is the city centre itself. It's heralded by the choking traffic on the quays and by the Georgian perfection of the Gandon-designed Custom House. There are glimpses of other buildings further from the water too: the Abbey Theatre on its shabby corner, close to the northern embankment; and the classical columns of the General Post Office a little further away on O'Connell Street. The curving façade of the old parliament building – now the Bank of Ireland – gleams near the southern bank of the river; beyond it is the austere West Front of Trinity College, its main adornment being the two statues of Burke and Goldsmith that flank the main entrance. Students and tourists swirl past these two statues by the thousand each day and probably few stop to think of their association with Dublin's 18th-century heyday, when they rubbed shoulders with other musicians, philosophers and writers – Handel and Arne and Swift – in the tiny city centre. I passed them daily for years and I scarcely so much as glanced at them.

However, the tourists certainly notice the other statue hereabouts: just beyond Trinity and a little further from the river stands Molly Malone herself, wheeling her wheelbarrow and sporting vast breasts that resemble a brace of butternut squash. Dubliners seldom notice her, of course, and maybe those that do are a little mortified at this monstrously well-endowed girl exposing herself so shamelessly at one of the city's busiest junctions, but visitors love her – and why not.

Neil Hegarty, Waking Up In Dublin (2004)

✳ ✳ ✳

Even when you're feeling down and prone to see the ugly side of city life, the weather can suddenly change, lifting your spirits by showing you a very different Dublin.

The quays, with their muddy square-setts, are noisy and dirty as usual, and in the dimming light the waiting buses are dull blobs of blue and yellow and red against the dull buildings. The Liffey is at lowest ebb, and its subaqueous population of forsaken buckets and weedy stones increases as I go rattling and banging up-stream on a wet tram-top. I return to the mud at Grattan Bridge, feeling I am rapidly approaching the stage of dejection which drives the strong-minded to a public-house, when from low down in the western sky there comes a gleam of yellow light, rapidly broadening and brightening. And then suddenly five great swans appear, flying down the centre of the river. In perfect formation, long necks outstretched, broad wings beating in unison, they sweep by majestically, a vision of pure beauty, gleaming plumage all snowy against the old houses opposite. While I still watch their receding forms fading into the smoky mist, a low red sun bursts out from underneath the last bank of cloud. It floods down the river; the long vista of dull houses lights up in a dozen lovely shades through a faint pink haze; the spires and towers behind stand up transfigured; the dirty water turns to gold and silver. One gazes at a dream city, beautiful beyond belief. And while I stand, a breath of softer air, bringing with it hope and a lifting of the spirit, comes from the west; the wind has changed.

Robert Lloyd Praeger, *A Populous Solitude* (1941)

✳ ✳ ✳

In an early novel by William Trevor, the incorrigible photographer, Mrs Eckdorf, launches herself upon Dublin for the first time and quickly begins to learn something about the city and its inhabitants.

'I flew this morning from Munich, which is the city where currently I live. About the city we're approaching I know extremely little.'

'It's a good business town these days,' the man informed her.

'A fair city,' murmured Mrs Eckdorf more romantically. 'In Dublin's fair city: that's a line in an old-fashioned song.'

'Yes.'

'Some cities are fairer than others. In my work I notice that.'

Mrs Eckdorf went on speaking, saying she knew as little about the inhabitants of the city they were approaching as she did about the city itself. She had read somewhere that they were litter-bugs and disputatious, but she didn't at all mind that. Revolution had taken place in the city, she knew, and was glad that it had: it showed spirit to revel against *status quo*, it lent a certain pride to a people. She knew that the country of which the city was the capital was a land of legend and myth: she had seen a television programme about that, a programme that had shown old men talking and priests talking and children dancing in the stiff local manner. Vaguely at the time she had thought that she herself could have made more of it than the television people had, but it was not until years later, as a result of meeting with a barman on an ocean liner, that she had been moved to think about the city again. This man, telling her much besides, had said he hadn't been attracted by the place. He had walked through it in the rain, apparently, seeking solace and finding it hard to come by. A motor-car, moving gently in the night-time traffic, had struck him as he crossed a street and the driver had smiled and waved, as though the contact created a friendship between them. [...]

In St Stephen's Green that morning the woman called Ivy Eckdorf took a photograph of a floating duck. She wore the same cream-coloured hat that she had worn in the aeroplane, and was dressed otherwise in a suit of pale linen over a cream-coloured blouse with buttons of pearl. Her finger-nails were lengthy, meticulously painted to match the shade of her mouth; her stockings were fine, the colour of honey; her flat-heeled shoes had soft wicker-work uppers and soles of a flexible leather. She carried a commodious cream-coloured handbag and about her neck, suspended by a thin length of plastic, hung the camera with which she had photographed the duck. It was an instrument of Japanese manufacture, a Mamiya.

11

'How charming!' murmured Mrs Eckdorf, referring to the duck and to other ducks that floated on the water in the park. 'What a truly attractive city!'

A man going by, a projectionist in a cinema, had an obscene thought about Mrs Eckdorf standing there, for she was a beautiful woman in her tall, angular way. She saw the man glancing at her and she guessed that in his mind he had already placed her on a bed and was unfastening her clothes. She smiled at him, quite pleased that he had paid her the compliment. 'You naughty chap!' she cried, and noted scarlet embarrassment spreading all over the man's face. He hurried on, and Mrs Eckdorf lifted her camera and photographed his retreating back.

An old woman spoke to her, asking for alms, her hand held slightly out. She said she would pray for Mrs Eckdorf, who told her to stand back a bit, which the woman did, imagining that money would follow. 'There are social services to see to you,' said Mrs Eckdorf, smiling more. She photographed the woman, explaining to her that her face would now travel all over the world. She spoke harshly when the beggar woman again asked for alms. 'Get off to hell,' she ordered angrily.

The woman went, and Mrs Eckdorf consulted her map. She saw the way to Thaddeus Street lay along York Street, over Aungier Street, past St Patrick's Cathedral, along the Coombe and then on and on. She did not much care for the look of this route. An instinct told her that a more roundabout one would provide her with greater interest. She turned her back on York Street and set off in another direction, towards the river.

Twenty minutes later, in Bachelors' Walk, she encountered two card-sharpers, one of whom carried a large cardboard box which bore the legend *Kellogg's Cornflakes The Sunshine Breakfast*. He was a red-haired man, tall and heavily constructed, with evasive eyes. His companion was smaller and excessively dirty. She photographed them and then moved on, only to find herself pursued by the men, who demanded money with menaces, claiming that she had offered them money in return for permission to take their photographs. They reminded her that they had specially performed their trick on the cardboard box and had risked observation by plain-clothes police. All that, they said, they'd done to oblige her.

Mrs Eckdorf balanced her camera on the wall that ran above the river. She photographed two nuns crossing the Metal Bridge.

'Local interest,' she explained. 'There's local interest everywhere.'

'We're working men,' said the smaller man.

'You're local interest to me,' murmured Mrs Eckdorf, again setting her sights on the nuns.

'Excuse me, missus,' began the red-haired man in a threatening way, edging closer to Mrs Eckdorf, his shoulder actually touching her clothes.

'Buzz off,' said Mrs Eckdorf snappishly, thinking it was extraordinary the way people in this city were always asking for money.

'You promised us,' shouted the red-haired man. He took her elbow in his hand. He raised the cardboard box slightly in the air. 'You said a consideration, missus.'

Mrs Eckdorf stared into the eyes of the man and spoke while doing so. She told him to release her elbow and stand well back.

'I'm a professional photographer,' she said. 'I cannot possibly go paying out cash for every piece of local interest I find. You must see that.'

'I see nothing,' cried the red-haired man. 'We risked arrest standing up there, exposed for you –'

'There's a Superintendent in uniform,' said Mrs Eckdorf quietly, 'on the other side of the street.'

She waved at the Superintendent, who was strolling along, tapping the calf of his right leg with a cane. He was in the company of two members of his force, a pair of dignified Civic

Guards immaculately turned out. She lifted her camera and photographed the three of them. Then she trained her lens on the backs of the card-sharpers, who were sliding urgently away.

Having waved again at the Superintendent, she continued on her journey. She passed by the humped metal bridge and strode along Ormond Quay, occasionally snapping the shutter of her camera at people or vistas that took her fancy. [...]

All over Dublin that lunchtime people from offices and shops took advantage of the sunshine; children, tired of the good weather, waited for the cinemas to open. Youths in open shirts crept over the grass in St Stephen's Green, causing the girls they crept upon to shriek. The card-sharpers whose photograph Mrs Eckdorf had taken spent part of their gains in a bread-shop in Mary Street, and the twins that had been that morning born in Coombe Maternity Hospital passed their first midday asleep and in health. The Indian doctor who had delivered them stood in the Municipal Art Gallery regarding the face of Lady Gregory as represented by the Italian artist Mancini. 'God give me patience,' said the manager of the hotel where Mrs Eckdorf had been staying. He had just been told that in his absence the luggage of Mrs Eckdorf had been forwarded to an hotel in Dolphin's Barn. 'Are you half-witted?' he noisily demanded of the untrained clerk who was responsible for the action, and the clerk replied that a clear message had been received from the lady, and that for his part he had done his best. 'You said to be always civil, sir,' he reminded the manager, who replied by depriving him of his position.

In Reuben Street the woman who had said to her priest that she was not ungrateful for the life she'd been given was meas-ured by local undertakers. In a public house in York Street the old woman who had begged from Mrs Eckdorf poured the dregs from glasses into a can and thanked the publican for allowing her to do so. The cinema projectionist whom Mrs Eckdorf had called a naughty chap hummed to himself in the projection room of one of the cinemas which children were preparing to enter.

It was a day in Dublin as any other, except that, being a Friday, less meat was consumed than on other days. The sun glittered on the water of the river, seagulls stood quietly on walls and parapets. At half past one the banks were open for business again, later the public houses closed for their quiet hour. [...]

In Dublin the rain fell heavily that morning. Turf in public parks became soft underfoot and the unpainted wood of hoardings changed colour and soon could absorb no more. Water spilt from chutes, gutters ran, puddles were everywhere. Raindrops spattered on all the formal water of the Garden of Remembrance in Parnell Square and on the water in old horse-troughs, and on horses themselves standing drenched between the shafts of tourist jaunting-cars. Statues glistened: washed of their summer dust, gesturing figures seemed less jaded in their stance, eyes stared out with a liveliness. Rain ran on Robert Emmet and Henry Grattan, on Thomas Davis, on O'Connell with his guardian angels, and gentle Father Mathew, apostle of temperance. It dribbled from the moustached countenance of Lord Ardilaun and fell on Lecky and on William Conyngham, and on the empty pedestal of the Earl of Eglinton and Winton. It damped the heads of Mangan and Tom Kettle and the Countess Markievicz, it polished to a shine the copper-green planes of a tribute to Yeats, Moore and Burke, Wolfe Tone and Charles Stewart Parnell, Goldsmith and ghostly Provost Salmon: dead men of Ireland were that morning invigorated.

William Trevor, *Mrs Eckdorf in O'Neill's Hotel* (1969)

✳ ✳ ✳

If it's music you love, you'll feel at home in Dublin – along with some of the biggest names on the contemporary music scene.

Indicators of music, symbols of music – these cluster together to greet the ferry as it slows down and prepares to dock. Dublin seems to stretch out to welcome the visitor; long before the ferry arrives at its berth, the long arching coastline has embraced the ship and the traveller, the Dubliner coming home. On the port side of the ship, the high frowning wall of Bray Head gives way to the shelving shingles of Killiney beach, the spectacular houses at Sorrento Terrace and the medieval village of Dalkey on its rocky headland. In front of the village, wild goats roam on Dalkey Island and shelter in the shadow of its Martello tower. This stretch of coast is the home of Dublin's musical superstars, and the homes themselves are clearly visible from the ferries as they ply the route between Ireland and Wales. On this still evening, I can see the lights coming on over there too: in Bono's house which faces east on the edge of the sea, in the castellated mansion next door where Enya lives, well tucked out of sight. Lisa Stansfield has settled in Dalkey and drinks in Finnegan's pub beside the train station; I saw her there one warm night. Today, Dalkey's High Street is crammed full of restaurants, bars, deli-catessens and expensive cars too. Housing in the area is firmly out of reach of most Dubliners, so they settle for visiting on a Sunday afternoon instead. I visit too sometimes, fancying myself quite the cosmopolitan as I brunch in a gastrobar called IN on the main street, browse in the Exchange bookshop, fire down an espresso in the Queen's, or gaze in staggered astonishment at the prices listed outside the über-trendy Kish restaurant. After all, there are no limits to trendy living ...

Neil Hegarty, *Waking Up In Dublin:*
A Musical Tour of the Celtic Capital (2004)

✻ ✻ ✻

A 'must see' for the first-time visitor to Dublin is Trinity College, where the Old Library contains the magnificent, world-famous Book of Kells.

At Trinity, a guided tour included a visit to the third item I was interested in, so we decided it was worth the price of a ticket. The Book of Kells is perhaps the greatest treasure in all Ireland, the work of monks who fled to Kells (just outside Dublin) in the eighth century to escape the raids of Vikings. In it, the four gospels are illustrated by hand in exquisite detail: it's remarkable, and no matter how closely you look there's hardly any crossing out at all.

When the guide finally turned up for the tour, he had a distinctly un-Irish inflection. He told us that he was from Melbourne, Australia, but had been a student at Trinity for a couple of years. It made about as much sense as someone from Denmark conducting tours of the Sydney Opera House but at least we could understand what he said.

Then we got to the Treasury. If you love old books, really love them, go now, book a ticket to Ireland, and visit the Old Library in the Treasury of Trinity College, Dublin. Yes, the Treasury contains the Book of Kells in a glass case surrounded by people politely jostling for a look at the page that is open for that day. But after a nun elbowed me in the ribs I wandered upstairs to take a look at the rest of the place. That's when I found the Old Library, perhaps the most beautiful room in the world. In front of me, row upon row, shelf upon shelf reaching up to an arched ceiling two storeys high, were crammed with beautifully bound antiquarian books. When Twidkiwodm found me, all I could do was whisper 'Look at this place.'

The shelves were roped off from riff-raff such as me, but I would have given anything to reach out to a book at random and snatch a few moments hearing its author's ancient voice. Then we found a bust of Jonathan Swift at the end of one of the shelves. It was a bit like meeting a friend.

Among the other items on display was an aged harp thought to have belonged to Irish chieftain Brian Boru before it was used for the harp trademark of Guinness. There's also a copy of the Declaration of Independence that was issued during the Easter Rising of 1916. It was a little tattered, having survived street battles, the failure of the rising and the execution of the ringleaders. Then it had set in chain events that created a nation. Not bad for a tattered sheet of paper. While I read it a few people wandered up from the Book of Kells, glanced at the books and went back downstairs. They didn't know what they were missing. I couldn't help feeling the Book of Kells was only the tip of Ireland's literary heritage at the Treasury. Upstairs, there's a whole iceberg.

Evan McHugh, Pint-Sized Ireland (2001)

✳ ✳ ✳

A quick break from the city centre as Chris Binchy takes us to one of the wealthier suburbs as portrayed in his 2004 novel, People Like Us.

At a curve in the high road there was a viewing point with enough space for a couple of cars to park. At night the orange lights of the city spread below, north and south as far as could be seen and east to the edge of the water, the curve of the bay marked by bright white street lamps along the coast road. Planes circled above. Boats and ferries floated, islands of coloured light, towards the port. The towers of the power station rose together from the blackness of the sea. Across the bay was a peninsula, dotted with the occasional lights of houses, and above the highest house was an area, barely discernable, that was darker than the night sky above it. If you knew the city, you could fill in the gaps and make sense of it. You could say what was water and what was land, what was industrial and what was housing. But if you didn't, it was just a mess of darkness and light.

The viewing point was paved up to a grass verge marked by a fence. If you stood on the verge and looked down, you would see that the ground fell away and fifty feet below was a scrubby field, half of it dug up. There were six lorries and two JCBs parked in a row beside a Portakabin. Away to the left was a road and there were large hoardings facing the traffic, advertising the new development, selling the houses and apartments, when the foundations had yet to be dug. Straight ahead, beyond the lorries and the disturbed earth, beyond what was left of the field was a wall, lined on the far side with a row of trees. They were tall enough to be seen, but not yet thick enough to block the view to the backs of the houses behind the wall, transplanted while still saplings for the older estate, to mark it, delineate it and to hide it.

The name of the estate was painted in Gothic script on a flat, two-foot-square piece of wood attached to a large rock and was visible from the main road. That rock stood on a green area in the middle of a circle of sixteen houses, ten years old. All of them were the same when built, the same size, same number of rooms, detached, painted white, wide at the front, two storeys high and each with their own driveway. All came from the same plan. They were built when space was cheaper, when living out here on the edge meant that the owners were missing out. Unserved at the time by a proper road or shops or transport or schools. A small community away from everything that was happening until the city spilled out and sprawled around them. A wise investment, the residents said to each other now, as if they had known all along what was coming. As if they had been waiting for the rest of the world to catch up. [...]

Paul had gone to work early. He preferred to leave the house at seven and get a seat on the train. It was a fifteen-minute walk from the station to the school. If he left later, there would be pupils in front of him, looking over their shoulders and laughing at him, running by, shouting as they passed.

That morning he was able to walk in peace, taking the longer route through the park. The smell of damp leaves and earth, the tarry pond and the broken graffitied benches in the morning calmed him. He sat there for ten minutes. He watched people as they passed him carrying cups of coffee and brown bags. He watched two women jogging together, their breath visible in the morning air, Americans from the hotel that backed onto the park. Three young office guys stumbled in silence together in the direction of the bank centre, bleary-eyed and sullen at the prospect of another day. They were scarcely older than his pupils, only a year or two of work behind them, but he felt the same way. All he wanted was to go back to the station and get on an empty train back out to the suburbs. He stood up and went to school. [...]

He liked where they were. It was near everything. There were parks and you could see the sea and there were restaurants and bars and shops where they called you by your name. Or they would if you wanted. They smiled vaguely at Paul in the butcher's and the vegetable shops as if they were supposed to know him, which was the way he wanted it. Free-range eggs and organic beetroot and beef from a farm in Wicklow. Their own farm. In the supermarket, where the girls on the till knew Lou and talked to her, they looked at Paul like he must be great. One hundred types of cheese. The smell of bread and coffee and the deodorant of the happy kids sweeping the floor in front of him, waiting in case he needed them. There was the train into town or buses for the kids. There were cafés with girls from the area working on Saturdays, all nice vowels and talking to each other about hockey matches and how drunk they got the night before and how they were so hungover. Shiny eyes and fresh skin. They never looked tired. There was a newsagent's where the paper that Paul read sat on the counter by the till for the convenience of people like him. Where the magazines that he wanted were in a row on the shelf, one after the other. There were bookshops and hardware stores. A Garda station where they would sign the photos for your passport without even asking if you were who you said you were because you wouldn't be there if you weren't. Not someone like you. They stopped cars at checkpoints on the main road on Saturday nights looking for drunks. Protecting their own from other people passing through their area on the way to somewhere else. Somewhere different.

There were pubs for the sailing-club boys, the rugby-necked shouting young fellows with Volkswagens and blonde girls and striped shirts. People who knew where they were going, never too far from here, and nobody was going to say no to them on the way. Sitting at tables outside in the summer in big hissing groups. Laughing. Drinking pints. Sunglasses and watches and phones and Marlboro Lights for everybody. There was nowhere else that they wanted to be. Everybody they knew would pass by some time. Lofty and Dunnie and Hugh. All the boys.

And away from it. Only ten minutes. Across the main road and up along by the big houses with cypresses and Land Rovers and gravel, around the corner onto their road where the houses were smaller but not small. An avenue between two side roads. Paul knew that they were built in the 1930s and before that the land had been a part of an estate, the one they named the shopping centre after. But the road felt like it had been there for ever, the trees as big as the houses, the houses settled and grown into the street, like a living organic unit. As if it would die if you changed it. Solid, grey- and red-brick houses with bay windows. Small front gardens with driveways. A road that was for people to live on. No traffic ramps because nobody ever came down here too fast. They couldn't. It would be rude.

Neighbours who knew just enough about each other. Enough to be polite. Never prying. A respectful distance maintained always. The same conversation every time that Paul met one of them on the road.

'How are you? And how is–?'

'Ruth?'

'Ruth. Of course, Ruth. How is she? And the children?'

21

'They're fine'

They were always fine. Everything was always fine. Because this was not the kind of place where things went wrong. Nice people living their lives quietly, tidily.

Chris Binchey, *People Like Us* (2004)

* * *

And from the twenty-first century, a leap back in time – though the city is still entirely recognisable – to Dublin through the eyes of the novelist W. M. *Thackeray (1811–63).*

The entrance to the capital is very handsome. There is no bustle and throng of carriages, as in London; but you pass by numerous rows of neat houses, fronted with gardens and adorned with all sorts of gay-looking creepers. Pretty market-gardens, with trim beds of plants and shining glass-houses, gives the suburbs a *riante* and cheerful look; and passing under the arch of the railway, we are in the city itself. Hence you come upon several old-fashioned, well-built, airy, stately streets, and through Fitzwilliam Square, a noble place, the garden of which is full of flowers and foliage. The leaves are green, and not black as in similar places in London; the red brick houses tall and handsome. Presently the car stops before an extremely big red house, in that extremely large square, Stephen's Green, where Mr. O'Connell says there was one day or other to be a Parliament. […]

The hotel to which I had been directed is a respectable old edifice, much frequented by families from the country, and where the solitary traveller may likewise find society: for he may either use the "Shelburne" as an hotel or a boarding house, in which latter case he is comfortably accommodated at the very moderate daily charge of six-and-eightpence. For this charge a copious breakfast is provided for him in the coffee-room, a perpetual luncheon is likewise there spread, a plentiful dinner is ready at six o'clock: after which there is a drawing-room and a rubber of whist, with *tay* and coffee and cakes in plenty to satisfy the largest appetite. The hotel is majestically conducted by clerks and other officers; the landlord himself does not appear, after the honest, comfortable English fashion, but lives in a private mansion hard by, where his name may be read inscribed on a brass-plate, like that of any other private gentleman.

A woman melodiously crying "Dublin Bay herrings" passed just as we came up to the door, and as that fish is famous throughout Europe, I seized the earliest opportunity and ordered a broiled one for breakfast. It merits all its reputation: and in this respect I should think the Bay of Dublin is far superior to its rival of Naples. Are there any herrings in Naples Bay? Dolphins there may be: and Mount Vesuvius, to be sure, is bigger than even the Hill of Howth; but a dolphin is better in a sonnet than at a breakfast, and what poet is there that, at certain periods of the day, would hesitate in his choice between the two?

With this famous broiled herring the morning papers are served up; and a great part of these, too, gives opportunity of reflection to the newcomer, and shows him how different this country is from his own. [...]

The papers being read, it became my duty to discover the town; and a handsomer town, with fewer people in it, it is impossible to see on a summer's day. In the whole wide square of Stephen's Green, I think there were not more than two nursery-maids to keep company with the statue of George I, who rides on horseback in the middle of the garden, the horse having his foot up to trot, as if he wanted to go out of town too. Small troops of dirty children (too poor and dirty to have lodgings at Kingstown) were squatting here and there upon the sunshiny steps, the only clients at the thresholds of the professional gentlemen whose names figure on brass-plates on the doors. A stand of lazy carmen, a policeman or two with clinking boot-heels, a couple of moaning beggars leaning against the rails and calling upon the Lord, and a fellow with a toy and book stall, where the lives of St. Patrick, Robert Emmett, and Lord Edward Fitzgerald may be bought for double their value, were all the population of the Green.

At the door of the Kildare Street Club, I saw eight gentlemen looking at two boys playing leapfrog: at the door of the University six lazy porters, in jockey-caps, were sunning themselves on a bench – a sort of blue-bottle race; and the Bank on the opposite side did not look as if sixpenceworth of change had been negotiated there during the day. There was a lad pretending to sell umbrellas under the colonnade, almost the only instance of trade going on; and I began to think of Juan Fernandez, or Cambridge in the long vacation. In the courts of the College, scarce the ghost of a gyp or the shadow of a bed-maker.

In spite of the solitude, the square of the College is a fine sight: a large ground, surrounded by buildings of various ages and styles, but comfortable, handsome, and in good repair; a modern row of rooms; a row that has been Elizabethan once; a hall and senate-house, facing each other, of the style of George I; and a noble library, with a range of many windows, and a fine manly, simple façade of cut stone. The library was shut. The librarian, I suppose, is at the seaside; and the only part of the establishment which I could see was the museum […]

Among the curiosities is a mask of the Dean – not the scoffer and giber, not the fiery politician, nor the courier of St. John and Harley, equally ready with servility and scorn; but the poor old man, whose great intellect had deserted him, and who died old, wild, and sad. The tall forehead is fallen away in ruin, the mouth has settled in a hideous, vacant smile. Well, it was a mercy for Stella that she died first: it was better that she should be killed by his unkindness than by the sight of his misery; which, to such a gentle heart as that, would have been harder still to bear.

The Bank, and other public buildings of Dublin, are justly famous. In the former may still be seen the room which was the House of Lords formerly, and where the Bank directors now sit, under a clean marble image of George III. The House of Commons has disappeared, for the accommodation of clerks and cashiers. The interior is light, splendid, airy, well-furnished, and the outside of the building not less so. [...]

The view along the quays to the Four Courts has no small resemblance to a view along the quays at Paris, though not so lively as are even those quiet walks. The vessels do not come above-bridge, and the marine population remains constant about them, and about numerous dirty liquor-shops, eating-houses, and marine-store establishments, which are kept for their accommodation along the quay. As far as you can see, the shining Liffey flows away eastward, hastening (like the rest of the inhabitants of Dublin) to the sea.

In front of Carlisle Bridge, and not in the least crowded, though in the midst of Sackville Street, stands Nelson upon a stone pillar. The Post Office is on his right hand (only it is cut off); and on his left, "Gresham's" and the "Imperial Hotel." Of the latter let me say (from subsequent experience) that it is ornamented by a cook who could dress a dinner by the side of M. Borel or M. Soyer. Would there were more such artists in this ill-fated country! The street in exceedingly broad and hand-some; the shops at the commencement rich and spacious; but in Upper Sackville Street, which closes with the pretty building and gardens of the Rotunda, the appearance of wealth begins to fade somewhat, and the houses look as if they had seen better days.

William Makepeace Thackeray, *The Irish Sketch Book* (1843)

✻ ✻ ✻

Like Thackeray, novelist Elizabeth Bowen sees both the grand side of Dublin and the aspects that are less impressive. Yet even the less than beautiful elements

> *of the city have one particular saving grace to capti-*
> *vate the visitor ...*

At the first glance, Dublin nearly always delights the visitor by its grand perspectives and large light squares, its at once airy and mysterious look. Then there is a less happy phase in getting to know the city – when it appears shut-up, faded and meaningless, full of false starts and dead ends, the store plan of something that never realized itself. The implacable flatness of the houses begins to communicate a sort of apathy to the visitor: after her first smile and her first grand effect, Dublin threatens to offer disappointingly little. This stale phase in the stranger's relations with the city can only be cut short by imagi- nation and vigorous curiosity. Dublin is so much more than purely spectacular; she is impregnated with a past that never evaporates. Even the recent past, the nineteenth century, leaves on some outlying quarters of the city a peculiar time-colour. Every quarter – from where the two cathedrals stand in the maze of side-streets, to the latest ring of growth, where red villas struggle into the fields – has, in fact, got a character you could cut with a knife.

Elizabeth Bowen, Collected Impressions (1950)

Streets broad and narrow

Dublin with its wide central street, its statues and its time-darkened buildings, has a dignity such as one associates with some of the southern towns in the United States – a dignity of memories and manners. Its squares, its railed-in areas, its flights of steps, its tall houses of brick richly-coloured as wine, give it the air of a splendid relic of the eighteenth century. It is unforgettably a capital. Soldiers appear and reappear like monotonous red toys, under the shadow of the low classic temple that is now the Bank of Ireland, but that once was the Irish Parliament House. It is as though they were there in temporary occupation: the Parliament House has an air of permanency, of solemn patience, that makes them look like impudent unrealities. Opposite to it stands Trinity College with its dingy walls – fortress in chief of the strong masterful colonists, against which wave upon wave of the national desire has beaten and broken, leaving its tide-marks as upon an old rock. Dublin, indeed, is a kind of ambiguous capital partly of a colony, partly of a nation; it never decided which. It is not without significance that the far-famed Dublin Castle is not much more noticeable in the scheme of the city than a shop in a back street. The Dublin that impresses itself upon the eye and the imagination is the Dublin of the Parliament House and Trinity College ...

Robert Lynd, *Home Life in Ireland* (1908)

* * *

It's easy to fall in love with Dublin's Georgian archi-tecture, and, as Iris Murdoch observes in this extract from her novel about the Easter Rising, The Red and the Green, *the beauty of it shines through even those buildings that were at one time allowed to fall into disrepair.*

The Dumays' house stood at the upper end of Blessington Street, a wide, sad, dirty street due north of the Pillar, which crawled up the hill and ended at the railings of a melancholy little park. It had, under the pale bright sky, its own quiet air of dereliction, a street leading nowhere, always full of idling dogs and open doorways. Yet in form it closely resembled the other great Georgian arteries of Dublin, with its noble continuous façade of sombre blackened red brick which seemed to absorb, rather than to be revealed by, the perpetual rainy light. Looked at closely, the bricks of these houses showed in fact a variety of colours, some purplish red, some yellowish grey, all glued together by a jelly of filth to form a uniform organic surface rather like the scales of a fish, the basic material of Dublin, a city conjured from the earth all in one piece by some tousled Dido. Iron railings guarded deep cave-like areas where dandelions and young saplings flourished, and a few steps led up to each front door, above which was a graceful semicircular fanlight. The ornate pillars which flanked the doors, battered and flattened by

28

time, had the air of Grecian antiquities. The windows alone were, the length of the street, handsome and elegant as upon their first day.

The doors varied. They were serious affairs, solid and many-panelled, and if well painted and provided with handsome knockers and a brass plate or two could sufficiently announce, even here, the residences of substantial citizens, well-bred reticent professional men. But by now many of the doors in the street were broken-down, their paint peeling off, chequered with mysterious holes, and lacking their knockers so that visitors had to shout through the letter-box. Various strange activities had meanwhile developed in the basements, such as a bicycle shop in one, a carpenter's workshop in another, and in one area a man sat all day mending cane chairs. While through grimy glass the fanlights displayed, besides the usual gaudy little figures of Christ the King, the cards of hairdressers and of chimney sweeps. At the end of the street there was even a house which had a sweet shop on the ground floor.

Yet the street had a spirit above these matters and in the evening when the lamp-lighter was just going his rounds, or on certain soft days when the sun shone through cloud, making everything vivid and exact as in a print, the street looked beautiful, with that particular sad, resigned, orderly beauty of Dublin. Those squared, cliff-like, blackened Dublin streets, stretching on and on, still had some inkling of perfection, even though the terraces sometimes looked more like warehouses, even had become warehouses, or in the poorer streets had gaping holes for windows and doors. Even then they seemed to know that they represented, they still in their darkened condition were, the most beautiful dwellings which the human race had ever invented.

Iris Murdoch, *The Red and the Green* (1965)

❊ ❊ ❊

29

And, of course, in their heyday, the most beautiful of the streets were inhabited by the rich and famous. But if you need an antidote to the splendour of places like Merrion Square, maybe a good old-fashioned pub crawl will reveal another side of the city ...

The next day embraces a stroll around the beautiful Georgian buildings of Merrion Square and its surreal array of brightly coloured doors. The jaunty little statue of Oscar Wilde leaning provocatively against a rock at one corner of the park, plaques to the former homes of eminent residents, such as Daniel O'Connell, Austrian Nobel Prizewinner Erwin Schrödinger, painter George Russell and, two doors away from the current offices of the Football Association of Ireland, W. B. Yeats. Just a bit further along you find the splendid Irish traditional Music Archive with its glorious library and a vast archive of mouth-watering recordings of many old legends of Irish music that are seldom heard. I feel almost pious being in among all this literary and cultural splendour, but that's nothing to the feeling on a return to Merrion Square later on for the Dublin murder walk. Apart from the obvious trips to the Guinness factory and the open-topped bus around the city, any number of alternative walking tours await your attention. The literary pub crawl, the James Joyce pub crawl, the musical pub crawl, the pub crawl, the ghost tour ... ultimately it really doesn't make much difference which one you choose, they all end up with you getting slaughtered in some bar at the end of it.

Colin Irwin, *In Search of the Craic* (2001)

❊ ❊ ❊

Like any city streets, those of Dublin are both ever-changing and yet visibly imbued with their history. Even when whole streets disappear, the mists of the past cling through its preservation in literature. Can the Dublin of James Joyce's Ulysses *ever really die?*

Dublin escaped the Second World War and the city of *Ulysses* is still there, forlorn, dishevelled and available. But only just available. Many of Joyce's streets have keeled over quietly, lanes have been suffocated, houses are lying, wounded and dying, on the kerbside. Only the big streets have survived and not always as Joyce utilised them. Even Mr. Bloom's house, Number Seven, Eccles Street, the most famous address in English literature, is on the verge of disappearing under the developer's pencil. Other areas have changed utterly. In fifty years from now it may well be that, public buildings and principal streets apart, the Dublin of *Ulysses* will be no more.

Yet Joyce's mist clings. It is to be found in the dingy lanes off the quays, in the web of streets leading to the river, through the railings at "Trinity's surly front", in Grafton Street still "gay with housed awnings", in the National Library, at the Martello Tower, preserved with dignity at Sandycove, behind the cypresses in the cemetery at Glasnevin. Like old glass jars, parts of the city have bottled Joyce's smoky vapours. [...]

Leopold Bloom, Joyce's Common Man, leaves his home at eight o'clock on a Thursday morning in June, 1904, to buy his breakfast and returns finally, and sleeps at approximately two o'clock the following morning. In the hours between, he lands on the shores of many streets, endures misadventure and delight, tastes gall and honey before, as Homer's hero did, he regains the sanctuary of his terraced Ithaca where his wife spins at her loom of dreams. His voyage has taken him through the streets broad and narrow of Dublin on a parallel to one of the greatest adventure tales ever described – for the Isles of Greece read the streets of Dublin.

Frank Delaney, *James Joyce's Odyssey* (1981)

❋ ❋ ❋

Ever changing – always the same. In the early 1950s, novelist Elizabeth Bowen wrote a whole little book about Dublin's famous Shelbourne Hotel, still recognisably the same as it serves a sophisticated twenty-first century clientèle.

The Shelbourne faces south, over Stephen's Green – said to be the largest square in Europe. Tall as a cliff, but more genial, the hotel overhangs the ornamental landscape of trees, grass, water; overtopping all other buildings round it. It gains by having this open space in front: row upon row its windows receive sunshine, reflect sky, gaze over towards the Dublin mountains. The red-brick façade, just wider than it is high, is horizontally banded with cream stucco; there are cream window-mouldings. Ample bays, two floors deep, project each side of the monumental porch – above, all the rest of the way up, the frontage is absolutely flat. Along the top, a light-coloured parapet links up the windows of the mansard; from the centre of the roof rises a flag-pole.

All in all the effect is striking. A width of roadway, between the hotel and the Green's railings, permits one to step back and take in the whole.

The present-day Shelbourne occupies, like its predecessor, a corner site, filling the angle formed by the junction of Kildare Street with Stephen's Green. The hotel, to the west, thus flanks on the narrow street, down which it runs for a considerable way, staring eye to eye at the Georgian houses opposite. This portion is called "the Kildare Street Wing"; from its upper rooms one looks over a sea of roofs into the misty distances of Dublin. The part of the city in which the Shelbourne stands is not ancient, but already is old enough to be dense with memories and to contain history.

Gazing up at the Shelbourne's south-west corner, one might imagine the building to be one great cube, four-square. Actually, the wing and the main block, about equal in size, compose an L. Inside the L the scene changes – the back windows over-look a silent, aerial, craggy world: from beneath them every-thing drops away. Streets are out of hearing as they are out of view. Far, far below is a network of sunken courtyards, also the roofs and skylights of the functional outworks of the hotel – kitchens and offices, laundry, the heating plant with its smokeless chimney. Fire-escapes zig-zag down. This outlook is in its way not less romantic than any the Shelbourne offers: in the mornings the angle fills up with early sunshine, into which steam from the bathrooms curls. Gulls, in from the river, drift and plane on the air; a clock on the nearby dome of the Government buildings provides time for guests who have forgotten to wind their watches.

But we return to the Green and the frontal view. On its east side the Shelbourne façade is joined to that of its eighteenth-century neighbour, 32 Stephen's Green, once Lord de Montalt's town house. The hotel – though from outside this cannot be guessed – has incorporated into itself No. 32; and also, more recently, No. 33. No. 32 has something unusual – under the drawing-room floor is an archway high enough to allow the loaded big-wheeled country wagons of Lord de Montalt's day to pass through into the backyards. Thus was the peer supplied with produce from his outlying estates. The aristo-cratic frontage of the house was planned to accommodate this feature: the front door, for instance, is stepped up so as to bring its fanlight into line with the top of the arch; and the windows accordingly are a half level higher than those of corresponding windows of the hotel. There is something pleasing about the slight disparity; as there is, indeed, in this fearless juxtaposi-tion of two styles. For the Shelbourne is nothing if not Victo-rian. Architecturally it is a cuckoo in the nest; Stephen's Green knows nothing else of its kind.

Seldom, however, can an intrusion have been conducted with better manners. The Shelbourne has the merit of being blandly true to itself; conspicuous it is, but not self-assertive. Without abating its size or colour, it has somehow gained favour with its surroundings.

Around it everything else seems set back in time. The eighteenth-century spirit broods over this quarter – which still looks residential, though it no longer is. The lavishness of the trees in the Green itself creates, even in winter, an air of mystery. All round a graceful mellowness can be felt – in the brown-brick houses whose underlying tawniness glows at sunset, the classical doorways, the dark-watery polish of old glass. This Georgian part of Dublin is full of half-tones: sometimes, by a trick of the shifting light, it looks strangely delicate, at once misty and clear-cut, all but transparent. The Shelbourne never looks anything but opaque. More than eighty years of hard weather have not dimmed the garnet-red of its brickwork, the dairy-cream freshness of its stucco relief. Did it not give the impression of having been here always, one could take it to have been built only yesterday. It *was*, in fact, completed in 1866. [...]

For the born Dubliner, the Shelbourne has always been there: how is he to recall how or when it first loomed on his infant eyes? Of those who do, consciously, look their first on the Shelbourne, there can be few who have not already heard of it. For the Irishman in general it is a symbol, a legend – only not a myth because, happily, its existence in time and place is so exuberantly apparent. It stands for grandeur – which, in Ireland, we have not yet become ashamed to like. It stands for a certain social idea of life; it is the image of style and well-conductedness. For me, who was a Dublin child, the Shelbourne remains the prototype of all large hotels – I cannot help comparing all others with it. Perhaps, indeed, in no other capital city does any one hotel play such an outstanding rôle.

Elizabeth Bowen, The Shelbourne (1951)

✳ ✳ ✳

> *Having enjoyed the luxury of the Shelbourne, we*
> *can keep up the mood of indulgence by sampling the*
> *wide variety of foods available in the 'newly cosmo-*
> *politan' Dublin.*

If, like me, you are an intrinsically greedy person, 'engaging' with a newly cosmopolitan Dublin tends to mean one thing: shopping for food, cooking food, devouring food like a maniac. Browsing through the vastly greater choice of new food on offer and then lugging it home in large shopping bags – these are the new pleasures of Dublin life. Ten years ago, even five years ago, the choice for consumers was still pretty limited: even good delis were still fairly difficult to come by, except in well-heeled south Dublin suburbs. Middle-eastern and African food shops were non-existent. If you wanted a certain spice – tough luck. Well, it ain't like that today.

In the last few years, a genuine foodie culture has grown up in Dublin. Ireland, of course, always produced exceptional food – not surprising in a country where agriculture remains the economic driving force. But in the city today, you can stop off at specialist Irish cheesemongers to buy all your heart's desire, before heading to any number of little Italian delis to stock up on olives, salami and olive oils. Up on Thomas Street, amid the clattering of street markets selling pyramids of cheap toilet rolls, a shop has opened selling Bosnian food; while the Russians have grocery stores amid the fruit markets of Moore Street. You can check out the stalls at the open-air food market in Meeting House Square. Or, if you're like me, you can round off a satisfying Saturday morning of hunting and gathering in the Middle Eastern shops along the Grand Canal at Portobello.

Neil Hegarty, *Waking Up In Dublin* (2004)

✳ ✳ ✳

But it isn't just new foods that are the mark of the new Dublin. Its streets also sport some more controversial signs of modernity ...

First thing I see on setting foot in O'Connell Street this time round is a dirty great silver white pole in the middle of the street stretching into the sky as far as the eye can see. I stand there gazing at it in dumbfounded shock for several moments when a group of equally bemused Japanese tourists all going 'What the feck!' I mean, it wasn't that long ago I was in Dublin, and I don't remember this thing being there then. 'It's Bertie's pole!' says Joan McDermott, singer with the band Providence over a pint later. 'Bertie Ahern. We reckon it's his phallic symbol. See, he wanted to build some sort of sports stadium, Bertie's Bowl, ... but in the end they decided on a spire instead, so we call it Bertie's Pole.'

Fair play to the Dublin pirate radio station that offered a million euros to the first person who could successfully lasso the spike with a bicycle tyre. The last time Dublin built a monument as a 'symbol of the future' was in the 1950s, when a 'Bowl Of Light' was stuck on O'Connell Bridge. Essentially a pretend glowing fire encased in a giant goldfish bowl, it was there just two weeks before a bunch of students from Trinity College decided to liberate it at the dead of night as a rag-week jape and it was last seen doing the back stroke down the Liffey into Dublin Bay. Those responsible were apprehended and taken to court only to be praised by the judge and given the unofficial freedom of the city. Bertie's Pole – alternatively known as 'Stiffy on the Liffey' – represents a bigger challenge but come on, you Trinity College students, you know your duty ...

Colin Irwin, *In Search of the Craic* (2001)

✱ ✱ ✱

Evan McHugh also has some humorous observations on one of the city's more recent monuments.

O'Connell Street, which I'll call a fine boulevard for the time being, had several statues of various figures in the Irish pantheon. At least I think they were. I have to admit some left me wondering what dictionary they'd used for the definition of the word 'fame'. The one of Catholic nationalist Daniel O'Connell made sense. So did the ones of various other martyrs for the Irish cause. But the statue of the bloke who put Dublin's water on was pretty doubtful. He had a name, but it's disappeared down the S-bend of forgotten information along with all the other pioneers of sewerage I've ever heard of.

Then I discovered O'Connell Street doesn't just have one statue with aquatic associations. It's got two. Maybe the Irish have a thing about fluids, which might explain why they've erected a statue with the Liffey, the river that flows through the city, as its subject. It's called the Anna Livia Millennium Fountain and it was commissioned to mark the 1,000 years since the Vikings settled what became the city of Dublin. As milestones go, 1,000 is pretty significant. So it's reasonable to expect something special as a memorial. To be honest, Anna looks like the sculptor caught her at a bad moment, but she does provide two valuable lessons for sculptors:

1 Think very carefully before agreeing to do a sculpture of a waterway.

2 A reclining figure may be the goods, but a figure lying in the bath is really stretching things.

Locals dismiss the work as 'the floozie in the jacuzzi', and yet, had Irish Olympic swimmer Michelle Smith won the back-stroke, they would have had a statue ready-made. Who'd have been any the wiser? [...]

We'd just saved a fortune on phone-calls, so we were more than ready to pay the anticipated fee at the first proper sight we wanted to see, the Ha'penny Bridge. It sounded like a bargain.

To our pleasant surprise they hadn't been charging any fee at all since 1919.

Built in 1816 for pedestrians, the Ha'penny was originally named after the Duke of Wellington, who was born in Dublin. The name was eventually changed perhaps because, when he was teased about his Irish birthplace, he is supposed to have replied, 'Being born in a stable does not make one a horse.'

The bridge also gave us our first glimpse of the much-vaunted Liffey. Here was the stream to which odes had been written and sculptures carved, one of the city's great founts of inspiration. So we stood in the middle of the bridge and looked down with appropriate awe. There was a mass of swirling grey murk sweeping quickly past. Almost as quickly our awe gave way to the feeling that the Anna Livia Fountain was looking better all the time.

Perhaps we needed to be on the bridge on a cold dark night, when it was more atmospheric. I could see myself wrapped in a long coat, collar turned up to ward off the chill, my face occasionally lit by the glow of a cigarette. Snakes of light were slithering towards me on the surface of the river.

Evan McHugh, *Pint-Sized Ireland* (2001)

✲ ✲ ✲

There are plenty of novels set on the streets of modern Dublin, but here are two extracts from one of the best of them – Emma Donoghue's Hood. *The first extract is the opening of the novel, the second comes about two thirds of the way through.*

Mayday in 1980, heat sealing my fingers together. Why is it the most ordinary images that fall out, when I shuffle the memories? Two girls in a secondhand bookshop, hands sticky with sampled perfumes from an afternoon's Dublin.

Up these four storeys of shelves, time moves more slowly than outside on the quays of the dirty river. One window cuts a slab of sunlight; dust motes twitch through it. I shut my eyes and breathe in. 'Which did I put on my thumb, Cara, do you remember?'

No answer. I stretch my hand towards her over the Irish poetry shelf, as if hitching a lift. 'All I can smell is old books; you have a go. Was it sandalwood?'

Cara emerges from a cartoon, and dips to my hand. She wrinkles her nose, which has always reminded me of an 'is less than' sign in algebra.

'Not nice?' I ask.

'Dunno, Pen. Something liquorishy.' Her eyes drift back to the page.

'I hate liquorice.' All I can make out now is vile strawberry on the wrist. I offer my thumb for Cara to smell again, but she has edged down a shelf to Theology. My arm moves in her wake and topples a pyramid of *Surprising Summer Salads*.

I'm sure to have torn one. I have only ninety-two pence in my drawstring purse, and my belly is cramping. It occurs to me to simply shift my weight on to the ball of my foot and take off like a crazed rhinoceros through the door. Then, being a responsible citizen, even at seventeen, I put my mother's spare handbag down beside the sprawl of books, and kneel. The princess who sorted seeds from sand at least had eloquent ants to help her. All I get are Cara's eyes rolling from the safe distance of the Marxism shelf, and a snigger from some art students over by the window. Luckily the black-lipsticked Goth at the till is engrossed in finding a paper bag for an old atlas; in any other bookshop a sales-woman would be pursing her lips and planting her stiletto heel six inches from my fingers. The tomb of *Surprising Summer Salads* I build is better neat, no one can make me buy a copy. If it were *Astonishing Autumn Appetizers*, now, I might consider it.

I'm blithering, amn't I?

Cara is over by Aviation pretending not to know me, so I set off downstairs, trying to soften the slap of my feet on the wood. Ragged posters for gigs and therapies paper the winding stairwell; their sellotape fingers flap in my breeze. Between the third and second floors the blood wells and I think I may be going to topple. Familiar clogs hit the steps behind me.

'Cup of coffee?'

Cara doesn't seem to hear, as her shoulders poke past, but when we have come out of the bookshop on to the dazzling quay she says, 'I'm off caffeine, Pen, I thought I told you.'

'Since when?' I shout into a surge of traffic.

'This morning.'

I let out my sigh as a yawn. 'A glass of water and a doughnut?'

'As you wish.'

I pause for a second halfway along the Ha'penny Bridge, to feel it bounce under the weight of feet. I refuse the first and second cafés we pass, as rip-offs. Cara wipes a dark red strand off her eyebrow. 'Pen, you know I've got plenty.'

'I'd choke on a bun that cost thirty-five pee.' It sounds like a point of principle, but is based on the ninety-two pence remaining in my purse.

We thread our way through the crowd on College Green in what I hope is a companionable silence. Town is full of twelve-year-olds in limp minis and pedal pushers; their shoulders are peanut-red, scored with strapmarks. I have often wondered if the Irish consider it ungrateful to use sun block. As we head up Grafton Street the light is like a splash of lemon juice in my face. I turn my stiff neck to find Cara, but she is ahead of me. Five yards ahead, in fact, sprinting. How odd. I scan the mass of shoppers for a familiar face, but then I realize that she is not running up to anyone, just running. Her head is down. Her fringed purse is smacking from rib to rib. I stand still and lose her.

When I catch sight of her narrow body hurtling past the flower barrows, a great weariness comes over me. It occurs to me, by no means for the first time, to let Cara go. But while that thought is worming its way down the nerves, through the labyrinths of flesh, to reach my feet, they are already flailing a path up the street. When I get past the cluster of tourists around the mandolin player, I grip my handbag under my elbow and gather speed. Cara is nowhere in sight, but I trust that even lanky footballers run out of energy when they've eaten nothing all day and their clogs are heavy. [...]

On a long wall on Leeson Street was stamped, over and over, *Dublin's beautiful keep it clean*. I thought of adding *Language is beautiful, keep it punctuated*, then sighed at my teacherly intolerance and looked away. Dublin was undeniably beautiful today, the sun bringing out the red of the brick terraces, catching the fan-lights over the Georgian doors. Even the odd burnt-out building looked rather decorative, as if left over from a film set.

I decided to cut through Stephen's Green, something that, being a driver, I hadn't done in years. I had forgotten that bronze of the Three Fates placed just inside the gates; I stopped short to look at it. A toddler bumped into the back of my knees, then stumbled on, its mother twitching the reins. The Fates sat holding the inch-thick rope of life, one behind another, their black eyes gloomy but by no means malevolent. Their hands were palms outermost, as if to ask, what do you people expect of us anyway? Water gushed from the rock they were sitting on. The youngest one had a drugged smile; scissors idle in her lap, she seemed to be absorbing memories from the frayed end of the rope which trailed against her skirt.

Jazz was booming from the bandstand as I walked farther into the Green. The tune was familiar to me, though I couldn't put a name to it. The only jazz I knew was from those afternoons Major to Minor used to play in Sachs Hotel, and I mostly went to those to eye up the women in sensible shoes who surrounded the piano. Here in the Green no one was paying the trumpet solo much attention. Couples cuddled sleepily on the bumpy lawn between beds of late roses. I nodded to Con Markievicz as I passed; her bronze head was almost hidden in holly and purple leaves. I had always loved the story of her setting her citizen army to dig trenches here in 1916 without thinking how easily they would be gunned down from the windows of the hotels that overlooked the Green. Or no, maybe I was underestimating her. Maybe she knew what would happen, but wanted to keep her men busy, like the games I made up for my Immac girls on sleepy afternoons.

The generous fountain was spurting in three plumes, making me thirsty. My mouth was dry from the coffee and pastries that my stomach was struggling to reconcile. At the edge of the meandering pond, a toddler stood casting strips of bread at the ducks with such vigour that I thought he might topple. Keeping one eye on him, I looked at the island in the middle where two swans were digging at the weed. There was an overgrown path up around the pond, I remembered now. Cara had dragged me up here once to kiss on the bend in the path where just for a moment you were screened from view. I strolled up that way now, to see what nostalgia would do to me. When I turned at the bend there was a couple on the grass; I doubled back immediately.

Emma Donoghue, *Hood* (1995)

✳ ✳ ✳

One of the liveliest quarters of contemporary Dublin is the Temple bar district. Neil Hegarty tells us a bit about it.

Facing the boardwalk is Temple Bar on the southern bank. If dastardly plans hadn't gone awry, the whole old quarter of the city would have been levelled in the '80s to make way for a huge bus station. That was the plan and as it had been all drawn up and arranged, any self-respecting business got the hell out of the area while it could, leaving tiny shops to mushroom, and musicians and artists to colonise the area, by taking advantage of cheap rents and joining the old bars which had existed for generations in this district of tangled and cobbled streets. Soon enough, Temple Bar developed a distinctive energy of its own: the artists and musicians were joined by others and soon enough again, the government saw what was going on and resolved to create Dublin's very own Left Bank, right here. Right here. The cobbles were taken up, cleaned, and laid again. The buildings were cleaned and repaired on the outside; inside, stucco work on magnificent Georgian ceilings was restored gorgeously, old timber was sanded and varnished, stained glass windows were removed, repaired and reinstated. The whole fabric of the area was taken up and replaced, in fact, and Temple Bar set about reinventing itself creatively too.

But it has only worked up to a point: the artists are still there, or some of them are, hanging on by their fingernails as the rents spiral. The smoky old bars were soon demolished to make way for superbars which seem now to stretch for miles and which trample on the very idea of character and vibrant life. On the other hand, some studios and galleries thrived, and exquisite cafés opened. People returned to live in the area and were joined by the Irish Film Centre, which took over the old Quaker Meeting House and fashioned two cinemas, a bookshop, and a café out of its ruins, and grouped them around a glazed plaza. Open-air food markets moved in too, taking over the new public square that was created in the heart of the district; they sell organic vegetables and meat, focaccia, and cheeses each Saturday. The Project Theatre rebuilt itself and the Contemporary Music Centre took over a tall, thin Georgian townhouse and set up a focus for art music in Ireland. A pastry shop and café called Queen of Tarts was set up on the edge of the area, introducing a whole new aspect of pleasure to my life. And U2 moved in too, buying up the old Clarence Hotel, shunting on the hookers who had seen the old ramshackle building as something of a home from home, and creating in the process the city's sleekest hotel.

Neil Hegarty, *Waking Up In Dublin* (2004)

❊ ❊ ❊

A city's streets are defined, above all, by the people who use them. Dublin has its fair share of eccentrics and 'characters', and in this extract from Sean O'Reilly's The Swing of Things, *we meet just one of them. Like the father in Anne Enright's story 'The Brat' (see the 'Dubliners – old and new' section), this half-destroyed human being still manifests a proud knowledge of his national literature.*

Between the steep cliffs of glass and brick, the crowds on Grafton Street were moving slowly. Security guards radioed from nook to nook, door to door; bank, shoe shop, chemist's, jeweller's, multinational, chocolate shop, multinational. They're on their way up towards you, Jamesy, three of them, white tracksuits, watch out for the girl, she'll take the eye out of your head. Cameras buzzed high on the lampposts as Boyle moved through the sweating glut and the gulls cried out their bin-day song in the narrow bridge of sky. There was an Arabic theme to the display in a department-store window, turbans and floors of furs and sand. At an intersection with a side street Boyle stopped to watch a street-performer, a man sprayed in gold who stood to attention on a pedestal with an old rifle on his shoulder and a gold balloon on a string over his head which he would take aim at when a coin was put in the slot at his feet. A few yards further on a trio of sad-faced Romanian men begged for joy with their accordions.

Boyle bought a sandwich and decided to make toward St Stephen's Green and sit himself down on the grass in the sun, like others did, like he had the right to do, and to go so far as to roll up his sleeves and take off his shoes if he found the right place and nobody was near. As he passed the flower-seller's stall he spotted a character he had listened to on a few occasions before, who was making a meal out of the struggle with his sandwich board. Boyle watched him wipe the sweat from his head, cross his arms Egyptian style and raise his face to the sun. The girl from the flower stall cut a stem with her scalpel and inserted the bloom in the buttonhole of his filthy shirt. Another minute must have passed, and at least a hundred sluggish people, before this character opened his eyes and his arms and cried out to the summer throng.

Poetry on tap, the great classics of Irish literature. Joyce and his chamber pots, Wilde and his twilight balconies. Yeats and his randy ghosts. I'll take you turf cutting with Heaney or onion eating with Jonathan Swift, lamenting the earls with O'Leary, into the monasteries and out on the misty hills, I've got ballads of the Easter Rising and odes to autumnal hussies, Sam the merciless, and brawling Behan, poets from the North and the South, Bobby Sands and Lady Gregory, bohemians and rednecks, dreamers and believers, wasters and wotnotters, scavengers and squanderers, a poem for everybody alive and dead, for the yawning refugees and pale-faced gunmen, the new Spanish armada and the Russian angsters, your mammy in heaven and your daddy in bed all the livelong day. Ah now, ah now, sure we'll get there in the end, we're all headed the same way but there's nothing like a poem to hit the spot on the way, you can't beat a poet to scratch your back on a bright sweaty day like today, or lower down there, a bit lower, right down, down in the pit, in your damp mossy bog, and further down, down as far as you dare go ...

He went after two women in he crowd, dancing at their backs, heckling with poems – Your narrow brows, your hair like gold, lady with the swanlike body, I was reared by cunning hand – until one relented and span round in a swish of hair to face her seducer in open-mouthed delight. What she saw was the yellow eyes of the wolf, the leer, the slight frame, the torn green shirt and she screamed, a loud shriek of warning down the centuries of women.

In the commotion, Boyle lost sight of the ragged proclaimer. The two women held on to each other like they had seen a ghost. A security guard pushed his way towards them. People were laughing. Then, there he was again at the sandwich board: I am the lad of ceaseless hum, it's enough to make you broken hearted, thousands of legs and none of them parted.

The flower-stall girl rushed over and gave him a piece of her mind. The chanter flapped his arms like a starving carrion bird. Shortly after, some tourists stopped, Italians, then a few Americans, and he fired words at them, sometimes putting on actions: pleading, slapstick fury, starving peasant, man against the wind, dying warrior, and hunting around the sandwich board where the names were written in gold paint on a white background scrolled with green Celtic snakes and birds.

Then there was an old woman who appeared out of nowhere. She stood quietly in front of the reciter while he seemed to be explaining something to her, joining his hands with promises. He delivered another speech to the street and yet she was still there, in an old tweed coat in the heat, small, slight, dusty with years of loneliness, no, poverty, clasping her handbag. The reciter made more promises to her, wringing his hands desperately until he covered his face and went down on his knees behind the board, a penitent on the street even after she had gone her quiet way.

Up again he cried out, flapping his wings: Myself unto myself will give, this name Katharsis-Purgative. Name your poison. One from the forest smoke of the ancient bothy or a moan in the rickety air of the bedsit still. I was a listener at the street corner. I was wild with frolic in the mead-hall.

The flower girl threw a coin high in the air, a livelier one come on please, a funnier thing, lighten it up, and the reciter went after it, wings a-flapping, skinny pinions, his tongue hanging out, but he made a mess of the catch and the coin disappeared under the feet of the crowd. Shocked, fascinated too, Boyle watched the lunatic go after it, a dog now on his hands and knees scuttling between the legs. He seemed immune to any type of shame. Some of the passers-by found it funny and most wanted to kick him out of the way. The barking grew more desperate and was broken by howls; going round in circles, sniffing, the reciter was licking at the feet of those who had stopped to watch. Meanwhile, the flower girl was calling to him, Leave it, leave it, a bucket in her hand. The street was choking up. Boyle spotted the Guard making a beeline for the commotion.

Sean O'Reilly, *The Swing of Things* (2004)

❊ ❊ ❊

And while we're on Grafton Street we briefly join young American student, Meghan Butler, visiting Dublin for the first time and seeing the world more vividly as a result.

Umbrellas pop as the rain starts to pour on Grafton Street. I don't know how all of these people and all of these umbrellas can fit in such a crowded area, and they don't really fit at all. Umbrellas hurtle into each other and spin upon contact, sending beads of rain flying in all directions. The sidewalk below you, made of slippery squares, was not designed with the rain in mind ...

My first walk through St. Stephen's green ruins every park I have ever seen before. When the elusive sun appears people sprawl themselves out all over the park to soak up as much of it as they can before it hides away again. Exotic birds I have never seen before trot regally on the green. I see a little boy doing somersaults on the pristine grass no one is supposed to walk on without inhibition or fear of reprimand. I don't think even an overseeing Garda would dare stop him anyway. The twangs and tongues of many languages hit my ears and blend together in the wind, the most prominent being the Irish accent which carries a little more girth. The warm grass smells the way grass is supposed to smell that is watered by rain. Some of the popcorn I am eating is taken from my hand by the wind and given to the pigeons. ...

Not all of Dublin is as fancy or flourishing as Grafton Street or St. Stephen's Green. Like any large city it has areas that could be considered seedy. But these places hold a deep-seated charm not found elsewhere. ... One of the houses in the poorer areas had a bunch of colourful clothespins hanging on the clothes-line outside. I was just staring at them thinking how pretty they looked. I thought about the person who bought them and how they went to a store to buy clothespins and were faced with the choice between bland wooden ones and colourful plastic ones. And it felt as if, at that moment, I really began to understand the soul of this city. Everyone always says that Dublin is a colourful city, but here were the colours staring me in the face. It made me sad that I never noticed small details like that in my own city but also excited that this experience might allow me to go home and seek them out.

Meghan Butler, 'Travels with my father' (2008)

✳ ✳ ✳

Though it's the main shopping area, a stroll down Grafton Street doesn't have to involve spending lots of money: there are plenty of other pleasures to be had, especially if you view the street through the eyes of a five-year-old ...

Joe took Nicola shopping, which involved hobbling up and down Grafton Street with the follower following and Joe trying to pick an argument with his daughter. Who was five. Or six. He wanted to give out to her for wanting branded products – for wanting Barney or Barbie or Pokémon things, for wanting Nike trainers or a Hilfigger bum bag or a McDonalds burger, or something of indeterminate function from Japan with which she would age him. He wanted to educate her about all of that, tell her of the evil in the world and how it operated. But she was happy enough to look at pretty flowers and listen to the buskers, and when asked what she wanted to eat, she insisted that a little cake in Bewleys would be lovely.

Keith Ridgway, *The Parts* (2003)

✳ ✳ ✳

In this short extract from The Light-Makers, *Mary O'Donnell further explores the lively diversions on offer along Grafton Street.*

Grafton Street streams with mid-afternoon shoppers and drifters, cars and buses having been long banished to surrounding road-systems. Bookshops where Dan and I browsed twenty years back are stuffed with luminous clothing. Benetton, Oui-set, Ton-sur-Ton, colour co-ordinated Escada, Laurel, Blackie. Part of the pleasure of any trip from Clonfoy to Dublin for the day was the inevitability of ending up in some bookshop or other with Dan, when half an hour would pass easily as we turned pages in silence, Today, what was once the Eblana bookshop is a hairdresser's, full of flouncing, busy-looking young men and women.

Crowds obstruct. Street-musicians attract them like bees near flowers. At least three different types of music compete for attention. The nearest source is a blues trio using the acoustics of an overhanging shop façade to make their sound more impressive. Billie Holliday, throttled again. People stand about, looking bashful. Some throw silver into the box and pass on.

Just above Bewley's a guitarist makes a mess of Scott Mackenzie's "San Francisco". The man's fingers have not mastered the intricacies of the piece but he battles on regardless. Meanwhile his girlfriend moves smilingly around with a cap in hand, a gormless young woman who no doubt believes she's supporting a great artist. Why hasn't she got her own guitar? And why isn't lover boy collecting for her?

The Diceman stands stick-still, his face painted in gold lustre, his entire head shorn and also golden, the eyes emphasised by purple kohl, lips exaggerated by cupid points in bright red. Arms folded across his chest, he wears the attire of an exotic sultan, minus turban. People press close and try to distract him but he never flinches. Occasionally he winks and they draw back, briefly unsettled by the fact that he is alive, that he observes, that he can choose such control.

Mountebanks, troubadours, dancers, beggars, mutants. A woman with a twisted face in Johnson Court, aware of shoppers with money to spend, shoppers with change. They create the ambience so beloved by tourists the world over, lend what people imagine is spontaneity to the proceedings. Everything has its price, can be straight-jacketed and sold as the original of the species. Authenticity to whet the appetites of the sated.

Mary O'Donnell, *The Light-Makers* (1992)

❊　❊　❊

Eccentrics and entertainers may be a normal part of city street life, but in Flann O'Brien's hilarious novel, The Dalkey Archive, *Mick has an even more engaging and surprising encounter in the very centre of Dublin.*

First he made his way to St Stephen's Green and sought a seat there – easy enough so early in the morning. The Green is a railed-in square pleasure ground near the city centre, an extravagance of flower beds and fountains. A pretty lake, spanned at the centre by a bridge and having little islands, was the home of water fowl, many exotic and matching the flowers in hue and life. And the green was constantly travelled by a great number of people since it offered a short cut diagonally between Earlsfoot terrace, where University College stood, and the top of Grafton Street – the portal of busy central Dublin. Curiously, this haven of hubbub (for that is what it sometimes seemed) was a good place for reflection and planning, as if all its burbling life was an anæsthesia, perhaps in the manner of finding loneliness in crowds.

He leaned back, closed his eyes, and meditated on what seemed to be his portion of things to be done. There were several things but, if big, they were not really complicated or unmanageable. He rather admired his own adroit manipulation of matters which, in certain regards, transcended this world. He would put a stop to the diabolical plans of De Selby, for instance, but by means of what was no less than comic-opera subterfuge. Again, Mick had been the one to be in a position to demonstrate that James Joyce, a writer and artist of genius, was not dead as commonly supposed but alive and reasonably well in the country of his birth. [...]

Coming in through the green towards the hospital, Mick's eye penetrated the tracery of shrubs and iron railings. Yes, Joyce was standing there, and Mick paused to appraise him soberly in the wan evening sunlight before he knew he was observed. He was by now no stranger, yet in his solitary standing there he was still a bit surprising. He looked a mature man, at ease, iron-grey hair showing from a small hat, symbol of life's slow ebb-tide: also experience, wisdom and – who knows? – adversity. He was neat in person, clean, and had a walking stick. A dandy? No. The carriage of his head in the fuss of traffic and passing people gave notice that his eyesight was uncertain. If a stranger were to try to classify Joyce socially, he would probably put him down as a scholarly type – a mathematician, perhaps, or a tired senior civil servant; certainly not a writer, still less a great writer.

Flann O'Brien, The Dalkey Archive (1964)

* * *

Fun. Variety. Entertainment. The chance to 'shop till you drop' … Yet at one time, despite the elegant lives of the lucky few, Dublin – like any city – was known for the insecurity and appalling conditions in which the poor lived. We take a look at this other side of Dublin with Eric Newby, Brendan Behan and Samuel Beckett.

What I remembered most about Dublin was the poverty. The poor lived in what were sometimes large eighteenth-century houses that had once been among the most elegant in the British Isles, but in Victorian times had become rookeries, teeming with inhabitants; what O'Casey described as 'a long drab gauntlet of houses, some of them fat with filth … long kennels of struggling poverty and disordered want … the lacerated walls, the windows impudent with dirt.' The poor swarmed in the street markets, filling the air with the adenoidal noises which rose to almost supersonic levels during their violent quarrels, called narks. They were to be found in the food markets high up around Thomas Street, and Meath Street, and Moore Street west of O'Connell Street, and around St Mary's Abbey, and in the junk and antique markets off Cornmarket and down on the quays. The big Christmas market was in Cole's Lane and there were second-hand books behind Bachelor Walk, where a minor massacre of Dubliners by British troops took place in 1914. Second- and third-hand boots and shoes and clothing were on sale in Anglesea Market and Riddles Row – markets more like oriental souks, where some still wore, and you could still buy, the black crotcheted woollen shawls that had been since time immemorial the uniform of the female poor, and were now soon to become collector's items.

The streets of the poor are almost certainly not now as they were then: there were doorways like the entrances to rock tombs in Chambers Street and in Crompton Court; shrines high on the vast walls with the lamps burning, just as in Naples; there was the vast cobbled expanse of Smithfield, as big as an airfield; whitewashed cottages with half doors in Camden Row and Sarah Place that looked as if they had been flown in from County Galway. They were beautiful streets, poverty-ridden but full of vibrant life: children swung on ropes from the lamp posts, or skipped with bits of rough cord; washing fluttered everywhere in the breeze; men wearing suits and caps, never without a jacket, sat on the kerb stones waiting for something to happen, watching the horse drays putting the motor traffic into disarray.

Eric Newby, *Round Ireland in Low Gear* (1987)

* * *

We said more nor our prayers in the slums of North Dublin, where I was born – less than an ass's roar from Nelson's Pillar. I come from the same area as Sean O'Casey about whom I don't intend to say anything for the simple reason that it would be like praising the Lakes of Killarney – a piece of imperti-nence. As far as I'm concerned, all I can say is that O'Casey's like champagne, one's wedding night, or the Aurora Borealis or whatever you call them – all them lights. At the time I was young, this area was pretty bad but that's one thing I must give the Government credit for – they built lovely flats for the people. You wouldn't see anything in Dublin now like the slum parts of Westbourne Park in London or some parts of Glasgow. Mind you, it was pretty bad while it lasted. I was born in a Georgian house that had gone to rack and ruin as a tenement, so I should know. It's been knocked down since but without any remorse on my part, much as I admire the Georgian Society whose activities are all right as long as they're confined to the houses of wealthy doctors in Fitzwilliam Street. [...]

You find the people I like on both sides of the river but, mainly, they live more or less along a line that you might draw between the Custom House and Glasnevin Cemetery – between birth and death, come to think of it. The Custom House is a remarkable building – though, to tell you the truth, I'm not particularly knowledgeable about architecture, Georgian or otherwise, possibly due to an architect friend solemnly informing me at some stage in a very austere voice: 'Good architecture is invisible.' The Custom House, as far as I'm concerned, is notable mainly for the fact that it was there I used to get false birth certificates in order to get false passports when I was in the I.R.A. It was burned by the Volunteers in 1921 and that's what brought British administration in Ireland finally to a standstill, for all local government records were housed there. Across the way from it stood Liberty Hall, the headquarters of the Irish Transport and General Workers' Union, where the Irish Citizen Army had it headquarters in 1916. It has been knocked down now and they're building a skyscraper block on the site.

Not far away is the General Post Office which was the headquarters of the 1916 Rising. The story of the Rising is too well known to go into it all again, but during that week an aunt of mine went down to the G.P.O. to look for her husband who was in there fighting. Shells from a gunboat on the Liffey were falling all around the place and my aunt was asked with some urgency to go away. (She had a baby son in her arms who was afterwards killed in France while fighting with the British Army in 1944.) She refused to get away and kept demanding to see her husband who finally came to a sandbagged window and roared: 'Go away, Maggie,' and she shouted back: 'I only wanted to know if you were going to your work in the morning.'

Turning down Bachelor's Walk at the Liffey by O'Connell Bridge where British troops fired on the people of Dublin in 1914, you come to the Metal Bridge or, as it is sometimes called, the Ha'penny Bridge. It's known as the Metal Bridge for the very obvious and unIrish reason that it's made of metal, but in my father's day it was better known as the Ha'penny Bridge because you had to pay a halfpenny toll to cross it. Further along there is the Four Courts where the Anti-Treaty forces dug in in 1922. I remember the man that was more or less second-in-command there told me that during the attack on the building, a young I.R.A. man from the country – a boy of seventeen or eighteen – was going up the stairs carrying the Chancellor's large wig. 'Hey, where are you going with that?' he called and the boy answered: 'I'm only going to take the kettle off the fire.'

Near by is O'Meara's pub – the 'Irish House', though why it should be called that in Ireland, I don't know. [...]

The area where Tone was born, and the area across the river immediately south, are two of the oldest parts of Dublin. They used to be the fashionable areas, but the opening of O'Connell Street, further down the river, drew the wealthier parts of the population down to the Georgian squares that were built about the same time – Merrion Square, Fitzwilliam Square, Parnell Square and the rest. South of the river, in the area I'm talking about, there is the old bastion of British rule in Ireland – Dublin Castle, in the dungeons of which so many died. Near by there is Christchurch Cathedral and St. Patrick's Cathedral where Dean Swift is buried. He was always a great defender of the Dublin poor. Behind the cathedrals, there are a few old type markets; the principal one is the Daisy market. It's mainly a second-hand clothes market but it has other stuff too. I remember principally going through it one day and hearing a stall-holder remark: 'Keep the baby's bottom off the butter.' I've bought decanters there. Very good ones, at a very cheap rate – I'm very fond of decanters, having a slight weakness for what goes into them. In the early thirties, when people still marched in great numbers to the First War Memorial at Island-bridge, soldiers used to repurchase their medals there – Mons stars, General Service Medals and indeed anything from the V.C. backwards – for a small amount of money – and march into the Park wearing them.

There's another market over at Cole's Lane where I bought a

massive chair which was carved from Burmese teak. I also bought a picture which hangs over my mantelpiece. It is of a bearded gentleman whom I give out is my grandfather though actually I don't know who the man is. There is also the Iveagh Market which is named after the Earl of Iveagh who gave the ground for it or something like that. The Guinness family have always been very good to the people of Dublin but as some wag remarked: 'The people of Dublin are very kind to the Guinnesses.' The Guinness Brewery at James's Gate is a huge place – almost a little town in itself. Although they have spread their wings very much in recent years, the fame of the Brewery still rests on its two traditional products – stout and porter. Porter is a lighter drink than stout and there's not all that much of it sold nowadays; but I recall my father telling me that before the First War, when it cost a penny a pint, it was so good that the glass it was in used to stick to the counter.

Brenda Behan, Brendan Behan's Island (1962)

✽ ✽ ✽

Belacqua made off at all speed in the opposite direction. Down Pearse Street, that is to say, long straight Pearse Street, its vast Barrack of Glencullen granite, its home of tragedy restored and enlarged, its coal merchants and Florentine Fire Brigade Station, its two Cervi saloons, ice-cream and fried fish, its dairies, garages and monumental sculptors, and implicit behind the whole length of its southern frontage the College. Perpetuis futuris temporibus duraturum. It was to be hoped so, indeed.

It was a most pleasant street, despite its name, to be abroad in, full as it always was with shabby substance and honest-to-God coming and going. All day the roadway was a tumult of buses, red and blue and silver. By one of these a little girl was run down, just as Belacqua drew near to the railway viaduct. She had been to the Hibernian Dairies for milk and bread and then she had plunged out into the roadway, she was in such a childish fever to get back in record time with her treasure to the tenement in Mark Street where she lived. The good milk was all over the road and the loaf, which had sustained no injury, was sitting up against the kerb, for all the world as though a pair of hands had taken it up and set it down there. The queue standing for the Palace Cinema was torn between conflicting desires: to keep their places and to see the excitement. They craned their necks and called out to know the worst, but they stood firm. Only one girl, debauched in appearance and swathed in a black blanket, fell out near the sting of the queue and secured the loaf. With the loaf under her blanket she sidled unchallenged down Mark Street and turned into Mark Lane. When she got back to the queue her place had been taken of course. But her sally had not cost her more than a couple of yards.

Samuel Beckett, *More Pricks Than Kicks* (1934)

* * *

When every square metre of Dublin offers something to interest the eye, the mind, or the spirit, you feel you want to shake a person like Eleanor in this next extract – from Sean O'Reilly's The Swing of Things. *Was it just all too familiar to a Dublin girl? Or had she never really opened her eyes?*

It was only nine o'clock; hours to get through before lunchtime. He set out on another long walk, over into the park and down towards the river [...].

He followed the river into the city centre. It was going to be a warm day. His face was already itching in the heat; maybe he should go for a trim, or even have the beard shaved off altogether. He might duck into a barber's if the whim took him; anything was possible. Although it was still early, the streets were lively, that word bustling. He drifted around, Wicklow Street, Westmoreland Street, Nassau Street, South Great George's Street. The pubs weren't open yet. A man was hosing down the inside of a van out the front of a butcher's. Girls smoking outside a hairdresser's, the first coffee of the day.

The sky was high, tantalising like a warm sea in the distance. The seagulls complaining, always the lamenting seagulls over Dublin, the lonely echoing accusations from above the narrow streets, adherents of a hardline sect. Lest we forget. Summoning his courage, Boyle stopped outside a café, a place he had never dared go into before at the edge of a covered market. The walls were layered heavily with posters for gigs and films. He sat at a big wooden table with a rake of people who all looked like they had been out on the tear the night before. Through the window young foreign ones were having piercings done.

He sipped at a coffee, and smoked, and warned himself to be careful. Eleanor was only visiting; she had another life elsewhere. When was the last time he had felt this kind of excitement about someone? His mind had always been on other things. He was entering new territory, breaking down walls in himself. That was the thing he had to hold on to; it was enough just to feel something for a change. It was proof he had it in him, the capacity.

As he was sitting there, Con came in with a girl, a new one. They had obviously just got out of bed together. Con sat down with him for a few minutes and they talked about Fada, then about Fiacra who had been kicked out by his girlfriend.

Boyle was at St Stephen's Green an hour later. He walked the paths, under the trees, over the footbridges and round the lakes. He stopped beside a man with his child who were feeding bread to the swans and ducks. The man spoke about the child as though Boyle had one himself. He sat on a bench and watched three winos having a laugh together. As the time approached, he began to worry about what he would talk about with Eleanor, how they would fill an afternoon together, whether he could make her laugh. Women liked that in a man he had heard, a sense of humour. He tried to sort through some topics in his mind – childhood, books, London – and then gave up. The city would feed them. They would talk about what they saw. No, don't go near the past, he warned himself. Try to keep the talk light. Be confident, optimistic. He wouldn't get moody or angry. He wouldn't try to tell her everything.

There she was, waiting at the crossing, a head above most of the women, smiling plaintively.

They went down Dawson Street, past Trinity and across the river to O'Connell Street. Boyle found the pavements were too crowded for much conversation to develop. Then Eleanor happened to mention she had once lived in Drumcondra. Boyle asked if she wanted to go and have a look at the area again. Eleanor shrugged: If you want, she said. So they passed the statue of Larkin with his arms spread to the workers and under the portico of the GPO to the Parnell monument. He took her into the Garden of Remembrance for a break from the noise of the street. The birds of freedom broke free at the far end of the shallow tomb of water. Eleanor closed her eyes, unimpressed, no, simply uninterested. A young junkie lad came up, trembling, drooling and asking for some money. Boyle rolled a fag for him. Eleanor kept her eyes shut through that as well. To get her attention, he mentioned the university, that he was a student there. She said she had never been inside the gates.

And you a Dublin girl? [...]

She took his hand as they went into Trinity.

What about the Book of Kells? Have you ever seen it?

She shook her head – was it proudly? No, freely, like she was enjoying it, the not knowing, or maybe the swing of her hair.

He told her about it as they stood in the queue with Americans mainly. It's one of the oldest books in the world. The monks used their own blood to illustrate it. Hitler had wanted it, like the Spear of Destiny.

She smiled at him hazily while he spoke.

We don't have to see it if you don't want.

No it's ok, she said. Why not?

He wanted to kiss her; it would take away the nerves.

That's the library over there, he pointed to the row of windows. At the same time he saw the Dove coming out of the arts building: he had not even considered the possibility of running into her. She stopped when she saw him but he threw himself into another speel about the Book of Kells and some of the intellectual tramp characters that hung around the university, anything at all until the danger was passed. The Dove had gone on her way. Students were eating sandwiches around the grass square.

Are you hungry? We could go and get something to eat and come back later.

She nodded, too eagerly he thought.

You should have said if you didn't want to go in, Boyle told her. You decide, she said.

They walked around in the lunchtime crowds and the heat in search of a café. Nowhere seemed right for them. He suggested a quiet pub but on the way he came up with the idea of a picnic. They could sit on the grass in Merrion Square. Eleanor agreed.

Sean O'Reilly, *The Swing of Things* (2004)

❋ ❋ ❋

Sometimes it takes an outsider to appreciate the place
– though the German visitor in this short story extract
by Eilís Ní Dhuibhne is perhaps a little too keen on
her guidebook.

Mutti wrote to Erich. She would like to visit him in May. It had been two years since his last holiday in Bad Schwarzstadt and she was missing him. Beside, she was longing to see Ireland. [...]

She was a real old battle-axe. Hard as nails. More demanding than a two-year-old Ayatollah. More conservative than Maggie Thatcher. A dyed-in-the-wool Lutheran. More puritanical than John Knox.

I would have to move out.

It was only temporary.

She didn't realise he was living with me and the shock would be too much for her. Her only son. It was only for two weeks. Why make an issue of it? For a mere fortnight.

What about my mother? I politely enquired. She was a dyed-in-the-wool Catholic, more conservative than John Paul the Second, more puritanical than Archibishop McNamara. She'd had to turn a blind eye on the fact that her daughter, her favourite daughter, her fifth daughter, was living in a state of mortal sin. [...]

Mutti was sixty-eight. She had severe arthritis of the hip. It was only for two weeks. For heaven's sake.

On the thirteenth of May, I moved in with Jacinta who lives around the corner. On the fifteenth, Erich invited me up for a cup of tea, and I was introduced to Mutti. [...]

A month prior to her visit, Mutti had borrowed a guide-book from the public library in Bad Schwarzstadt. The work of one Heinrich Müller, it was entitled *Ein kleines irisches Reise-buch*, and she had studied it with single-minded diligence until she knew its contents by heart. It was to be her inseparable vade-mecum during her holiday, and her main criterion for enjoyment in sightseeing was that the sight had been referred to by Herr Müller.

Therefore she had merrily and gratefully limped through the litter of O'Connell Street ('oh! the widest street in Ireland!'), but the Powerscourt Centre had failed to arouse the mildest commendation. The Book of Kells had won her freshest laurels, but to the 'Treasures of Ireland' Exhibition, her reaction was one of chilled disappointment. 'Please, what is the meaning of the word "treasure?"' she had asked Erich, coming out of the museum onto Kildare Street. 'We did not have it in class, I believe.'

Herr Müller had spent the greater part of his *Reise* in Spiddal, and had devoted more than half his book, ten whole pages, to a graphic account of that settlement and its environs. Few corners of the western village were unfamiliar to Mutti, and she anticipated her sojourn there with the greatest of pleasure.

Unfortunately, it would occur at the end of her stay in Dublin and last for no more than two days.

I arrived at the flat on the following morning, having taken a day's leave from my job in the Department of Finance.

'We'll go through the Phoenix Park,' I recommended brightly, determined to get value for my time. 'It's much more interesting that way, and only a bit longer. The President lives there. It's the biggest park in Europe.'

'Ah, yes,' responded Mutti noncommittally, as she settled into the passenger seat and opened a map. 'Can you show me where it is?'

I tried to lean across the brake and locate it for her, but Eric beat me to it, and, from the rear, indicated the relevant green patch. Mutti took a pencil from her handbag, held it poised in mid-air, and smiled: 'Are we going now?' On, James.

I drove to Charlemont Bridge.

'That's the canal,' I exclaimed brilliantly, waving at it as we turned off the Ranelagh Road.

'Canal?'

'You know, Mutti. Canal. Not a river. Made by man. *Ein Kanal.*' Erich proffered the translation with caution: Mutti had decreed that no German be spoken in her presence, since this might sabotage her chances of commanding the language.

'It's called the Grand Canal,' I continued, pedantically. 'There are two canals in Dublin, the Royal and the Grand. This is the Grand. It's quite a famous canal, actually. Poems have been written about it. Good poems. Quite well-known poems.'

Alas, it was not the leafy-with-love part of the canal, it was the grotesque-with-graffiti bit, and Mutti stared, bemused, at peeling mildewed walls and disintegrating furry corpses. Even if it had been picturesque, I don't think its high-falutin associations would have pulled any weight: Kavanagh had the misfortune to be post-Müller.

We drove towards Kilmainham in silence. The looming jail flooded my spirits with enthusiasm. The Struggle for Freedom was a favourite theme of Heinrich's, and Mutti, I had gathered from a few comments she had made, had also fallen victim to the romantic nostalgia for things Irish, historical, and bloody.

'Look!' I cried, 'there's Kilmain ... '

But she had glimpsed the portico of the boys' school, which is impressive. And fake.

'Oh, Erich! How nice! Is it medieval, do you think?'

'Oh, yes, I think so, Mutti,' replied Erich, in his most learned voice. He knows nothing about Dublin, or architecture, or the Middle Ages.

'It looks like some of our German castles.'

'Look,' I pressed, 'that's Kilmainham Jail. The 1916 leaders were imprisoned there.' The light turned green. 'And shot,' I added, optimistically.

'In Bad Schwarzstadt we have two castles dating from the thirteenth century, Eileen, Marienschloss and Karlsschloss. They are so nice. People come to look from everywhere.'

'Really? I'd love to see them some day!'

The hint was ignored. I turned into the park by the Islandbridge gate.

'This is the Phoenix Park,' the guided tour continued.

'Oh! A park. And we may drive in it. How nice.' Her tone was deeply disapproving. 'In Germany, we have many car-free zones. You know. Green zones, they are called. It is good without cars sometimes. For the health.'

At that moment, a Volkswagen sped around one of the vicious bends which are so common on the charming back-roads of the Park. It took me unawares, and I was forced to swerve in order to avoid it ... Swerve very slightly, and the Volkswagen was at fault.

'Oh, oh, oh, oh!' screamed Mutti, clapping her hands across her face. Through bony fingers her gentian eyes glared vindictively at me. I gritted my teeth and counted to fifty. Then I repeated fifty times 'a man's mouth often broke his nose,' a proverb I had come across in *The Connaught Leader* a few weeks previously. Meanwhile, Mutti ignored the Pope's Cross, the clever woods, the flocks of deer gambolling in the clever woods, the American Embassy, the troops of travellers' ponies bouncing off the bonnet, the polo grounds and Áras an Uachtaráin.

'What town will we come to next?'

'Castlenock,' between one 'a man's mouth' and the next.

Scratch, scratch, went the pen on the map. Scratch, scratch ...

Eilís Ní Dhuibhne, *Blood and Water* (1988)

❊ ❊ ❊

And a final taste of the grittier side of Dublin's streets from Keith Ridgway.

Cars, houses, streets. The wind whip, the slap, the hunkered down temper of the traffic. Growling under the negative lights, the darkroom lights, at the corners and the intersections, the blood red lights. By the glow holed dwellings, the rows of windows – lined up, occupied or empty, who knows? They go up and they go across. Grid work. The clattering concrete and the stained pavements, collecting footfalls and litter, vomit and phlegm, money, dogs, children, shoe parts, animal shit, debris, bad air, car smoke, scraping, minor infestations, little wispy nothings that we drop and don't miss. The huddles, the doorways, the single palm, the invocation. The blanket and the chewing gum box. The sleeping bag and plastic cup. You know them. The mild roar of the weekend drinkers. The clump of hormones at the corner – all crotches and dribble, all gagging for it. The confused, the queues, waiting for the bouncer to give them the once over – no work clothes, no sports gear – mixed nerves and bravado, all smelling the same – cheap, hopeful, scared. Shirts, skirts, jeans, seams, skin, hair, scents, mouths, slap, tickle, snatch, tackle, come on, c'mon, you on for it, you up for it, you out for it, you in on it? That's the crunch, the hope of violence. That's what they're all after, a fight or a fuck, something howled out, vicious, bitten. It's the weekend. It's Dublin. It's showtime.

Keith Ridgway, *The Parts* (2003)

Dubliners – old and new

Dublin is good at celebrating its famous sons and daughters – in statues, songs, poetry, and annual events. We start with one of the most famous ...

Dublin's big on statues. They've even got one to Father Matthew, who apparently persuaded five million Irish people to take a pledge of teetotalism in the mid-nineteenth century. Just think of the legless stag parties dancing around the statue on a Saturday night as the revenge of the immoral majority, Father Matthew. Worst Statue Award, though, goes to the one of Molly Malone – 'tart with a cart' – in Grafton Street. It depicts her with saucy expression and suggestively low-cut dress, giving credence to the legend that while Molly sold cockles and mussels by day, she sold more intimate favours by night. I always thought the whole Molly Malone, cockles and mussels thing was a bit of a laugh. A ludicrously melodramatic song for schoolkids to sing and a story without basis in reality. A song also credited with having been written by James Yorkstone, a Scotsman. But you can't keep the Irish away from a good legend and they take her tale seriously enough in this neck of the woods, claiming church records show the baptism of a Mary Malone on July 27, 1663, and a subsequent burial of the same person 36 years later are proof of her existence. Some academic even researched the story and reached the conclusion that the real Molly Malone was actually Peg Woffington, the mistress of Charles II, and cockles and mussels were really metaphors for ladies' naughty bits.

Colin Irwin, *In Search of the Craic* (2001)

* * *

Dublin is, above all, a city of writers, and everyone likes to claim a connection with the most famous of them. The mother of Brendan Behan (himself a well-known Irish writer) had been a maid in the house of Maud Gonne. This passionately republican actress was regularly visited by W. B. Yeats – regarded by many as Ireland's greatest poet – with whom she had a long and turbulent involvement. Behan's mother was in a position to provide some unusual insider information on the great man.

My mother was a maid in the house owned by Madame Maud Gonne MacBride, and she knew Yeats quite well, but I never heard her advert to his drinking. He used to visit that house which was in St. Stephen's Green, and he used to call her 'Kitty' which she disliked for her name is Kathleen. He arranged his entrances to the house so infallibly that he was there just as she'd be coming up the stairs with a tray of tea and cakes and sandwiches for the visitors, and he'd stop and talk to her for a couple of minutes. I think it was probably an inverted form of snobbery to show the guests that he'd as leave talk to the housemaid as the lord. But this didn't excuse my mother from Maud Gonne's tongue when she scolded her for having the tea cold.

My mother also told me that at lunch, where she often served Yeats, he was absolutely impervious to what he ate, as he didn't know what he was eating half the time. He absent-mindedly would put sugar in the soup and salt in the coffee and all sorts of peculiar things like that. The one dislike that he had in the way of food was parsnips. Once he was served parsnips by some mistake and he remarked: 'This is a very peculiar pudding.'

I was in the 'Deux Magots' in Paris one time and an American that I was introduced to asked me if I had known James Joyce. I said that I hadn't had that honour, but I told him that my mother had often served a meal to W. B. Yeats in Maud Gonne's house on Stephen's Green and that the poet turned his nose up to the parsnips. 'He didn't like parsnips?' said the American reaching for his notebook, 'You're sure this is factual?'

'It is to be hoped,' I replied, 'that you are not calling my mother a liar?'

'No, no, of course not,' he said, 'but she might have been mistaken – it might have been carrots,' he added hastily.

'You must think I'm a right fool to have a mother that can't tell a carrot from a parsnip,' I said nastily.

'No, no, of course – I mean I'm sure she could but it is very important … ' He wrote in the book: *Parsnips – attitude of Yeats to.*

'And you say he didn't like Stephen's Green either – now what kind of vegetables are they?'

Brendan Behan, *Brendan Behan's Ireland* (1962)

✳ ✳ ✳

Someone else who remembers Yeats is the novelist V. S. Pritchett, who found Dublin an inspiring city for the young, would-be writer.

Living among writers who were still at their good moment added to my desire to emulate them. I had the – to me – incredible sight of the beautiful Mrs W. B. Yeats riding a bicycle at St Stephens Green; and of A.E. (George Russell), also riding a bicycle and carrying a bunch of flowers. I had tea with James Stephens one Sunday at that hotel at Dun Laoghaire where people go to day-dream at the sight of the mail-boat coming in from England, that flashing messenger to and from the modern world. This gnome-like talker sparkled so recklessly that one half-dreaded that he might fall into his teacup and drown. One afternoon I took tea with Yeats himself in his house in Merrion Square.

It was a Georgian house, as unlike a hut of wattle in a bee-loud glade as one could imagine. To begin with, the door opened on a chain and the muzzle of a rifle stuck through the gap. A pink-faced Free State soldier asked me if I had an 'appointment'. I was shown in to what must have been a dining-room but now it was a guard room with soldiers smoking among the Blake drawings on the wall. Yeats was a Senator and he had already been shot at by gunmen. Upstairs I was to see the bullethole in the drawing-room window. Presently the poet came down the stairs to meet me.

It is a choking and confusing experience to meet one's first great man when one is young. These beings come from another world and Yeats studiously created that effect. Tall, with grey hair finely rumpled, a dandy with negligence in collar and tie and with the black ribbon dangling from the glasses on a short, pale and prescient nose – not long enough to be Roman yet not sharp enough to be a beak – Yeats came down the stairs towards me, and the nearer he came the further away he seemed. His hair was bird-like, suggesting one of the milder swans of Coole and an exalted sort of blindness. I had been warned that he would not shake hands. I have heard it said – but mainly by the snobbish Anglo-Irish – that Yeats was a snob. I would have said that he was a man who was translated into a loftier world the moment his soft voice throbbed. He was the only man I have known whose natural speech sounded like verse.

He sat me in the fine first floor of his house. After the years all that remains with me is a memory of candles, books, wood-cuts, the feeling that here was Art. And conversation. But what about? I cannot remember. The exalted voice flowed over me. The tall figure, in uncommonly delicate tweed, walked up and down, the voice becoming more resonant, as if he were on a stage. At the climax of some point about the Gaelic revival, he suddenly remembered he must make tea, in fact a new pot, because he had already been drinking tea. The problem was one of emptying out the old tea pot. It was a beautiful pot and he walked the room with the short steps of the aesthete, carrying it in his hand. He came towards me, receded to the bookcase. He swung round the sofa. Suddenly with Irish practicality he went straight to one of the two splendid Georgian windows of the room, opened it, and out went those barren leaves with a swoosh, into Merrion Square – for all I know on to the heads of Lady Gregory, Oliver St John Gogarty and A.E. They were leaves of Lapsang tea.

V. S. Pritchett, *Midnight Oil* (1971)

* * *

And now a picture of the relationship between Yeats and Maud Gonne as beautifully recreated by Orna Ross in A Dance in Time.

So to Dublin, where the poet awaits his muse. He arrives to her hotel, the Crown in Nassau Street, for breakfast on her first morning. They eat together in the morning-room which has an agreeable view northwards over the cricket greens of Trinity College. Careful to keep their voices low so as not to shock the respectables at the tables nearby, they discuss, across eggs and toast, with crumbs falling unheeded onto Willie's waistcoat front, their occult interests.

Afterwards, they stroll together up Kildare Street to be at the National Library of Ireland when it opens at ten. That day and the one following and the next, they pore for several hours over ancient tomes and recent research, progressing their work on their Castle of the Heroes – and the Celtic mysteries that will sustain it. These rituals must, in their main outline, be the work of invisible hands, brought into being not by conscious thought but through invocation and meditation and a holding open of the soul. What this library research fills in are details: Gods and Goddesses, heroes and romantics, objects and symbols that confirm their direction and add substance to the rites.

For eight days they work together. Mr Lyster, the Librarian, is a friend of Willie's father and permits them to work in rooms that are off-limits to others. Thus they have privacy behind their library stacks. Maud is careful to be her most charming and in the afternoons and evenings, they go about very much as a couple, meeting friends and political and literary connections and often, then, back to her hotel for a night-cap. Day, afternoon or evening: there is nothing to impede a declaration. Yet no declaration is forthcoming.

On the ninth morning of her visit, Maud sits to her bureau after breakfast, the dilemma coming between her and her correspondence. Instead of writing, she sits staring out the window, the stub of her pen in her mouth, recalling the previous day when, in handing him a book, she allowed her hand to gently graze his. The touch reached its mark, for he blushed like a girl, but all he did was open the book at the desired page and point her towards what to read.

Contrary boy. So often she has discouraged him; now that she wishes him to speak: nothing.

What is she to do?

She turns to the letters before her: quite a pile, forwarded from France, including a dear little missive from Iseult. A picture fashioned in blue crayon of a tall lady and a little girl, *maman et fille*. They are hand-in-hand beside a bushy green tree with red apples. Underneath she has written in her dear, unformed hand: *Chere Moura, J t'aime. Xxxx Iseult*. Clever girl. Maud has begun her reply – a sketch of the sea-shore at Howth Head where she went walking on Sunday, complete with fish and seagulls – when a knock comes to her hotel-room door.

Opening it, she sees immediately that he is greatly excited. His eyes flash, his fingers clutch each other and he looks more than ever like a skinny, dishevelled demon. Only one thing could bring about such fervour at this hour. 'I went to you last night,' she says, ushering him in. 'Did you find me in your dreams?'

'Yes, yes, that is what I have come to tell you. I woke with the fading vision of your face bending over mine. With the knowledge that you had just … '

'Just … ? Just what? Oh do go on, Mr Yeats.'

'That you had just … kissed me.'

She moves a step closer but still he talks, in his volatile, over-excitable fashion, of how he has often dreamt of kissing her hands, of how once in a dream *she* had kissed *him* but now this was the first time that the kissing had been mutual. She lets him talk, and lets him finish, and lets the ensuing silence grow as she feeds him a look, with eyes open and limpid, for as long as is seemly.

Until such a look can be borne no longer.

The moment passes. 'Come,' she says, a little weary. 'Let us go down for breakfast.'

They spend that morning as they have spent every other morning, in the National Library and in the afternoon they visit the old Fenian leader, James Stephens. All day she is at her most charming and affectionate to him, even in front of others: another change in her that he disdains to notice. In the late evening, when dinner is finished and they are in her room, she moves to try again.

'Let me tell you now what happened last night,' she says. 'When I fell asleep I saw standing at my bedside a great spirit. He took me to a great throng of spirits, and you were among them. All at once, everything got very full of light and I began to see forms and colours more distinctly than I had ever seen them with my ordinary eyes and I knew that I was in the middle not of a dream but a vision. My hands were put into yours and I was told that we were married.'

She pauses, waits.

'Go on,' he says, with vehemence. 'Who told you this? What else was there?'

'I saw enormous multitudes of birds and in the midst was one very beautiful bird wearing a crown, a bird like a great white eagle. By now I was aware that I was out of my body, seeing my body from outside itself. I was brought away by Lugh and my hand was put into yours and I was told that we were married. Then I kissed you.'

She leans forward in her chair, close enough to see the hairs on his face, a small tuft on the underside of his chin that he missed in his morning shave. At least he has stopped wearing that ill-judged beard.

'I kissed you and all became dark. After that I remember nothing. I think we went away together to do some work.'

He assumes the air he always assumes in their most secret, symbolical dealings. 'What were you wearing in this vision?'

'Wearing?'

'Yes, when you came to me?'

'A white dress.'

He frowns. 'In my dream you wore the red dress with the skirt of yellow flowers.'

'I don't attribute much importance to this, do you?'

'In my dream the flowers gradually grew and grew until all else was blotted out.'

She has had enough talk. The moment is come and if he is too shy to initiate it …

Well …

She leans a little more out of her seat, stretches her neck to place her lips on his. There. There, Mr Yeats. Your dream come true. She strengthens the kiss, makes it full and unmistakable in intent. His lips are cool under hers, and unmoving.

How much she has to teach him, about private and public case. He makes life so difficult for himself and all around him. She sits back and opens her eyes to him, expectant, and finds his mouth shocked. Slack. His eyebrows frozen into an unmistakable expression of alarm.

She has misjudged her move. 'You had better leave, Mr Yeats,' she says.

'Miss Gonne ... Please ... '

'I beg of you, do not speak. Go from here.'

'I must –'

'Please, Mr Yeats, I *entreat* you. Put all thoughts of me from you. If you care at all for me, go. Go now.'

Orna Ross, *A Dance in Time* (2008)

✳ ✳ ✳

For a student of literature, what more inspirational city to find yourself in than Dublin? Here's Mary Colum in the early twentieth century ...

A lot of young people must have got off trains in Dublin that autumn day to pass four years as students. One of them, a boy of about my own age, travelling in the same railway carriage, was armed with a large book about Dublin which had pictures of the eighteenth-century squares and the Georgian houses and Dublin Castle and St Patrick's Cathedral. He was to study what, for me then, was a mysterious branch of learning – architecture – and he pointed out to me in a knowledgeable and superior way the points of interest in the picture of St Patrick's and the part of Christ's Church that had been in built in the time Sitric the Dane was king of Dublin. My interest in St Patrick's was that it was Swift's church, where he was buried with the '*saeva indignatio*' epitaph written on his stone, where fierce indignation could tear his heart no more. The boy had his own dream; I had mine, and as for him, a few minutes after he stepped off the train, the Georgian houses he longed to see presented themselves to his gaze, so for me also something of a dream came alive. The drive on an outside car to the university residence house where I was going to live led all over the city from the north to the south side, so I passed through all the well-known streets. But it was not the stately eighteenth-century houses or the statues or Parnell's monument that held my attention. I just noticed them as I went by, but what awoke me to excitement was the figure of a down-at-heel, trampish-looking man walking slowly across O'Connell Bridge with a billboard attached to him back and front – a sandwich man.

On the billboard was printed in large letters on a sort of orange ground a notice that thrilled me so that I nearly fell off the swaying jaunting car: Irish Plays for One Week. *Riders to the Sea*, by J. M. Synge, *Kathleen ni Houlihan*, by W. B. Yeats, *Spreading the News*, by Lady Gregory. My companion on the train was stepping into his beloved squares and streets, but I was stepping right into the Irish Revival. I asked the jarvey to walk his horse slowly so that I could read again the magic names, the magic titles, from the back of the sandwich man. Yeats, Synge ... They might be walking the street that very minute.

Mary Colum, Life and the Dream (1928)

✻ ✻ ✻

... and a young American student of literature, Caitlin Gerrity, visits Dublin in the twenty-first century.

I knew that Ireland had a number of authors undoubtedly celebrated within the culture, but I hardly expected to be constantly surrounded by the evidence of their influence on the country. The house we are staying in for the month we are here is located on the prestigious Merrion Square. If entering our vine-covered Georgian manor with its high ceilings, crown moulding, and sparkling chandeliers for the first time was not overwhelming enough, then realising we live just down the street from Oscar Wilde's former abode certainly made the experience surreal.

On any given day I can stroll down the path in Merrion Square that smells of damp earth, flora, and a hint of tobacco from the sauntering, hand-holding couples who decided Ireland's air is far too clean for them, past the statue of Wilde. He is posed languidly, coolly, with a smug, knowing smile directly across from his former residence. A monument across the path is inscribed with some of his famous, witty quotes. "Who, being loved, is poor?" it asks – who could argue with that. A short walk past the prestigious Trinity College, where boys dressed all in white play cricket on the green, perfectly manicured lawns bring me to Davy Byrne's café, to enjoy a cup of coffee in a place James Joyce frequented.

The constant presence of literary giants of the past and the way they live on in present day Dublin has an astounding effect on the way I perceive myself. Solely to be in a city with such reverence for literature makes me feel more confident in my decision to major in English – a choice I was apt to doubt in America, where how much money you will make with your degree is valued more than whether or not the career it leads you to will truly make you happy. Here, I am reminded of my love of literature on a daily basis, and comforted in my decision to pursue what I truly love by those whose work inspires me – and with whom I happen to share my heritage.

Caitlin Gerrity, 'The Travelling Identity' (2008)

❊ ❊ ❊

While on the subject of Dublin students, here's a passing reminder of one of Trinity College's most famous prod-ucts – the great Jonathan Swift (1667–1745), known to many as Dean Swift, or simply 'the Dean'. Ewan

*McHugh recalls the power of Swift's writing to impress
even a twentieth-century schoolboy.*

On the other side of the bridge we made our way through the
pubs and restaurants of Temple Bar to the entrance to Trinity
College. I may not have known much about Ireland but I knew
about this place. Or, more accurately, I knew about two of its
former students and one of its books.

The first former student, Jonathan Swift, was something of a
rarity among famous Irish writers in that he actually lived and
wrote in Ireland. Most of the others, like Joyce, have tended
to shoot through and then rhapsodise or bitch about the place
from afar. Swift was born in Dublin in 1667, went to England
in 1689 to pursue a political career, but when that was a fizzer
he returned to Ireland and took to religion. He also turned his
pen to political satire and instead of bitching about Ireland he
bitched about the English.

When I was about 13 or 14, an English teacher read my
class a satirical essay of Swift's called 'A Modest Proposal'. In
it he suggested that the English landlords take to eating Irish
babies, since they'd committed every other imaginable atrocity
upon the place. It may be one of the earliest examples of 'biting
satire'. At any rate, I've never forgotten it, particularly because
the language was direct and neither scholarly nor smug.

Evan McHugh, *Pint-Sized Ireland* (2001)

✳ ✳ ✳

*Dublin's student population has long contributed to the
city's character, just as the city has left its mark on the
students who have studied there. Nuala O'Faolain recalls
what life was like for Dublin students in the late fifties.*

I remember Dublin as dark and dramatic then, at the end of the
1950s, the streets drifting with smoke and rain. I see it in my mind's
eye in black and white. Pubs and cafés were thrilling, because light

and warmth spilled from them. The students moved like guer-
rillas around the centre of the city. They walked everywhere. They
borrowed each other's coats. They lent each other books, and ate
egg-and-onion sandwiches and chips with mince sauce and if they
had money, at three o'clock potato cakes came on the menu in
Bewley's. You ate them slowly, a whole pat of butter on each one,
sometimes accompanied by the snuffles of Myles na Gopaleen,
toying with a white pudding on toast at the next table.

Middle-aged or young, city people lived alone in cold bed-
sitters that smelt of gas, with stained curtains, and dripping
bathrooms down lino-covered halls. There were hundreds of
these lairs, and young men and women walking and getting
buses from one to another. Even Trinity students, supposedly
patrolled by proctors, could disappear into a network of rooms
in Kenilworth Square and Waterloo Road and under pavement
level in Leeson Street and up in the attics of Nassau Street and
over the shops in Baggot Street. Couples went into the musty
beds in the afternoons, by silent agreement – she in her jumper
and skirt and suspender belt, he pushing down his trousers
under the blankets. The fumbles led to this and – ugh! ouch! –
that. Buddy Holly serenaded Peggy Sue on the Dansette so that
the fellows playing cards next door wouldn't hear.

Nuala O'Faolain, Are You Somebody? (1996)

✳ ✳ ✳

*Sex, poetry, ambition and poverty – the themes are
continued in Anne Enright's short story, 'The Brat'.
The father of the title's 'brat' is a Dubliner through
and through, steeped in poetry and a complex use of
language that might seem at odds with the difficult
circumstances of his life. He and his daughter, Clare,
are unforgettable Dubliners.*

She was a brat. It wasn't that she was good-looking – she could
be, but she wasn't. She wore her ugliness like a badge. Her

clothes were tight in all the worst places, but she pushed her body forward as she spoke. She had fat arms and small breasts. She wore bovver boots and cheap pink cotton trousers. She was all wrong. Her eyebrows were plucked bare and a thin, brown line was pencilled in over the stubble. There was a flicker in her eye that told you she knew that she was being watched, and every gesture took on the slight edge of performance. It made her unpopular, except with new acquaintances, whom she seduced casually and then annoyed.

Clare was fifteen. She had been drunk once in her life, with a girl from school who had filled two pint glasses with the top of every bottle on her parents' cupboard. They drank it all in one go and Clare noticed nothing until she sat down in the bus and discovered that her legs were numb. The rest of the night was spent throwing up in the queue for a toilet, and kissing a boy who took her home. When she woke up her eyes were swollen, and her father had left without his breakfast.

Clare's father makes his way from the Customs House to O'Beirne's on the Quays, crosses the Liffey by means of a bridge, so sited as to add to the distance between the two buildings a length of nearly three hundred yards.

'If I could swim now, I'd be right.' He is a man much given to speaking aloud when company is absent, and to silence when the nicer of social obligations might urge him into speech. Those contributions he does make are as counterpoint to the sounds of liquid consumption only, the sweetest of which is the sound of a pint drawing creamily at the bar, a music only those born with the gift, or those who spend a minimum of three thousand hours acquiring the gift, can hear.

O'Donnell was doubly blessed. He was born with a magic thumb, the sucking of which enabled him to discern the music of a good pint from the discord of a bad, before a head had even begun to form; but being a man of diligence and application (those same qualities which, combined with tenacity, ensured his promotion to the rank of Under-Manager, Grade Two of Dublin Corporation, Sanitation Section, despite the vagaries of political influence, which was never behind him, the unenlightened reservations of his superiors, cognisant as they were of his talents, and thence careful of their own interests and tenure, and the constant whingeing begrudgery of his fellow workers, craven in the envy of a magnitude only the true culchie could muster, with the smell of dung still clinging to their boots, the stripes of the diocesan fathers still stinging their palms and the sly post-colonialism still giving the edge of flattery to every utterance of a personal nature that crossed their lips), he distrusted the gifts of nature and concentrated the subtle power of his intelligence on discerning, without the aid of his cool, Fenian thumb, that crystalline hum, that black, creamy noise, of a pint just waiting to be drunk.

The river is at an ebb, its green is black in the early evening. 'It's not green. See?' he says to a passing young woman, who ignores both him and the complexity of his literary allusion. He pivots his body and fixes his eyes on her receding back, its cheap, smart blue coat, her black hair and the hurried motion of her tights, with a pattern of skin disease, arranged in bows along the seam.

'Golden stockings she had on,' he says loudly, in the interests of the general good. A sharp sniff, and the air stings his nose, outside and in. Three fingers he counts, tapping them one after the other on the interstice of his right nostril.

'Most high, most pure, most sweet … ' Black hair, blue coat, and flesh-coloured legs – don't forget the bows. He stands, swaying slightly against the flood of people crossing the river to the northside of the city and strains to hear the broken clack of her shoes on the pavement. He sees her opening cans in a bedsit in Drumcondra. The shoes are loose, and a raw, reddened heel emerges at every step.

'There will be peace in the valley,' he assures her and all the other backs now interrupting his view of her, as a benediction, then turns to square himself against the tide.

'I wouldn't spit now,' he says, 'at a pint. If it was handed to me.' He was a man who could not abide spit.

O'Donnell avoids the snug in O'Beirne's, likely as it is to contain Elements. He takes his place with the dockers at the bar.

'Stevedores.'

There is no need for another word, his order is known. The brown suit strains tightly against the yoke of his back as he places the elbows, long stained with old porter, carefully on two beer-mats equidistant from the apex of his nose. His head is loosely cupped in two large hands.

'There's one for the drip,' says the barman, slapping a mat under the point of his snout. O'Donnell stares at the wood of the counter, his feet broadly placed on the brass rail. His air could be interpreted as one of dignified rebuke.

'Larry,' he says, from the cavern of his crouched torso, 'would you ever hinge that elbow in the way God intended.' And not wishing to disturb the barman by his tone, he adds the phrase, 'he says,' to allow a proper distance from the remark.

'Does he so?' says Larry, and places a small preliminary Bushmills on the central mat.

After many hours of similar silences, the air is punctuated by the word 'Nevermore'.

The barman gives the wink to a man in the snug, the long-suffering recipient of countless memos on the subject of parking meters: the cleaning thereof, embellished in O'Donnell's hand by the appropriate quotations from Latin.

'So they finally gave the old codger the push, eh?' The final syllable is terse, sympathetic, way-of-the-worldish; harsh, without interrogative cadence or function.

'Resigned, Larry. For God's sake, the word is "resigned".' He saluted the barman with his pint, and with one finger he taps, three times, on the interstice of his left nostril.

Clare was late home again. A boy came up to her at the dance and started asking questions. 'How are you?' 'What did the Da say?' It was the one she had kissed some weeks before and she found herself answering quite sweetly because of the shame she felt. She must have told him everything. 'You were crying,' he told her, 'and you said that you wanted to die.'

'I wanted to throw up,' she said.

'You did.'

'Well, that didn't stop you, anyway.'

'Shush,' he said, although the music was making them shout, and she started to kiss him again.

He had a good, strong accent and spoke very carefully. When the slow songs came on he just stood back and looked at her face. They only kissed again when the music changed.

Apart from that he had green eyes. 'Don't fucking worry about me,' Clare said, 'I'm clever.'

'I know you're clever.'

'My father is clever.'

'My Da's an arsehole,' he said. 'So what?' He was like a doctor, he asked questions that no one else asked. Whatever it was that made him sad made him kind as well and so she took her sympathy. He was a nice man. She felt obliged to tell him things, like she would tell any unicorn she met in the street.

Clare's father was sitting in front of the television when she got home, with his eyes closed. He looked away from her when she came in, and examined the curtains. 'Words,' he said, 'are for the radio. They should have stuck to silent films. Where were you?'

'Where were you?' she asked back.

'Your mother never left, you now … ' his voice trailed after her as she left the room, 'you have her accusatory tone to perfection.'

There was a smell in the house. Clare had never realised that the disinfectants, the carpet cleaners, the plastic boxes that were hung up in the toilet did any good. She had hated their stink, like an industrial version of all the fluids, lotions, perfumes and bath-salts that made it her mother's house. A stink of unnecessary work and hours spent in front of the mirror, of cleaning windows in pink fluffy slippers, of fits of hysteria when towels were folded the wrong way. Now the kitchen smelt of old fat, the hall of damp and urine, her bedroom of clothes come out of the rain, like the top deck of the bus on a bad morning.

She went across to pull the curtains and was shocked to see that the boy was still outside, his arms folded and leaning on top of the wall. He saw her, smiled and walked away.

Her brother came into the room, and she let the curtain drop. 'The old man got the sack,' he said. 'Where were you?'

Your honour, on this, the second occasion, the victim spent some hours with the accused outside her house. Interglottal activity was engaged upon and some saliva was exchanged. The couple embraced warmly and muscular tissue from the sacral region to the crown of the head was palpated. This was followed by both visual and tactile exploration of the upper limbs and face of the accused and there was a Verbal Exchange. On the evening in question the victim had his back to a wall and indentations made from the ornamental gravel in his buttocks and upper back took thirty minutes to diffuse.

A girl from up the road told Clare that she had seen her mother in town, walking down the street 'and Dressed To Kill'.

Kill what?

It was on the third occasion that the alleged murder took place. I will not offend the court with details save that there were several breaks for cigarettes, which were smoked in a car, the windows of which, much to the amusement of the accused, became steamed up, in the manner of comic sketches which can be seen from time to time on the television set. I have the assurance of the victim that no reproductive processes were engaged, although they were vigorously and callously primed by the frotteur.

(Objection your honour! The term 'frottage' implies guilt, I will not have my client tried by lexiphanicism, at the hands of a coprolalomaniac!)

(Objection sustained.) The appalling psychological damage suffered by the victim even before the fatal blow was struck, can only be imagined, and in happier times this frustration of biology might be viewed in the light which it deserves and sentence passed commensurate with the enormity of the crime.

He had left school young. He had a car and a job. He had taken his hand off the wheel and crossed his middle finger over his index and said 'I'm like that. You see? You can trust me. I'm like that.' The streetlamp outside the house made slits of his eyes, and Clare was shocked by the freedom she took. She was violent and tender and made herself cry again. He absorbed it all without surprise.

At three o'clock in the morning, she heard the sound of a dog barking and her father's voice. He was walking down the street with a Jack Russell at his heel. As she watched she saw that he was not kicking the dog but playing with it. He emerged from Mrs Costello's forsythia bush with only a few leaves in his hands, but he threw them defiantly, shouting 'Fetch!' The dog was confused and he bent down over it. Then he straightened up and addressed the street and its dog, in the grand manner: 'Bitch!' He buttoned up his coat and walked on.

'That's the old man,' she said to the boy in the car, who smiled.

'Does he have a shotgun?'

Clare had never seen her father look monumental. He staggered in and out of the light from the streetlamp and she lost all sympathy. He was not in any way normal.

'You should see mine on a good night,' said the boy in the car. He straightened his jumper.

'Do you want to go?'

Mr O'Donnell reached the car and vented a stream of buff-coloured puke on the bonnet, which was fresh and decorative against the biscuit-brown of the paint-work and the chrome. His meditation on the effect was disturbed by the cognisance that the vehicle was occupied and by intimations of a possible unpleasantness to come. He hinged his torso into the upright and carefully aligned the cuffs of his shirt below the line of his coat-sleeves, a gesture he had admired in his long observation of the British Royal Family, and one he reserved for the petty and the punctilious. His relief on finding the face that peered out from behind the windscreen familiar, mitigated to a great extent the indignation he felt on finding that she was not alone: that uncomfortably close to his daughter was a hairy young skelp. The contrasting paleness of his daughter's countenance, and the bar of shadow that fell from the framework of the car and caressed her mouth, made his throat constrict alarmingly, and the tragedy of generation burst in his chest. This was the entrance to eternity. No sound or movement greeted his thoughts as they took wing, but beneath his hand he could sense the dormant miracle of the internal combustion engine, and above his head stars, that had seen the continents rip, one from the other, wheeled and waited the light years it would take before they could witness his shame. He stood back. The moment called out for expression. With the flat of his palm, he banged the bonnet of the car.

' "I will tell you.

The barge she sat in, like a burnish'd throne,
Burn'd on the water; the poop was beaten gold,
Purple the sails, and so perfumed, that

The winds were love-sick with them, the oars were silver
Which to the tune of flutes kept stroke, and made
The water which they beat to follow faster,
As amorous of their strokes. For her own person,
It beggar'd all description ... " '

＊

And so beggar'd, he left the lovers, opened the gate with a creak
and entered his house.

Clare came into the kitchen at four o'clock in the morning
and found her father sitting at the kitchen table. There was
a smell of drink in the room but she couldn't see any bottles.
The record player in the living room was left on and the record
on the turntable was finished. The sound of the needle going
round and round reminded her of the scene in the car and the
feeling in her insides.

'Your mother never left, you know. You have her guilty look
to perfection.'

She left her father where he was and went into her room
where she took down all the posters and started to write on the
walls. She wrote all the poems from the school curriculum so
that she would be able to study them every night, and so know
them off by heart.

'Had I the heavens' embroidered cloths.'

'Golden stockings she had on.'

'I wonder, by my troth, what thou and I
Did till we loved?'

No more dancing. On the other wall, she copied all her theo-
rems and the basic laws of Physics. Then she lay on the bed and
promised herself that she would not sleep for three days and
three nights before she closed her eyes and cried.

Anne Enright, 'The Brat', from *The Portable Virgin* (1991)

* * *

Dublin's profoundly literary culture, ensuring that even the O'Donnells of the city had a mind shaped by poetry, produced some of the greatest writers of the twentieth century. Although he chose to leave Dublin for mainland Europe, James Joyce's work focuses almost entirely on Dublin and, of all the writers associated with the city, he is the one whose presence is inescapable. As Joseph O'Connor points out in this next extract, the ghost of Joyce haunts the city ... and yet he can't help feeling sorry for him.

Freud said that the Irish were the only race who could not be psychoanalysed, because they were too much given to fantasy. And certainly, in Ireland, things which are not there are often much more important than things which are. Joyce's work reverberates with this knowledge. It is full of phantoms, apparitions, people who are not there any more. It is full of ghosts. Many of the most important characters in his work are dead. Parnell in *The Portrait of the Artist*, and 'Ivy Day In The Committee Room.' Young Rudy Bloom and old Paddy Dignam in *Ulysses*. Poor Georgina Burns and Michael Fury in 'The Dead.' And the spectre of Stephen's heart-scalded mother, so much more scary in death than she ever was in life.

Similarly, the ghost of Joyce is much more terrifying than anything he actually did, or wrote. I read *Ulysses* again recently and I mentioned this to a young Irish novelist I know. 'Oh really,' he said. 'Is it any good?'

It was a joke, I think. But it was an interesting question too. Is *Ulysses* any good? It's important, yes. It's a milestone, a turning point in twentieth-century fiction. But is it any good?

The problem for those of us who write 'Irish' fiction is that Joyce is so frequently described in superlatives. The greatest, the deepest, the most obsessive, the craziest, the funniest. He is always there, the line goes, always peeking over your shoulder, the monolithic spectacular superstar Joyce who tore up the rulebook and wrote the novel out of existence. But the notion that young Irish writers are lying awake in their beds worrying about James Joyce or Irish history is simply untrue. Young Irish writers are busy telling stories, writing sentences, busy with the grim and unglamorous work of writing fiction which says something to readers about their lives. When they are not doing this, they are worried about their German publishing rights, and who is making the movie of their first novel, and will the tax-free scheme for artists remain in place even under a Progressive Democrat government. For a young writer now, James Joyce is probably the biggest irrelevance in a history that is best ignored.

He left UCD, announcing that he was going off on the mail boat to forge the uncreated conscience of his race. It must have raised quite a laugh in the student bar at the time. Certainly, these days, if there is one single young Irish writer who thinks that he or she is forging uncreated historical consciences then I haven't met them, and I'm really not sure I'd want to.

Who can honestly say that if they met the snobbish, arrogant, prematurely aged Stephen Dedalus of *The Portrait of the Artist* they would have had any fun with him? Who can say that *Ulysses* does not contain long excruciating sections of unadulterated tedium? And as for his last book, 'I've even read *Finnegans Wake*,' says a character in an Aidan Matthews short story, 'although, admittedly, that was for charity.'

Modern Irish writers want to forget about Irish history. But Joyce tried to get vengeance on it, 'Oh Ireland, my first and only love,' he raged, 'where Christ and Caesar are hand in glove.' But modern Ireland has got its own back. Joyce is not a writer any more. He is a celebrity, a fitting subject for witty anecdotes and gas stories on chatshows. He appears on our postcards, on our stamps, on our banknotes, on T-shirts usually sold in the duty-free section of Irish airports. The last thing you will see, as you emigrate from an Irish airport, is a poster of James Joyce. He appears everywhere, but not, interestingly, on the leaving certificate English course, never mind the history curriculum. He is celebrated in summer schools and quoted by our political leaders, which latter phenomenon is almost always an accurate signifier of a writer whose work is rarely read by the general public any more. There is a statue of him in Saint Stephen's Green, and another one on the campus at UCD, just across from the new coffee bar, which has recently been renamed, in tribute I suppose, 'Finnegans Break.' There are Joyce key rings and boxer shorts and shaving mugs. Dublin pubs and restaurants and hotels are called after his characters. You will always know a really lousy Dublin pub, in fact, because it will be called after somebody in *Ulysses*, and have a faded poster of Georgian Doors sellotaped to the wall behind the bar.

So I feel sorry for James Joyce. When his friend Samuel Beckett wished the terrible curse of an honoured name on his enemies, he had a point. Joyce is respectable now. He is safer than de Valera ever was. He is beyond criticism. The extraordinary young visionary has become the grand old man of modern Irish writing.

Joseph O'Connor, *The Secret World of the Irish Male* (1994)

✳ ✳ ✳

So, a closer look at what Ulysses – *Joyce's great 'song' to Dublin – is really about. First, briefly, from well-known writer and broadcaster Frank Delaney.*

Ulysses is James Joyce's incantation to, for and of Dublin. It was designed by him as a detailed account of ordinary life on an ordinary Dublin day, and he planned each movement of each character on each street as though he were playing chess. He placed them in houses he knew, drinking in pubs he had frequented, walking on cobblestones he retraced. He made the very air of Dublin, the atmosphere, the feeling, the place, almost indistinguishable, certainly inseparable, from his human characters – Dublin *is* a character in *Ulysses*, the "womanicity" with her skirts lifted. [...] A journey through its pages is a glistening, aromatic, atmospheric voyage in the company of believable, likeable, culpable human beings with ordinary vices, virtues and traits – recognisable people, comic, tragic, vulnerable, uncertain, carnal, aggressive, defensive, passionate, aloof, romantic, cynical.

At its simplest – dare I use the word! – *Ulysses* is a story of some random ramblings through a large part of Dublin on a single day, Thursday, 16th June, 1904. Paths cross and criss-cross, characters pass by each other, knowingly and unknowingly. They greet, ignore, applaud and insult each other – their lives and the life of the city intermingle naturally and normally in the teeming streets. They are not remarkable people in any late-twentieth-century media-gilded way; few of these citizens would ever make the newspaper columns except by the announcement of a birth, marriage or death. But they are credible in their ordinariness, comic and tragic in their predicament and monumentally luminous, illuminating in their humanity. In the personalities of Leopold Bloom and his heaving wife Molly, Stephen Dedalus (Joyce himself at the age of twenty-two, the age he left Dublin) and various other assorted characters, Joyce drew, as he set out to, a map of human nature, a map whose symbols are everyday incidents, joys, tragedies, encounters, disappointments, boastings, betrayals, laughter and pain ...

Frank Delaney, *James Joyce's Odyssey* (1981)

✳ ✳ ✳

And now a more thorough exploration: the great Joyce enthusiast, Senator David Norris, is interviewed by Mark Harkin for the hundredth anniversary of the day on which Ulysses *is set.*

Every year in Dublin on 16 June, people celebrate James Joyce's 1922 novel, *Ulysses*, by re-enacting the journey of its central characters, Leopold Bloom and Stephen Dedalus. With many participants dressed in Edwardian period costume, the day has an eccentric, circus-like quality to it. The precise setting of the novel is 16 June 1904, so this year promises to be the most extravagant celebration yet.

Many might be tempted to ask why. The novel features one day in Dublin at a time when it was a depressed regional city of the United Kingdom. Nothing very extraordinary happens to its characters: Stephen Dedalus, a recently bereaved young man with a poorly-paid teaching job, gets drunk with medical students and then has a violent encounter with British soldiers; Leopold Bloom, an early precursor of the media sales executive, attends a funeral in Glasnevin, calls in to his newspaper office, has lunch in Davy Byrne's, gets into a row with some dreaded Dublin 'characters' and meets up with Stephen later on.

On the face of it it's hardly the sort of material that would light up the eyes of a commissioning editor in any publishing company. Readers who have cast this tome aside after the first couple of chapters constitute the majority of those who have picked up the book in the first place. 'Difficult' and 'boring' are the chief reasons for failing to finish. And yet this novel has stood the test of time, towering over modern literature, inspiring generations of lesser mortals. The question is 'why'?

One of Joyce's most vociferous and eloquent advocates in Ireland is Senator David Norris, former lecturer at the English department in Trinity College Dublin. For him, *Ulysses* is a constant source of wonder and celebration: 'It's probably the greatest novel written in the 20th century – certainly in English – and one of the greatest works of the creative imagination ever. It's a great humane, comic novel, which endorses wonderfully human values and celebrates the ordinary man.'

The ordinary man in this instance is Leopold Bloom. The title of the book derives from the Latin name of Homer's hero, Odysseus; every episode of Bloom's day corresponds to an event in Homer's *Odyssey*, thus making heroic an ordinary man's progress through mundane reality. One of the episodes in *Ulysses*, which Senator Norris points to as central to the construction of Bloom's heroism, is the protagonist's encounter with the barroom republican, the Citizen. Here, Bloom's argument against a myopic, bigoted world-view corresponds to Odysseus's strike against the one-eyed monster, the Cyclops. In the midst of a heated debate on world politics, Bloom states: 'It's no use ... force, history, hatred, all that. That's not life for men and women, insult and hatred ... Everybody knows that it's the very opposite of that that is really life ... Love.'

Senator Norris reads this statement as still depressingly relevant to Ireland today: 'It's the kind of message that we, in this country, are very slowly and painfully beginning to learn. Bloom is right: insult, injury, revenge, hatred – all these things are pointless and enmesh people in endless feuds and bloodshed. To understand the common humanity of people, struggling to make their relationships, their homes and families, to survive and create social networks and an understanding of the arts ... I think Joyce's message in that is very clear.'

Norris refers to the characters of *Ulysses* as 'down-at-heel Dubliners'. None of these people are prospering. As Norris explains, this was directly connected with Joyce's life in 1904: 'He was at the nadir of his experience in 1904. He'd been summoned home by his father's famous telegram – *Mother dying. Come home. Father.* – to linger around Dublin while she died in great distress of cancer of the liver. The father had drunk them into abject poverty, so life was very painful. Joyce somehow managed to cauterise these personal wounds, and out of that unpromising material gave us one of the great celebrations of the human spirit.

Bloom's defence of love against the forces of brutality is integral to the overall message of *Ulysses*. At the heart of the hero's experience of love is his thoroughly imperfect marriage to Molly, which is depicted with unflinching candour. Part of what makes *Ulysses* different to the novels which preceded it is that it shows the entire physical reality of what it means to inhabit a human body – eating, sweating, urinating, defecating, masturbating, copulating, etc. Joyce shies away from nothing in this snapshot of Leopold and Molly's life together. With their moribund sex-life and respective infidelities, the couple's situation is far from ideal, yet this imperfection is crucial to *Ulysses*'s theme, as Norris explains: 'Joyce doesn't expect people to be heroic in the ordinary sense. He's quite unlike D.H.Lawrence – in order to succeed as a hero in Lawrence's fiction, you have to be a very considerable sexual athlete. Leopold Bloom survives, but he hasn't had complete sexual intercourse with his wife in over eleven years, and he ends up, at the conclusion of the novel, upside down in her bed.'

In the middle of *Ulysses*, Molly Bloom has sex with a concert promoter, Blazes Boylan, while Leopold Bloom masturbates at Sandymount Strand, leering at Gertie McDowell. And yet, in spite of this sad and sordid carry-on, Mr and Mrs Bloom continue to meditate with affection on their pre-marital courtship. Senator Norris identifies a kind of union which transcends their current relationship difficulties: 'On the night of the day she has committed adultery with Blazes Boylan, she thinks about him almost as a kind of sex toy – 'that big red thing' – whereas she reflects on Bloom to the extent that Bloom is the last man in her thoughts as her eyes close in sleep. She thinks about him, that day in Howth, when they lay on the rhododendrons and savoured their first kiss ... it's the only moment in the novel where there is a shared experience, a kind of communion. Bloom also thinks about *kissing* Molly in the Lestrygonians episode, where exactly the same language system is used. There is a real meeting, not just of their bodies but also of their spirits.'

It is fitting that *Ulysses* should end on a note of romantic affection as Joyce chose its date according to his own courtship with Nora Barnacle. Norris explains: 'Joyce met Nora in a casual encounter in the street on 10 June 1904, and this led to him going walking with her on 16 June, just under a week later on the strand at Irishtown / Ringsend. From that, the romance blossomed and they eloped, which was quite a risk for Nora Barnacle. That date impressed itself on Joyce's mind and he celebrated it by making it the day on which he offered to the world a reduction of Homer's *Odyssey*.'

While most critics acknowledge *Ulysses*'s greatness, some wonder if it effectively 'finished' the novel, making anything 'new' impossible. Senator Norris has little time for such doom-laden theories: 'As to whether it's possible to write a good novel after *Ulysses*, Joyce went on and made it worse by writing *Finnegan's Wake*, and he left a mushroom cloud hanging over Irish writing. But after *Finnegan's Wake*, Joyce told a friend of mine that he was going to write something new and simple, about the sea. So why can't they do that? Human nature is inexhaustible. I'm not a mathematician, but once you go over seven items, the number of permutations and combinations gets pretty vast. Within the vast resources of the English language and the human situation, there's quite a lot you can write.'

What about the spawn of *Ulysses*, the fiendishly difficult novels that came in its wake decades after, those which weren't really worth the reader's effort? 'The dog is not responsible for its fleas,' answers Norris.

With all the controversy over *Ulysses* and the massive Bloomsday celebration to come this year, there seems a danger that this one novel will overshadow Joyce's entire oeuvre. *Dubliners* and *A Portrait of the Artist* were groundbreaking works in their day, yet now seem no more than an athlete's warm-up before the main event. Not so, according to Norris: 'Well, of course, I think Joyce wrote one enormously long treatise on humanity, which is *Dubliners*, *A Portrait*, *Ulysses* and *Finnegan's Wake*, and it's a continuous expansion. You can almost predict *Finnegan's Wake* from *Ulysses*, with its wonderfully subtle use of verbal patterning and so on. *Dubliners* is an immensely sophisticated book, considering the youth of the author. I think one of the reasons *Ulysses* has taken over is that it's difficult enough to be regarded as a Mount Everest, but at the same time it has been scaled by various mountaineers in the past, and now more and more people are doing it, so it's almost becoming a tourist destination. On top of that, a scandalous and controversial aura has attached itself to it – that's attractive to people and has led to its celebrity. Then of course it revolves around a particular day and that wonderfully romantic story, so it's become a kind of Dublin and international fiesta, so for all those reasons it has achieved a kind of pre-eminence, but it should not be allowed to eclipse the works on either side of it.'

Mark Harkin / Senator David Norris,
'James Joyce's *Ulysses*: Why the Fuss?' (2004)
www.threemonkeysonline.com

✳ ✳ ✳

Is Dublin's annual celebration of Bloomsday just a tacky tourist event? – or does it go deeper? Brian Lalor, general editor of The Encyclopaedia of Ireland *and himself an author, takes us around typical Bloomsday activities, the silly and the serious, the exhausting and the excellent, and reflects upon the value of this yearly literary carnival.*

Under a pale blue sky and against a backdrop of the ruffled grey waters of Dublin Bay, smartly dressed church-going couples hurry along the seafront at Sandycove, anxious not to be late for the service. Men in striped blazers, white ducks and straw boaters, women with pleated ankle-length skirts, lace blouses, flat, flowered hats and pale gloves, accompanied by children in sailor-suits all stride purposefully southwards, the shipping in the bay behind, trudging remorselessly in and out of the port, seeming to belong to a more mundane world. Each earnest soul carries underarm a thick and well-thumbed tome, a book of common prayer, missal or church hymnal. The chapel of ease which the crowd is approaching looks like no ordinary church, the featureless granite exterior wall sloping gently upwards to a high and bevelled parapet, already busy with heads bobbing in the early-morning light. This is the Joyce Tower at Sandycove, the volumes carried by the crowd are tattered copies of *Ulysses*, the occasion Bloomsday. [...]

My feelings about Bloomsday are ambiguous. Being a reader of Joyce rather than a worshipper, I usually dip my toe into the Bloomsday festivities, but balk at the obligatory Edwardian music-hall garb and prescribed pork kidneys for breakfast. This year I decided to succumb to total immersion; 16 June is both a Sunday and a day of glorious and uninterrupted sunshine, ideal for perambulations. At 8.30 the Martello Tower is already busy. [...]

The interior spaces of the Tower are small and tortuous (like being on the inside of a gorgonzola cheese), designed for the accommodation of a small garrison, armament supplies, a powder magazine. The rooms – sparse, functional and austere – have been overcome by Joycean memorabilia: the writer's embroidered waistcoat, his cane, correspondence and books. A tableau on the first floor, like a stage set, recreates the room as originally occupied by Gogarty, Trench and Joyce. On Bloomsday it is hardly possible to move between the bodies and exhibits, or communicate up and down the duodenum-like spiral staircase. [...]

In the centre of the gun-emplacement at the flagstaff / chimney, Barry McGovern, celebrated interpreter of Beckett, prepares for his reading [...] many of his audience following him in their own copies. Elegant-suited and waistcoated young men who look as if they might be more normally studying the Dow Index are absorbed in their texts. All around to the horizon, the sea now sparkles and the sky begins to brighten; the idea of holding a reading up in the air and enclosed only by sea and sky on a day of summer sunshine transforms the claustrophobic and often subversive-seeming atmosphere of many literary readings into something life-affirming and joyful; for such a life-affirmer as Joyce, this could hardly be more appropriate. [...]

Allegra and I feel the need for food, and follow the straw boaters back along the Sandycove seafront to the South Bank Restaurant, where a Joycean breakfast has been available since 6.30 in the morning. I ask a passing waitress, 'Did anybody come at 6.30?' She looks at me wearily, 'Oh, yes. Germans.' As we arrive, nineteenth-century parlour songs with piano accompaniment are being delivered. By the time we have been served with lavish plates of animal organs and puddings, a two-handed reading of the pub encounter between Bloom, the odious Citizen and his wretched dog, Garryowen, is in full progress. Somewhat later, a woman in period outfit who had been among the congregation at the Tower becomes Molly Bloom, and improbably exposes her most intimate thoughts to a roomful of hungry breakfasting strangers. *Ulysses* may be all things to all men, but I doubt that its contents are appropriate to every occasion, ' ... and yes I said yes I will Yes.' I thought rather, 'not while I am eating my pork kidneys, please.' [...]

I pass into Bewley's and go upstairs to the Café-museum (an archive of catering-trade memorabilia), where a reading of the Nighttown episode of *Ulysses* is about to take place.

The audience is composed of devotees: a German scholarly type with a fistful of papers, furiously taking notes even before the performance has begun; an undoubtedly American academic, deadly earnest, rapt in attention; a motley crowd of students, tourists, the curious, myself. The actors are lined up before the counter, facing the audience. Behind the counter a waitress stands, bored by the proceedings, her expression vacant.

The performers, a group of actors in period costume, each take a number of parts: prostitutes, the Madame, Bloom, Stephen, the soldiers, the crowd, Edy Boardman, a holly bush. The dialogue is fast and funny, well delivered with appropriate accents. German and American scholars are captivated, pencils poised, suppliants at the shrine. Behind the counter the waitress has woken up and is laughing heartily. The funnier the performance, the more she tries to stifle her giggles, yet more solemn become the listeners. Eventually, heaving with amusement and suppressed laughter, the waitress stuffs her apron in her mouth and disappears beneath the counter. The reading over, audience and academics applaud enthusiastically. The waitress resumes her post, her face suffused with pleasure. She has discovered Joyce. [...]

Despite the mammoth breakfast of inner organs at Sandycove, lunch (or a drink) beckons, and I move across the street to Davy Byrne's pub where Leopold Bloom paused in his 1904 rambles for a glass of Burgundy and a gorgonzola sandwich; the same fare is available for Bloomsday, in tandem with the conventional supply of pints and bulging triangular ham sandwiches served with enough English mustard to give the eater heart failure. In the dark interior, pub life is as usual: drinkers undisturbed by any particular date on the calendar hover expectantly over their pints in earnest conversation. I dutifully order my Burgundy and gorgonzola and place myself at the rear of the pub, where I have an appointment to meet some other journeyers. The Duke Street doors are wide open, the pub bouncers solidly silhouetted against the brightness outside; passers-by appear and vanish abruptly in the golden opening.

In the rear room of Davy Byrne's, a woman in a large feathered hat, whom I had not previously noticed, stands up from one of the tables. She seems ill at ease as she tentatively addresses the customers: quite clearly some of these people are not aware that it is Bloomsday; possibly they have never heard of Joyce. After some hesitation the woman – 'Molly' again, I presume – produces some letters from her crocodile-skin handbag. I am mistaken: this is not Molly Bloom but her alter ego, Nora Barnacle, who then proceeds to read out loud in a public bar the real letters written to her in intimacy by her actual lover, James Joyce.

The lunch-time crowd in Davy Byrne's are not impressed by this tabloid exposé; they have been talking about the prospects of Noble Lady winning the 4.15 at Down Royal, with Tim Tracy up; Ireland's chances in the World Cup; the latest Walrus and Carpenter quadrille of Northern Ireland's politicians. Jim's outpourings to Nora are not welcome. A thin man wearing a grimy woollen cap, with a grubby cigarette-butt permanently attached to his lower lip like an offensive mole, takes umbrage at the delivery. His voice intrudes on the reading like the hiss of a disturbed python.

'Would you feck off to the stage of the Abbey The-atre with your fecking oratorio, missus. I'm on me lunchbreak – this is a fecking bar, not a lit-ter-rary meeting.'

Undaunted, Nora reads on. Two young men in blazers and boaters appear, possibly a supporting cast of Jim and Gogarty. The objector decides, correctly, that a song would end the reading, and growls out a few bars of a tuneless 'The Oul Triangle'. Instantly the barman intervenes. 'That will do, Tony, the young lady is entitled to give her recimitation.' [...]

North Great George's Street is only a few streets away from Bloom's house [7 Eccles Street, now demolished]. The James Joyce Cultural Centre, rival omphalos to the Sandycove Tower, has been busy all day with similarly appropriate events. By the time we arrive there in the afternoon, it is closing to prepare for the night's Bloomsday Ball, a £60-a-head, costume affair. At this juncture, foiled by a closed door, I feel that a rest is required. I do not think that I can listen to another 'Stately plump Buck Mulligan' without violently attacking the speaker. [...]

The Mansion House, residence of Dublin's Lord Mayor, has also been busy throughout the day with Bloomsday events. The evening's offerings are musical interpretations of Joyce's period, Edwardian songs, both the appropriate and the banal. One group of songs, part of a song-cycle by Maureen Charlton, takes Jim and Nora to a further plane of encounter, and comments wittily on the period. Alas, there was much of the banal from other contributors. This is the point at which Bloomsday might be decently abandoned, as the event nose-dives into the anything-will-do bracket of bad poetry, inaudible delivery and uncomfortable chairs.

The Mansion House is deserted in favour of a sprint around the corner to Buswells Hotel, where more serious business is in progress. Gathered in a darkened room (with two doors to the bar) are assembled the hard men of Bloomsday, serious Joyceans, reading *Ulysses* with passion and cunning. Instead of, as in our previous port of call, people talking about Joyce, here are those who know his work intimately: David Rose, director of the Oscar Wilde Autumn School, poised to be painted by Whistler; Robert Nicholson, curator of the James Joyce Museum, in impeccable if slightly raffish whites. We might have been in the *Els Quatre Gats*, circa 1900, young Picasso intense in the corner, Erik Satie drunk under a table. People from the floor go to the front of the room and read their selected pages; the main performance is a simultaneous English / French reading with thunderous (French) piano accompaniment. All this is delivered with extraordinary gusto and involvement, the proximity of the bar enormously assisting delivery. The Edwardian clothing, previously dapper, is now decidedly frayed. Straw boaters lie in piles like empty biscuit tins, bonnets are askew, bow ties have swivelled under the ear. One of the readers goes round with a bowler hat, soliciting contributions to pay for the room. We stagger out through the bar into the night, vastly relieved – Ms Bloom had not been mentioned. [...]

In recent years critics have begun to lament that the phenomenon of Bloomsday is in danger of trivialising Joyce's work, that honouring his achievements is becoming submerged in fancy-dress parades and farce. Never! Without doubt the trivia abounds, yet what is more important is that Bloomsday has wrested *Ulysses* and *Finnegans Wake* from the exclusive possession of scholarship, and brought them a wide and appreciative readership. All the end-of-Bloomsday crowd, irrespective of the amount of drink taken, know both their *Ulysses* and their Dublin. Joyce's work is being celebrated for his love of language and affirmation of life's multiplicity, his image of Dublin confirmed by reciprocity. There are few themes in current Irish life which Joyce failed to touch on; the language, culture, humour and foibles of his fellow citizens have totally changed, yet changed not at all.

Brian Lalor, *The Laugh of Lost Men* (1997)

✳ ✳ ✳

Another Dublin literary ghost is that of poet Patrick Kavanagh (1905–1967). Though coming from rural Ireland (as a young man he regularly walked the 80 miles or so to Dublin to meet leading literary figures there), the second half of his life was spent in the capital. You can sit beside him in sculpted but life-like form on a bench overlooking the canal. Poet Eavan Boland introduces us to the great man himself.

I met Patrick Kavanagh in a café at the end of Grafton Street in Dublin. It was the middle sixties. He was within two years or so of his death. I sat at a small table, facing the door which opened out onto the street. I could see shop fronts and passersby. He sat with his back to the street: a man in early old age, wearing a coat and spectacles and a soft felt hat. I doubt if we talked for more than half an hour, forty minutes at the most.

In a simple sense, he was a man trying to eat his lunch in peace on a winter afternoon. I was callow enough to introduce myself; he was courteous enough to show no surprise and no irritation. I remember some details clearly; others have faded. I remember he wore a soft felt hat at a rakish angle. But his coat will not come clear in my memory. It might have been a gabar-dine raincoat. Then again I may have reinvented that from familiar photographs. I do remember that we ate hamburgers, which were then still new in Dublin. They were served on green plastic plates, on a dimpled paper napkin. As Kavanagh spoke – and he was short of breath from a lung operation – the paper fluttered under the hamburger.

His style of speech was shy and apocalyptic. He had a distinc-tive register of amazement, and impatience and dismissal. He spoke with real irritation about certain characters, "poetas-ters," as he would have called them. And shortly afterwards he told me with real pleasure that he had seen a golden eagle – in the States, I think – and that it was followed by "a retinue of little birds." But the connection is mine, not his.

By then Kavanagh had lived in Dublin for more than twenty years. I knew a little about him: that he had left Monaghan at the end of the thirties, that he had come to Dublin in search of literary fellowship. And that he regretted the decision. "No man," he once wrote of his townland, "ever loved that landscape and even some of the people more than I." Dublin, however, was another matter. He had come to the city in the aftermath of the Literary Revival. He was scathing about its rhetoric and its preconceptions. "When I came to Dublin," he had written, "the Irish Literary Affair was still booming. It was the notion that Dublin was a literary metropolis and Ireland as invented and patented by Yeats, Lady Gregory and Synge, a spiritual entity. It was full of writers and poets and I am afraid I thought their work had the Irish quality."

He finished lunch, drank a cup of tea and got up from the table. [...]

Gradually the city was catching my attention. Not far from my flat was the canal. At night the water glittered under streetlamps, the grass of the towpath took on a livid color and the wooden bulk of the locks turned into hunches of shadow.

Patrick Kavanagh had come here in the mid-fifties. He had sat by the water within sight of the bridge and the traffic. There was nothing particularly beautiful about the spot he had chosen. It was a noisy inch of city, shadowed by poplars and intruded on by passersby. He had been a sick man then, disillusioned and estranged. And with his foot on that inch, he had written a visionary sonnet. I never passed the canal at that point without thinking of it. *O commemorate me where there is water.*

Eavan Boland, *Object Lessons* (1995)

✳ ✳ ✳

Before moving on from Dublin's writers to its political figures, a quick tribute to an institution that works to help and encourage the city's up-and-coming writers today. Even an established writer like Nuala O'Faolain was grateful for their help.

In the centre of Dublin, just up from the neon and burger joints of the wide main street, there are terraces and squares of tall Georgian houses that have become homely over the centuries and are warrens now of different uses. One of these is the Irish Writers' Centre. Before I could get my autobiographical introduction started, I had to sit on a plastic chair under the elegant stucco ceiling of what, in the eighteenth century, would have been a reception room, gazing morosely at the teacher's wonderful shoes on her shapely legs, a reluctant enrollee in a six-session writing course. My fellow students looked at me a bit closely the first day because they knew who I was – as far as they were concerned I was a writer already.

Nuala O'Faolain, *Almost There* (2003)

✳ ✳ ✳

Dublin's writers have often been involved in the political battles that have been part of the city's history. But probably the best-known name in the region's political past is that of Charles Stewart Parnell (1846–1891), the champion of Irish Home Rule. Though he died of a heart attack aged only 45, he is regarded by many as one of the greatest political figures of the nineteenth century. The visitor to Dublin cannot fail to notice his memorial, standing at the junction of O'Connell Street and Parnell Street. As a young Irish landlord, he'd taken his seat in the House of Commons in 1875, to all intents and purposes a typical product of the English public school system – but his American mother's grandfather, an admiral in the American Navy, had fought the British during the War of Independence and the Parnell house in Dublin often played host to veterans of the American Civil War who had come to Dublin to participate in the Fenian rising. This no doubt fired his defiant nationalism. In his novel-style autobiography, Sean O'Casey – known principally as a playwright – recreates the night when news of Parnell's death reached the ordinary people of Dublin.

An October sky was black over the whole of Dublin; not a single star had travelled into the darkness: and a bitter rain was pelting down on the silent street. The rain had the still and unresisting city to itself. No one was out to feel it, and it seemed to pelt down harder in rage because there wasn't a soul out to shiver under its coldness and its sting. Even the heavy-coated and oil-caped police were hidden back in the shelter of the deepest doorways, uneasily dozing the night hours away, lulled into drowsiness by the slashing rain's pelting murmur falling on the spray-swept pavements. Everyone else was fast asleep in bed. Safe and sound oul' Dublin swept itself to sleep, well watched over by God and his Blessed Mother, assisted by the glorious company of the apostles, the goodly fellowship of the prophets, and the noble army of martyrs; each man, woman, and child having as well a guardian angel leaning over the bed, watching, with a well-cocked eye, the charge left in his care; so safe and sound and well oul' Dublin slept. Sound she was in sleep, and safe she felt, for God was there, and they were here, and the night was passing silently away, and soberly, except for the rain dancing a savage dance all over the city on the patient pavements. Behind heavy silken curtains, in happy-looking beds, slept the nicely night-gowned; behind tattered and tumbled curtains, on muddled mattresses, gowned in paltry calico or faded flannelette, slept the sisters and brothers of the nicely night-gowned. But the poor Protestants turned up their noses at the guardian angels, for they didn't believe in them, and felt sure and safer stuck in the arms of Jesus, their rock of ages and their morning star.

Between two narrow sheets, thickly ribbed with patches, under the eyes of God, among the prophets, apostles, and martyrs, in the midst of the valley of sleep, slept Johnny in his skin, for he had neither calico nor flannelette to decorate his rest. Under a few old coats and several big squares of buff felt, showing the inky imprint of the *Daily Express*, pinched by Archie from the stereotypers' room, Johnny lay snug, for the fire of the day lay half awake still in the grate and the room was still warm; while his mother slept in the little room opposite, in a fast sleep, too tired to feel cold, finding in sleep the one glamour of a hard day. […]

He raised himself up on his elbow, rubbed his eyes, looked over at his mother who was now putting some cups and saucers on the table; while Archie was tugging on his trousers standing by the old horsehair sofa which was a stately seat by day and Archie's narrow and nettlesome bed by night.

Now Johnny heard the patter of feet in the street mingling with the patter of the rain upon the pavements, and the sound of voices crossing and recrossing each other, crying Stop Press, Stop Press! He could hear the hasty Archie cursing querulously that a fella could never get his trousers on quick when he wanted to, and his mother muttering, half to herself, We'll get to know all about it soon enough; and the noise of the windows and doors opening, and the murmur of the kettle singing her song, panting it out, panting it out, and she sitting in the midst of the flames rising from the glow of the fire.

– What's wrong, mother? asked Johnny, his sleep falling from him, his eyes opening wider, his ears hearing heartily the sounds in the room and the sounds outside in the street.

– You lie down, you lie down, replied his mother, an' go asleep again.

– Why've you lit th' fire, an' why've you made tea?' inquired Johnny.

– Poor Parnell's dead, said Archie, busy with his boots.

– It may be only a rumour, murmured his mother.

– We'll soon know for certain when we get a paper, muttered Archie.

Parnell! What had this man done that all the people were so upset about him, one way or another? The mention of his name always gave rise to a boo or a cheer. The Roman Catholics who wouldn't let a word be said against him a while ago, now couldn't pick out words villainous enough to describe him; while the Protestants who were always ashamed of him, now found grace and dignity in the man the Roman Catholics had put beyond the pale.

Well, they could all breathe in peace now that he was dead. His Ma said his Da often said the first chance the priests ever got, they'd down Parnell. And there he was now, down among the dead men.

The pattering of the feet went on in the streets outside, mingling with the patter of the rain on the pavements. Archie, safe now with his breeches and his boots on, whipped up his cap, and hurried out to try to get a copy of the Stop Press telling that a golden bowl was broken, a silver cord loosened, and a wheel broken at a mighty cistern.

For fiddling with a woman or something, the Catholics had turned away from him. Kitty O'Shea it was who had brought the anger of the righteous overmuch upon him. [...]

Now Parnell was dead, and they were crying it in the streets; and fear came upon them that the one man they had was gone. A great thing had been taken, and a lot of little things had been left. They'd have to go now through the valley of the shadow of life alone; and they divided, and moved by every wind, unstable as water. The pillar of fire that had led them so long and so bravely and so brightly had died out; and they were all in the dark.

Sean O'Casey, *Pictures in the Hallway* (1942)

* * *

Important as its writers and political figures are to the identity of the city, Dublin and Dubliners are about much else besides – including a particular brand of humour. We have a taste of this from novelist Joseph O'Connor (b.1963) as, returning to the city of his birth after a spell abroad, he introduces us to some fellow Dubliners – not the best of them ... but one can meet the same types just about anywhere.

It was a happy day for me, seeing the city of my birth and boyhood again. But one thing you notice on returning to

Dublin after a spell abroad is the inexplicable but undeniable fact that there are more crashing bores strolling the avenues of our capital then there are caps on a debutante's molars. I do not say that all Dublin people are bores. Not a bit of it. Most Dubliners are great company, full of jizz and strange mischief. But Holy Mother in Heaven, do we have our share of fellows – and usually they *are* fellows – who would make you want to sprint out and purchase a gallon of emulsion purely in order to slap it on a jacks wall and watch it dry rather than engage them in even a millisecond's intercourse?

You have met, I assume, The Man Who Knows All About RTE? '*That* place? Hah. Pull, pull, pull, that's what gets yeh up the shaggin ladder above in that kip, sure that's well known. DID YEW NOT KNOW THAT, begob, I'm surprised at yeh, and yew a college man. Sure, the fingers udd be worn off yeh with the pullin, oh yeah. It's no wonder yer wan, Olivier O'Leary upped and offed ourra the gaff.' And his cousin, The Man Who Didn't Get Into The Civil Service? ('Ah well, I didn't have the right connections, if you get me drift. Them buckos look after their own. If you're not in The Knights you may forget about it.')

Quite ubiquitous these days is The Man Who Followed Irish Football For Years But Wouldn't Go To A Match Now If You Paid Him. 'No, I would *not*, are yew jokin' me? Sure Janey, it was great years ago below in Glenmanure Park, ye'd be there all be yerself in the stand and the gaiters bein freezed off yeh be the cold, ah yeah, yer balls'd be the size of peanuts, but now that was fookball. And that's not fookball they do be playin now, sure it's gone too poplar now, all them yuppies, all them Ole Ole-heads, sure they're not real fookball men ... '

Then, horrors of horrors, there is that unspeakable creature: The Man Who Has A Good One For You. 'Is it yerself? C'mre to me, I've a good one for yeh now. I went to a pub on the moon one time, burr I didn't like it, no atmosphere, dja geddit? The wife, right, she's a face on her like the supreme feckin cours, no appeal, ha ha ha. She has teeth on her like the ten command-ments, all broken. HA HA HA. No. C'mre to me. These three thick culchies, right, they go into a bar in Jerusalem, HA HA HA, and the first culchie says … '

Next we have The Man Who Does Impressions at Parties, The Man Who Thinks Charles Haughy Should Be Persuaded to Come Back (For The Good of the Country), The Man Who Does Not Want You To Get Him Started About The Farmers, The Man Who Invites You To Guess How Much Them Slacks Cost Him in the Sales ('No, go on, have a guess, they're corduroy mind, none of your rubbish'), The Man Who Told His Boss A Thing Or Two, The Man Who Thinks We Should Hand The Country Lock Stock and Barrel Back To England (And Pray To The Holy Mother They'd Take It), The Man Who Thinks Christmas Has Gone Fierce Commercialised, The Man Who Thinks There Is No Need At All For the Bad Language in Roddy Doyle's Books (a close relative to The Man Who Is Not A Prude, But). Also, we have The Man Who Knows That Mary Robinson Is Not What She Seems, The Man Who Was Beaten To A Pulp Every Day of His Schooling Be The Brothers (And Divil The Bit of Harm It Ever Did Him) and The Man Whose Friends Have Been Telling Him For Years That He Should Write A Book About His Life (Only Nobody Would Believe It). He is among the worst, this last monster. He is to be feared. 'I could tell yeh stories about yours truly now pal that would raise the fookin hairs on yer beck. But yeh know what? Yeh wouldn't believe them!!'

Trotting after these chaps is The Man Who Would Feck Off Out Of This Priest-ridden Country If Only He Was Ten Years Younger, The Man Who Knew Brendan Behan Well, The Man Who Still Has His Health ('sure that's the main thing, isn't it?') and The Man Who Misses the Old Days When Chizzellers Had To Make Their Own Fun. ('I got a ball of silver paper for me birthday every year until I was twenty-seven, and I was happy as a pig in shite.')

The king of Dublin bores, of course, is the talkative taxi driver, the withering pox be upon him and his. How many of us have had to endure the following turgid monologue?

'Taxi? Hawya boss, sit in there and take the weight off yer brains. Purr on the auld seat belt, willya like a good man. Where are yeh gointeh? Ratmoines? Game ball. We're off. Listen, do yeh know any jokes? C'mere, I've got a good wan for yeh. I wouldn't say the auld wan is ugly rich, but she fell asleep in the gairden wunst and the dog buried her. HOOHOOOHOOO. Did yeh see that article on the paper there about Ballymun? Towerblocks? Are yew jokin me? Don't be talking. *Ballymun deproived*? Me bollix. On the pig's back up there. Don't talk to me about deproived, when I think abou' that place I want to gawk. Hot weather? Way ourra that don't make me laugh. Leave it flowin all day up there. Don't pay a bean for it. And free heat. Up there once, wait till I tell yeh, collectin a fare I was. Middle of winter, and do you know wha? Guess. Strippin the feckin clothes off themselves with the free central heatin. Like the beach or sumpin. Like shaggin Rimini it was. Deproived me howl.

'Darndale, that's the same. Deproived. Yer man from the Labour Pairty is never off the television abour it. And what that prognosticatin' bowsie would know about deproived now you could write on a stamp. I seen him ownee the other night outside Lillie's Bordildo and him bein lurried into a joe maxi blue mowldy with the dhrink and singin Sean Southa Garryowen and the hair on him like a madwoman's fanny and a nurse with him and the frock on her up to her wishbone. Oh Jem Larkin is back in the saddle right enuff. But no, deproived is the latest. Jaze it would make you throw the head together. I mean, them houses above in Darndale is lovely. The ones with the arches. They're after winnin' every award in the bewk. The arkitexture is ownee bleedin rapid in them. And so yeh think *I* can afford arches? I can not, not even in me fookin shoes. Far from arches that shower was rared. Lovely houses. But fallin apairt now a course. Anywhere else they'd be grand, but it's the Woild West up there. Mad Comanches they are. You would need your tomahawk up there.

'Some people are just ignorant. Jairseeful Mazes, yeh can give them nuttin. The wild dogs that do be roamin around up there, sure they'd take a lump ourra yer arse yeh wouldn't fit in the yer hat. Yeh see a thing or two now Boss, in the taxiin' trade, I don't mind telling yeh, but up in shaggin Ballymun beejaze yeh'd see characters dandcrin' about the place that'd straighten the hair in yer oxters. And as for the smell up there, in the lifts, don't get me stairted. Disgoostin. No respect for a pairson's feelings.' (Pause while driver enthusiastically evacuates contents of nostrils into dubiously stained kerchief.)

'And I wouldn't mind ownee they're *set up* out there. They are laughin at the rest of us, they are *scutterin themselves* laughin, I'm telling yeh. Free heat, free butther and free yew name it, firin' the free grub I themselves good-oh, me same poor deproived buckos beyond in Ballymun, oh bedad, every last wunna them on the rock and roll and havin childers left and right to get money and you never hear about *that* from the arty-farty Labour Pairty, oh no. They wudden know *how* to work. Wudden know what to *do* with a tool. And there they are, feckin themselves over the balconies! Nuthin else will do them bar leppin the balconies. The ingratitude of it. I was ownee sayin to the war department there last night, Monica, sez I, the *ingratitude* of them hop-o-me-thumbs beyond the Ballymun is what gets me, sure it's no wonder this country is a laughin stock. They do break their howls laughin at us in England you know, Monica. They think we are bleedin hilariousness pairsonified.

'And do you now what she sez to me? *DO YEH*?!!! Sez she, they ARE deproived. Annoyin me, yeh know? Hoppin the ball she was, ourra badness. Moi Grandfather fought for Urland, sez she, and I'll tell yeh this Jack, he never thought when we gor our freedom we'd put up places like Ballymun. *When* did your grandfather fight for Urland, sez I. Wasn't he in the post office in 1916, sez she. He *was* alright, sez I, he was buyin a fookin stamp. Ah well, don't be talking. Here we are anyway, Ratmoines wazzen it? What's this is the damage, sure we'll call it the even fiver, yeah. Tankin yew. Listen, c'mere to me, I hope I didden bore yeh to bleedin tears, did I? Wake up. WAKE UP YEH EEJIT!!!'

Something should be done about this pantheon of Dublin superbores. Perhaps we could round them up and export them to Holland, as vengeance for knocking us out of the recent World Cup? Although, come to think of it, I've been to Holland and over there, you know, bores are actually ... oh, never mind.

Joseph O'Connor, *The Secret World of the Irish Male* (1994)

✳ ✳ ✳

In Standard Time, *novelist Keith Ridgway describes the experience of another 'returner' – so much has changed, and yet the heart of the city is the same as ever.*

We came in over the sea, we came in the morning, just after the sun, coming low out of the east across the flat sea, on time, the two of us. We watched boats scratch the surface, we put our seatbacks in the upright position, we called for more drinks, but they were having none of it, they were cross with us – they wouldn't let us toast your first sight of Dublin.

We crossed the panel sea, the grey-blue web of waves and routes and trawlers, across the humming radioactive sea, over submarines and the drowned, over the cables and the pipes and the deep connections, and we craned our necks and looked for the city. It came at us as islands, small islands which I could not name, and the two pencil-thin chimneys then, which I had forgotten, and finally the bulk of it, split by the river, a huddle of colours and a shadow in the foothills, a gathering of times, a city on the edge of Europe, on the edge of the world, a city from the back of our minds, shot suddenly forward, in front of us, offered in the early sunshine, the clouds rolled back for us, the whole place gazing upwards for us, waiting. [...]

We descended over housing estates and motorways that I had never seen before. We skimmed the tops of call centres and warehouses, distribution networks and technology parks, software development clusters and the green belts tightened by a future that I had missed.

The plane hit the ground.

'Welcome home,' you said. [...]

Our taxi took us on roads which I didn't recognise, past homes and businesses which I didn't fully see, so perplexed was I by the traffic and the look of the people and the voices on the radio, all familiar, somehow, but altered as if by special effect, which is I suppose, what time may be. My confidence that I had the measure of you here was a little dented, until we reached the city centre and I saw that, fundamentally, although the streets were crowded and the sun was out, and the faces were healthy and varied and the money was obvious, fundamentally I knew where I was.

Keith Ridgway, *Standard Time* (2001)

* * *

And another Dublin arrival. Someone a little more special. When Pope John Paul II flew in, Dublin life was put on pause. Journalist Nell McCafferty describes the event. Although another part of her article records the disappointment and alienation felt by many Irish women as a result of his tradition- alist message to them, the extract below captures the population's initial sense of excitement at his visit.

The Pope came out of the sky and descended into Ireland on Saturday 29 September 1979. It was a magnificently Messianic moment. The heavens had been cleared for it, and the earth brought to a standstill. All airports were closed, so that no man but John Paul could come down from above; all traffic had been banned in Dublin city so that pilgrims must walk to meet him; all workplaces had been closed, all over the country, that the people might be free to greet he who symbolised spiritual freedom.

No other place in the world had made such arrangements, but no other place in the world identified so strongly with the direct inheritor of the mantle of Jesus Christ. 'The Pope is infallible when he defines a doctrine, concerning faith or morals, to be held by the whole Church.' These are the words that echo and re-echo, unbidden in the mind, when all other words, learned off by heart, have faded away. Their meaning is awesome. The Pope knows what God thinks, and says what God means, and the Pope is absolutely right. When the Pope speaks, God is speaking.

The Pope, when we were first taught those words, was a figure unreal as the man in the moon. He lived far, far away. We would never meet him, nor did we expect to meet him, no more than we ever expected to meet God on this earth.

Then a man landed on the moon.

And going to Rome was as common, more common given the cost of a holiday in the West, than going to Killarney.

But still the aura of magic remained.

Men might go to the moon, and all of us might go to Italy, but the Pope would remain immobile and unmoved, there in the Vatican, deep in the panting heart of Rome. Also, an Irishman would never be Pope. So we kept our distance and he kept his and the Godliness of it all was right and proper and seemly.

No wonder the nation came to a halt when he came over here. I mean to say, Jesus Mary and Joseph, who would have thought it, or wrought to think of it. I was in Blackrock when his plane appeared in the sky, suspended over Howth. As it came drifting closer, hearts stopped with the wonder of it all. 'There's the Pope,' we shouted, laughing and disbelieving and proud as a chosen people could be.

In the Phoenix Park a million people gathered, happy and carefree and innocent of evil intent as a bunch of babies. Goodwill and good cheer emanated like sunshine, and the sun did indeed shine from a cloudless sky. The ushers and orderlies and security men were redundant. A joyfully corralled nation behaved as if blessed, and thought itself blessed, and *was* blessed when he stood atop his Popemobile and was driven up and down and through our serried ranks, so that no one was far from him, and the Irish people felt as close to God as it was possible to be.

He looked the part: handsome, virile, gentle, happy and gorgeously dressed, in white silk, satin and glowing gems. We never heard a word he said, but no matter, for the words had been with us since birth, and the ritual of the Mass an automatic reflex genuflection.

Nell McCafferty, 'Next to Godliness' (*In Dublin*, 1986),
collected in *Goodnight Sisters* (1987)

❋   ❋   ❋

Another arrival from abroad. In Mary O'Donnell's short story, 'Little Africa', a Nigerian boy – receiving an excellent Irish education, thanks to the Jesuits – enjoys a taste of 'home' at a market in what has come to be a noticeably African area of the city.

Now, in Ireland, he was Mosi. Boys were not usually called after flowers. He must forget Hyacinth, Angela said. They had to make things as easy as possible for themselves.

But after a year in Ireland, Mosi still found it impossible to forget. His mother found it hard too, having to forget and

115

learn so much at once. He would watch her face across the small square breakfast table in their inner city attic flat and observe the determination in her eyes. Son, I need to think, she would often say. Sometimes, Angela's new man Colm stayed over at the flat. Mosi tried not to suspect him. He was white, his features as vague and unformed as most white people's. The only thing that distinguished him was his hairy nose. Mosi would peer with dislike at the small gingery hairs that grew inside his elongated nostrils and wonder if his mother had lost her mind from too much death and thinking.

While his mother was thinking, Mosi went to school in Denmark Street and afterwards walked through the north city. The school had taken him in as one of three boys from Africa and he was happy enough there. Before he had come to Ireland, he never thought about happiness, but in the past year it was a word he heard frequently from adults on the radio. Everybody in Dublin believed in happiness, but in his previous life it was not discussed. That did not mean happiness did not occur, merely that it was not a subject worth discussing.

Mosi grew accustomed to the rushing city. Many years before, he had once been to Kano with his father. There, everybody was black and ordinary. The fact was – and he could not admit this even to Kevo – that in Dublin he sometimes found it difficult to tell one white person from another. He had spent the first three months in school talking to people he only half recognised because they looked just the same as someone he had spoken to only a minute beforehand. Gradually, he developed codes that helped him. He began to observe hair, the shapes of heads, lengths of noses. Not all hair was as straight as he imagined. Some people had hair like wavy rivers and others had short, totally straight pale hair, worn very close to the scalp. He began to see that not all eyes were pale blue, but that there were various shades of blueness, and that there was light brown and dark brown too. Their teeth were small and they had small jaws. That did not help matters. But mostly it was the skin – chicken pale, bloodless looking, which they wore with such casual pride, not seeing anything remotely startling about themselves.

At school, they did not ask about Africa. It was understood that he might not want to talk about some things. But sometimes he spoke up. Sometimes, in class, there was an opportunity to describe how something had been or what a certain place looked like. In Geography, he had spoken about the equatorial climate and about the animals that came to the watering hole at sunset.

Many of the boys in his class were rich, but not all. They wore black blazers with an emblazoned crest, and so did he. His mother had not had to buy the uniform, because the Jesuits had taken him on and were looking after everything. Mosi made an Irish friend. For some reason, although he often spoke with the two other African boys in his year, he had no desire to play with them or to know about their previous lives. He was certain that they too had experienced awful things but he had no more room in his head for such sad furniture. [...]

At lunch hour, Mosi left the school and wandered down to Moore Street. He had two euros in his pocket. That street reminded him of his old home except that here they sold fish instead of dried dust dogs. All the vegetables in the stalls were like those he had seen in his other life. The air throbbed with voices and footsteps, with patient women calling out prices. People stopped and haggled over apples from South Africa, yams from Zimbabwe, over livid oranges and hairy kiwis. Finally, he saw what he was looking for. A ripe pineapple, deep yellow, notched with little brown patches from which leaked small droplets of syrupy sweetness. He stopped and examined it more closely. It was perfect. Of late, Angela had wanted as many sweet and dripping fruits as possible, but especially pineapple and mango.

The woman behind the stall reached over and held it out to him like a golden lamp.

'It's yours, love. Sixty cents,' she said in a smoky voice.

'Forty,' Mosi responded automatically.

'Fifty-five,' she eyed him knowingly, replacing the pineapple in its straw-lined box.

'Forty-five!'

'Fifty and not a cent less!'

She stood back and folded her arms as if daring him to answer back.

He nodded, then passed a euro coin into her hands. She handed him the pineapple and his change. He smiled, pleased at this compromise, then pushed the fruit into his rucksack.

A fog was descending as he made his way back to Denmark Street. The sun was gradually being soaked up, like yellow ink in the blotting-paper sky. Only a thin light touched the broad footpaths where people jostled and avoided collision, hunching shoulders, pulling scarves around their throats.

Mary O'Donnell, 'Little Africa', in *Storm Over Belfast* (2008)

* * *

And then there are the Dubliners from mixed backgrounds. In The Speckled People*, Hugo Hamilton writes about his mixed German-Irish parentage.*

My father pretends that England doesn't exist. It's like a country he's never even heard of before and is not even on the map. Instead, he's more interested in other countries. Why shouldn't we dance with other partners as well, he says, like Germany? So while he was still at university he started learning German and listening to German music – Bach and Beethoven. Every week he went to classes in Dublin that were packed out because they were given by Doctor Becker, a real German. He knew Germany was a place full of great music and great inventions, and one day, he said to himself, Ireland would be like that too, with its own language and its own inventions. Until then, he said, Ireland didn't exist at all. It only existed in the minds of emigrants looking back, or in the minds of idealists looking forward. Far back in the past or far away in the future, Ireland only existed in songs.

Then he started making speeches. Not everybody had a radio and not everybody could read the newspapers at that time, so they went to hear people making speeches on O'Connell Street instead. The way you knew that people agreed with what you were saying is that they suddenly threw their hats and caps up in the air and cheered. The biggest crowd with the most amount of hats going up was always outside the GPO for de Valera. Some people had loudspeakers, but the good speakers needed nothing, only their own voices, and my Uncle Ted says the best of them all was further up the street, a man named James Larkin who had a great way of stretching his arms out over the crowd.

My father wouldn't throw his hat up for anyone, so he started making his own speeches at the other end of the street with his friends. They had their own newspaper and their own leaflets and a party pin in the shape of a small 'e' for Éire: Ireland. He said it was time for Ireland to stand up on its own two feet and become a real country, not a place you dreamed about. The Irish people spent long enough building stone walls and saying the opposite. There were no rules about starting a new country and he wasn't interested in saying what everybody agreed with either. He had his own way of bringing his fist down at the end of a sentence, like he was banging the table. Hats went up for him all right. He had the crowd in his pocket when he put his hand on his heart, and he could have stolen all the flying hats from de Valera and Larkin and Cosgrave, but he started speaking in Irish and not everybody understood what he was saying. [...]

And then my father had the big idea of bringing people from other countries over to Ireland. After the war was over he met my mother in Dublin and decided to start a German-Irish family. He was still making speeches and writing articles for the newspaper and going around on his motorbike wearing goggles. But what better way to start a new country than marrying somebody and having children? Because that's what a new country is, he says, children. In the end of it all, we are the new country, the new Irish. [...]

My mother never imagined meeting someone, least of all an Irishman who could speak German and loved German music. She never imagined staying in Ireland for good, talking about Irish schools or making jam in Ireland and picking out children's shoes. My father asked her if she was willing to accompany him on a walk and correct his pronunciation. And because Germany had such great music, he wanted to tell her something great about Ireland, about St Patrick and about Irish history and Irish freedom. He told her he was not afraid to make sacrifices. He spoke quickly as if he was still making a speech and people were throwing their hats up in the air by the thousands and didn't care if they ever came back down again.

My mother said she had to go home to Germany because that was a country that had just got its freedom, too, and had to be started from the beginning. He would not emigrate or leave his own native shores. He said he had bought a house that was not far away from the seafront. There were no pictures on the walls yet. There was no furniture, only a table and two chairs in the kitchen and a statue of the Virgin Mary. At night, you could be lonely and you'd miss your people because it was so quiet and so empty, just listening to the radio with a naked light bulb in the room and the wallpaper peeling on the walls. But in the end of it all, you would be starting a new republic with speckled Irish-German children.

They got married in Germany at Christmas. [...] She didn't get a white dress but she got snow instead, thick silent snow.

They went on the train together along the Rhine. They talked about the future and he said she would always be able to speak German in her own home. She said she would try and learn Irish, too. The children would be dressed for Ireland and for Germany.

Hugo Hamilton, The Speckled People (2003)

✳ ✳ ✳

As in every big city, Dublin's attitudes to immigrants range from the welcoming to violent rejection. Yet if this next brief extract is anything to go by, it is traditional for Dubliners to accept and appreciate people who are different.

Trinity College, Dublin. At a party held in the rooms of an undergraduate acquaintance, an American actor, whom I last saw playing the Ghost in *Hamlet* at the Gate Theatre, relates how, returning home about two o'clock in the morning along O'Connell Street, he met an apparition playing on some kind of rustic pipe and every now and again leaping ecstatically into the air as it rushed along. It had a battered bowler hat, a beard, and it wore boots on only one foot, the other being bare. At first the American was under the impression that he had been reading too much James Stephens, but on questioning an enormous Metropolitan policeman discovered that it was only another of the curiosities of Dublin. 'He does be astray in the head,' said the policeman, 'but he does be doin' no harm' – whereupon the American, in relating the incident, went into ecstasies of appreciation of the innate sense of justice and individual liberty in a city and a country where such eccentricities were not only tolerated but were regarded as a break in the monotony of everyday living.

Denis Ireland, From the Irish Shore (1936)

✳ ✳ ✳

From Colin Irwin, another amusing portrait of a tolerant and welcoming Dubliner who has learnt that charm pays ...

The first time I set foot in Dublin twenty-five years ago, I got off the airport bus and checked in at the first hotel that crossed my path. Wynns in Abbey Street. I've been back to Dublin on numerous occasions since and stayed at establishments of varying vintage, but had never been back to Wynns. The only thing I remembered about it was the beggar who hung around outside and collared me each day with convivial chit-chat. 'Tell me, sir, would you be English?' Having spent the previous evening being accused of being an errant Dublin milkman, I freely admitted that yes, I was indeed English. 'Ay,' said my new chum, beaming fetchingly but swaying dangerously as he pushed his face close to mine, knocking me backwards with a pungent blast of something seriously toxic. 'Can I tell you something, sir?' I nod in the full knowledge that, whatever the answer, he'll tell me anyway. 'I've seen some things, sir ... ' That's nice. 'I've been all around the world, sir, I've met a lot of people.' You have? 'Oh, I have that, sir. I've met people from all over the world, sir and do you know something, sir?' I know nothing, I'm from Barcelona. 'I've met a lot of English people, sir ... ' Oh, here it comes ... hundreds of years of oppression and persecution, bastard landlords, Irish jokes, 'coloureds and Irish need not apply' signs ... I start to apologise for the sins of my nation but he's not listening. 'As God is my witness, this is the honest truth. No Englishman has ever let me down ... '

I dug deep and gave him all my change.

I was in Dublin five days then and each morning that beggar was waiting outside Wynns to greet me and we went through the same ritual and it always ended up with him emptying my pockets. That first pilgrimage to Dublin had been a major culture shock. The tiny children begging on O'Connell Bridge; the drawn, grey faces of the old women; the overt fierce drinking going on at every street corner; the religious zealots shouting the odds wherever you looked; the dark, dingy pubs that, once entered, offered disarming conviviality and top grade intellectual debate. 'You wanna know the trouble with the Brits?' confided one bar-stool philosopher. 'The Brits are all bastards. But never mind that, what are you drinking?' And that's the crux of it. You can despise the race, but in Ireland it's never *ever* personal. I've met hard-line republicans whose hatred of the Brits knew no bounds – and they didn't care who knew it – yet on a one-to-one were always wonderfully warm, genuinely helpful and unerringly entertaining. For all the ills, Ireland can't help itself. It's an inveterately sociable nation and you are indeed welcome here, kind stranger.

Colin Irwin, *In Search of the Craic* (2001)

* * *

Is there such a phenomenon as an 'essential Dubliner'? Playwright Peter Sheridan tries to define it when he talks to Deirdre Purcell.

Peter Sheridan's credentials as an 'Essential Dubliner' are impeccable, so he is the ideal person to give his view on what constitutes such a character. For the purposes of this book, this has to refer to the past; clichéd heart-of-the-rowl Dubliners are a rare breed in this era when most of the trading on Moore Street, the stereotypical Dublin thoroughfare, is carried on by people who are of African, Asian, East European or of Baltic origin.

'Openness and friendliness,' he says.

Himself, obviously.

'But a sort of perversity as well.'

Himself again.

'The Dub is always attempting to prove something to the world. We feel we've been made lesser because of the association with the bigger city, London, across the water. Maybe that's not just a Dublin thing but an Irish thing too. That feeling of having lost the language and all the kind of historical stuff that must be buried somewhere in the communal psyche. We use English but with a Gaelic consciousness.'

He gives an example. 'You have a definite "yes" and "no" in English but you don't in Gaelic, where it's "sea" and "ní hea". They translate as "Well, maybe it is and maybe it isn't." So you're saying "maybe to everything". And then there's that whole thing where you're paying someone a compliment by using the opposite. "Ya effing bastard!" means "you're a great guy" – but to call someone "a great guy" means you're a bit iffy about him.'

There's a First City sense of 'up yours' too, softened with subtle humour. [...]

'They're replacing flagstones outside the Gresham Hotel. You know how it is, a pile of cement, a couple of planks going over the mess so that people can still use the hotel, a couple of barrels to warn them. Ten guys there, nine leaning on shovels and one guy actually working, cutting and shearing and shrieking away with ancient cutting equipment. There's an engineering conference and the delegates are going in and they're looking at this and they can't believe it. The Spanish delegation goes in. The French delegation goes in. The German delegation is going in and one guy just can't hold himself back: "Who's in charge of the site?"

'"That fella down there –"

'So he goes down. "Are you in charge of this site?"

'"Yes, I am. I'm the gaffer."

'"You know, in Germany now when we cut the pavement we have a computer on the site. And everything is punched into the computer and we are correct to one ten-thousandth of a centimetre."

'And the Dublin guy says, "Well, that wouldn't do us at all. Because we have to be spot on!"'

Deirdre Purcell, *Follow Me Down to Dublin:*
The City Through the Voices of Its People (2007)

The Great Escape

Some people escape to Dublin, some can hardly wait to escape from it. Joseph O'Connor considers those who don't escape too far … just to the suburbs. And why.

I was brought up in Glenageary in the suburbs of Southside Dublin. The road we lived in had been a field, until 1963 the year I was born, the year my parents bought a new house there. Glenageary was a place that had no history. For years after my parents bought the house, Glenageary did not even appear on maps of Dublin. It was a place that did not exist in history. It was a place that first appeared in 1963, like myself, and like sexual intercourse in the Philip Larkin poem, and The Beatles' first LP. It was a place where you went to reinvent yourself and your future, by reinventing your past.

Glenageary was full of Dublin working-class people who, like my own parents, had made good in Sean Lemass's Ireland and become middle class. And it was full of country people who had migrated to Dublin to find work, then turned their backs on the land. The only echo of rural past was in the names they gave their houses. Mountain View, Glenside, River View. These people were living lives which were very far from the ideal which Yeats and de Valera had so incongruously shared. The maidens were not dancing at the crossroads. They were watching The Rolling Stones on the latest colour TV set. And if they were not exactly fumbling in the greasy till, they were certainly fumbling in the latest Zanussi washing machine from time to time. Glenageary was *Gleann nag Caorach* in Irish, the glen of the sheep, but the only sheep around when I was a child were the ones wrapped in clingfilm and deposited in the brand new freezers which hummed their hymns in every double garage.

Having BBC was very important in Glenageary. Having the odd pseudo-English accent that Southside Dubliners develop was very important. The connections with personal or national history were tenuous indeed. Of course we had our token suburban gaeilgeoiń family, who knitted things and insisted on ordering articles in Irish in the local shops, and who tended to shout '*bualadh bos*' at you for no apparent reason. But generally, as children, we had no interest in anything even remotely gaelic, except, perhaps, early Horslips records. We did not understand a single word of Peig Sayers, but we knew the words on '*An Dearg Doom*' off by heart.

Glenageary was full of people reinventing themselves by reinventing their notions of Irish history, and forming themselves around new notions of Irishness. This is what suburbia was for. You didn't have to go into exile any more to escape from the nightmare of Irish history. The good times were here. This was the new Ireland.

Joseph O'Connor, *The Secret World of the Irish Male* (1994)

✳ ✳ ✳

While many Dubliners moved to the city from the surrounding countryside in search of a better life, in Ita Daly's novel, A Singular Attraction, *Pauline can't wait to break free from the city she finds increasingly depressing.*

Pauline sat surrounded by maps of Europe. The prospective holiday had become much more than that. She now saw it as a means of escape, her personal salvation.

She would travel overland, taking the car, because of the artist's paraphernalia. She would take the ferry to Cherbourg and from there make her way down to Arles in easy stages. The prospect filled her with unease, made her nervous and edgy. But she felt also that if she could achieve it, she would have broken out of the cringing, restricted body that she inhabited, she would be – in some radical fashion – freed.

And there was the pressing need to get away. Dublin had begun to depress her; the filth of the city and the general air of dereliction seemed menacing, as if the society in which she lived was on the point of disintegration. Illiterate graffiti bloomed on hoardings, which in turn protected vast, cavernous stretches of waste ground. These areas awaited the attentions of developers, but they reminded Pauline of pictures she had seen of Berlin after the Allied bombers had done their work.

On the streets stray dogs roamed, defecating on the footpaths, so that one had to walk with eyes permanently on the ground. At street corners armies of youths lounged, their orange and pink hair bright, but their faces grey, their smiles splitting into decay.

Only inside her flat did Pauline feel safe, reassured by the shadowy spaces, the cleanness, the coolness. Even to look out of her windows was to glimpse decline. In the sterile tarmac which surrounded the flats little beds of earth had been dug out. Originally these had been planted with a variety of shrubs and flowers. The latter were now dead, choked with the detritus of weeds and multi-coloured plastic. Some of the shrubs still survived but looked yellow and ailing.

Nobody else seemed to have noticed, and maybe she, too, needed that sort of detachment. If she could drive herself down to the south of France, she should on her return be able to drive through the pock-marked city without fear rising, as it did now, to grab at her wind-pipe and press.

'If I can stick it out for the next six weeks, I'll be all right.'

[...]

She went to bed and dreamt of a pale, shining city, with empty streets and buildings of reflective glass. She walked in the streets and was surprised to find that she was in Dublin, then happy to see the transformation of her native town. She felt secure in the empty streets.

Ita Daly, *A Singular Attraction* (1987)

* * *

For some people, Dublin is a refuge from suffering and loss. The city's newer residents include many migrants, seeking safety and a new life. In Andrew Nugent's Second Burial *we meet Jude, a refugee from Nigeria.*

As he washed he reflected. Until four months before, Jude had never been farther than Anambra and the neighbouring Igbo states, what used to be called Biafra. He spoke Igbo fluently and English well, but it was the English of Igboland and the Delta, quite different in syntax and intonation to the provincial dialects of Dublin. He had a big problem of communication in a city whose natives seemed certain that the best, indeed the only correct English in the world, was as spoken by themselves.

Jude was no stranger to city living. He knew Onitsha like the back of his hand and he had spent three months in Lagos on his way to Ireland. Anyone who survives those maelstroms, friends had assured him, would survive anywhere in the world. Dublin by comparison was small, and calm to the point of being eerie. He could not quite believe it at first: the cars stayed on their own side of the road – the wrong side actually – and they always stopped at red lights, even when there was no Yellow Fever man standing by with his whip to torture the drivers, as there was at home.

He still felt far from secure. Although not particularly hassled by police or immigration officials, most of whom seemed quite human, he had far too much to do with them. Visa offices to visit, police stations to report to, forms to fill out, questions to be answered, all the time more and more questions, many that he had no idea how to answer. Immigration formalities were interminable, bewildering, and intimidating. From day to day, from week to week, he had no idea whether his case for a resident's permit was going forward or backward. There was the nagging fear all the time that they would come for him suddenly and send him packing. [...]

Jude knew the world of Dublin's Little Africa, that area from Parnell Square back towards the North Circular Road, increasingly colonized by Africans, who had come to hitch a ride on the Celtic Tiger. He was also fairly at home in the food markets down near the river, where people knew him and where, in typical Dublin style, everybody called him 'Judo'. He enjoyed walking back from there each morning, the huge basket of fresh produce balanced skilfully on his head. He could sense people looking at him. Sometimes he would flash pearly teeth at some pretty girl, who would immediately turn pink. Then he would go home happy, dreaming impossible dreams.

But outside the little circle of Africans frequenting Shad's restaurant, the mostly friendly neighbours in adjoining streets, his market pals at the church where he worshipped, Jude knew virtually no one and was shy of making contact. In the six weeks he had spent in Dublin he had not encountered much racial hostility. Incoherent taunts in his back a few times, once a glutinous yellow snot landing at his feet, and another time, from a pretty girl on the arm of an ugly lout, obscene gestures, which sparked disgust and even pity in his heart, more than anger or fear.

But he had heard stories of what had happened to other people, those who had strayed from the African ghetto and dared to compete in other sectors of Irish society. He was in no hurry to do likewise. He knew nothing south of the river bisecting Dublin, not to mention anywhere outside the city. He had not even learned how to take a Dublin bus, use a public telephone, or handle any but the simplest commercial transactions. It was a slender basis for all that he had to do now. [...]

'Hey, Blessed Martin, where do you think you are going?'

The manner of address did not surprise him. It was not the first time he had been called 'Blessed Martin'. The Dublin poor had a great devotion, going back over many years, to the black Peruvian Dominican saint, Martin de Porres. Even after the Pope had promoted Martin to being fully paid-up Saint Martin, Dubliners still called him what they had always called him, Blessed Martin, or even, Saint Blessed Martin.

When black boys first began to appear in the streets of Dublin, they were regularly addressed, with wry affection, as Blessed Martin, especially as the boxes used to collect pennies from the poor for the foreign missions used to have a little black boy made of plaster kneeling on top, who was wired to nod appreciatively each time a coin fell through the slot. Those humble boxes 'for the black babies' probably did more than anything else to prepare a reasonably enlightened reception for real-life black people when eventually they began to be seen around the city.

There was also a no doubt well-intentioned, but incredibly ill-conceived, luxury model of the black baby boxes. This box had the usual little black boy kneeling beside the money slot, ready to acknowledge subscriptions with grateful nods. But his gratitude did not stop there. The more money that went in, the less black in the face he became, until eventually, at around fifteen shillings and nine pence, his face had become shining white. A truly amazing combination of ingenious technology and ingenuous theology, and innocently racist to an appalling degree.

When the first prominent black football player was signed by a Dublin soccer club, the city took him to its heart as its very own black baby. Splendid in defense as in attack, he was above all a magnificent striker. The only problem was that the 'baby' had a name about fourteen syllables long and included unpronounceable combinations of x, y, and z. So each time his team moved in for the kill at Dallymount or Tolka Park, the cry went up from the bleachers, in the unmistakable cadences of Old Dublin: *Give it to Blessed Martin!!*

Andrew Nugent, *Second Burial* (2007)

✳ ✳ ✳

There's a double escape in Roddy Doyle's The Deportees. *The narrator, having escaped his homeland for what he hopes will be a better life in Dublin, finds himself, without a work permit, at the mercy of thugs from whose violent intimidation he is determined to extricate himself.*

My second job takes me to the place called Temple Bar. I walk because the bus is too slow, when other people are going home from work. The streets are busy but I am safe. It is early and, now, it is spring and daylight.

Temple Bar is famous. It is the centre of culture in Dublin and Ireland. But many drunk people walk down the streets, shouting and singing with very bad voices. Men and even women lie on the pavements. I understand. These are stag and hen people, from England. Kevin, my Irish friend, explained. One of these people will soon be married, so they come to Temple Bar to fall on the street and urinate in their trousers or show their big breasts to each other and laugh. Kevin told me that they are English people but I do not think that this is right. I think that many of them are Irish. Alright, bud? What are you fucking looking at? But Kevin wants me to believe that these drunk people are English. I do not know why, but Kevin is my friend, so I do not tell him that, in my opinion, many of them are Irish.

Here, I am a baby. I am only three months old. My life started when I arrived. My boss shows me the plug. He holds it up.

– Plug, he says.

He puts the plug into the plug-hole. He takes it out and he puts it in again.

– Understand? He says.

I understand. He turns on the hot water.

– Hot.

He turns on the cold water.

– Cold. Understand?

I understand. He points at some pots and trays. He points at me.

– Clean.

I understand. He smiles. He pats my shoulder.

All night, I clean. I am in a corner of the big kitchen, behind a white wall. There is a radio which I can listen to when the restaurant is not very noisy. This night, the chef's joke about the man in Belfast called Stakeknife. The door to the alley is open, always, but I am very hot.

– How come you get all the easy jobs?

I look up. It is Kevin, my friend.

– Fuck that, I say.

He laughs.

Food is a good thing about this job. It is not the food that is left on the plates. It is real, new food. I stop work for a half-hour and I sit at a table and eat with other people who work here. This is how I met Kevin. He is a waiter.

– It's not fair, he says, this night, when he sees my wet and dirty T-shirt. – You should be a waiter instead of having to scrub those fucking pots and pans.

I shrug. I do not speak. I do not want to be a waiter, but I do not want to hurt his feelings, because he is a waiter. Also, I cannot work in public. All my work must be in secret, because

I am not supposed to work. Kevin knows this. This is why he says it is not fair. I think.

The door to the alley is near my corner, and it is always open. Fresh air comes through the open door but I would like to perspire and lock the door, always. But, even then, it must be opened sometimes. I must take out the bags of rubbish, old chicken wings and French fries and wet napkins. I must take them out to the skip.

And, really, this is the start of my story. This night, I carry a bag outside to the alley. I lift the lid of the skip, I drop in the bag, I turn to go back.

– There you are.

He is in front of me, and the door is behind him.

– Hello, I say.

– Polite, he says.

I understand. This is sarcasm.

– Did you think about that thing we were talking about? he says.

– Yes, I say.

– Good. And?

– Please, I say, – I do not wish to do it.

He sighs. He hits me before he speaks.

– Not so good.

I am on the ground, against the skip. He kicks me.

I must explain. The story starts two weeks before, when this man first grabbed my shoulder as I dropped a bag into the skip. He spoke before I could see his face.

– Gotcha, gotcha.

He told me my name, he told me my address, he told me that I had no right to work here and that I would be deported. I turned. He was not a policeman.

He understands.

– Hey! Hey!

I walk away.

I walk out of the alley. To a narrow street that is always dark. I do not look behind. I do not hurry. I hear no one behind me. I do not think that I am followed.

I am now on Grafton Street. I am not a fool. I do not think that the crowds will bring me safety. If the man wishes to injure me, if he thinks that he must, he will.

I walk.

If he decides to hurt me, or kill me, because I have humiliated him in front of his colleagues, he will wait. He will not do it here. There are too many people, and too many security cameras. If he wants to teach me, and others, a lesson, he might do it here: nowhere is safe – *do as we say*.

I do not think that he will attack me here. Perhaps he knows: he can teach me nothing.

I am a fit man and I enjoy walking. Just as well – as they say here. I must walk all day.

Fuck that.

I know that I am smiling. It is strange. I did not know that I was going to. It is good. To find the smile, to feel it.

I pass a man who is standing on a crate. He is painted blue and staying very still. When somebody puts money into the bucket in front of him, he moves suddenly. Perhaps I will do that. I will paint myself blue. I will disappear.

– Fuck that.

A man looks at me, and looks away.

I am the blue man who says Fuck that.

I must walk. All this day.

I cannot sit. I cannot stop. I cannot go home. I must be free. I must keep walking.

I walk. Through Temple Bar. Along the river, past tourists and heroin addicts, strangely sitting together. Past the Halfpenny Bridge and O'Connell Bridge. Past the Custom House and the statues of the starving Irish people. I walk to the Point Depot. Across the bridge – the rain has stopped, the clouds are low – I walk past the toll booths, to Sandymount. No cars slow down, no car door slams behind me. I am alone.

I walk on the wet sand. I see men in the distance, digging holes in the sand. They dig for worms, I think. They look as if they stand on the sea. It is very beautiful here. The ocean, the low mountains, the wind.

It is becoming dark when I cross the tracks at the station called Sydney Parade.

I will go to work. I will not let them stop me. I will go to work. I will buy a bicycle. I will buy a mobile phone. I am staying.

Roddy Doyle, The Deportees (2008)

✳ ✳ ✳

A brief escape back to the joys of a thriving modern Dublin by a one-time resident who had obviously been away too long.

Signora got out of her bus and walked up the quays beside the Liffey to O'Connell Bridge. All around her there were young people, tall, confident, laughing, in groups. She remembered reading somewhere about this youthful population, half the country under the age of twenty-four was it?

She hadn't expected to see such proof of it. And they were dressed brightly too. Before she had gone to England to work, Dublin had been a grey and drab place. A lot of the buildings had been cleaned, there were smart cars, expensive cars in the busy traffic lanes. She remembered more bicycles and second-hand cars. The shops were bright and opened up. Her eye caught the magazines, girls with big bosoms, surely these had been banned when she was last here or was she living in some kind of cloud cuckoo land?

For some reason she kept walking down the Liffey after O'Connell Bridge. It was almost as if she were following the crowd, and there she found Temple Bar. It was like the Left

Bank in Paris when once she had gone there so many years ago with Mario for a long weekend. Cobbled streets, outdoor cafés, each place full of young people calling to each other and waving at those they knew.

Nobody had told her Dublin was like this.

Maeve Binchy, *Evening Class* (1996)

✻ ✻ ✻

In Pat Mullan's short story, 'Tribunal', amazement at the change in Celtic Tiger Dublin is recorded by another former escapee returning to the city after working in both the U.K. and U.S.A.

There's a buzz about the place. *Sure as hell wasn't here when I left fifteen years ago.* He remembered Dublin as the pits then. Dark, priest-ridden, can't-do culture, living on government handouts and money from the emigrants. A Godforsaken hole of a place. For himself, anyway. Edmund Burke. *Yeah, that's me. My old man had delusions. Thought if he named me after the great Irish statesman that the name would overcome the bad genes and the lousy upbringing.* Willie Burke had been a failure, failed at every no-risk job he ever attempted, and the old man had ended his days earning a mere pittance as a salesman in a tailoring shop that had seen its best days in the last century. Mass on Sunday was the highlight of his mother's week, a timid woman from the west of Ireland who'd never felt at home in the big city. An only child, Edmund had been conceived just as his mother's biological clock was about to stop ticking. She was forty-two when she had him.

All these things flooded his mind as he jumped into the taxi at Dublin Airport and told the driver to take him to Ballsbridge. He'd survived. Succeeded because his father's failure terrified him. Got into Trinity, earned a law degree, headed for England, stayed a year in a boring clerk job at a London legal firm as resident Paddy. Luck intervened. His mother's uncle in Boston sponsored him to the States. Decided he'd go by sea instead of air. Took a 28,000-ton liner out of Liverpool. Gave him a sense of being a pilgrim setting out for the New World.

Now he was back. Why? The Celtic Tiger! That's why. Well, one of the reasons. He was running away again. But that's another story. Taking a year off from his New York law firm. Had just about enough of his mob clients. As well as his ex who wanted to rob him blind. Oh, yeah, he'd stashed away a few dollars, but still hadn't made that million. Maybe Dublin's the place to be these days. Everybody's here. All these faces in Dublin on a Tuesday and you see them again in New York or LA on the weekend. Aidan Quinn. Gabriel Byrne. Liam Neeson. Colin Farrell. Michael Flatley now a household name with *Riverdance* conquering the world. And Michael O'Leary and Ryanair conquering the skies. The priests are scarce on the ground these days. Divorce is legal. The Bishop of Galway has a love child with an American lover, and the President of Ireland has crossed the religious divide to take communion in a Protestant cathedral. The IRA is about to call it quits and the border separating the Republic from Northern Ireland is gradually becoming an imaginary line. Money talks. And money goes where it's well treated. And the Celtic Tiger is treating it well.

Money! That's really why I'm here, he reminded himself. *Not here to feel sentimental. Still, the old city looks good,* he thought. New roads, new houses, construction cranes everywhere. Plenty of Mercs and BMWs. They're not taking the Liverpool boat anymore. No! They're in investment banking, working for McKinsey and Microsoft. Turning Ireland into the largest exporter of computer software outside the United States.

At Ballsbridge, Burke paid the taxi fare and walked up Shelbourne Road. Dublin 4. The most sought after neighbourhood in the city. Bright skies and the early morning briskness countered his lack of sleep. Old stately homes lined the streets. Surrounded by sturdy stone walls, they exuded wealth and power. As a kid this would have been an alien place to him. *Still is*, he thought, as he reached a modern four-storey apartment block in Ballsbridge Gardens. He already had a key, mailed to him in New York before he'd left.

Once inside, he realized that he could be anywhere. Luxury that would be right at home on Fifth Avenue. He dropped his bags, started the coffee machine, and minutes later sat in the large Jacuzzi bathtub watching the bubbles welcome him to Dublin.

Pat Mullan, 'Tribunal', in *Dublin Noir* (2006)

✳ ✳ ✳

Finally, the dream and the reality. Maeve Binchy's short story, 'Flat in Ringsend', shows us Jo, a determined young woman who has escaped from a backwater to work in Dublin – though real Dublin life proves a little tougher than the dream.

Jo knew what she should do. She should get the evening papers at lunch-time, read all the advertisements for flats, and as soon as she saw one that looked suitable, she should rush round at once and sit on the doorstep. Never mind if the advertisement said 'After six o'clock'. She knew that if she went at six o'clock, and the flat was a good one, she'd probably find a queue of people all down the street. Finding a good flat in Dublin, at a rent you could afford, was like finding gold in the gold rush.

The other way was by personal contact. If you knew someone who knew someone who was leaving a flat ... That was often a good way. But for somebody who had only just arrived in Dublin, there was no chance of any personal contact. No, it was a matter of staying in a hostel and searching.

Jo had been to Dublin several times when she was a child. She had been on school excursions, and to visit Dad that time he had been in hospital and everyone had been crying in case he wouldn't get better. Most of her friends, though, had been up to Dublin much more often. They talked in a familiar way about places they had gone to, and they assumed that Jo knew what they were talking about.

'You *must* know the Dandelion Market. Let me see, you come out of the Zhivago and you go in a straight line to your right, keep going and you pass O'Donoghues and the whole of Stephen's Green, and you don't turn right down Grafton Street. Now do you know where it is?'

After such a long, helpful explanation, Jo said that she did know. Jo was always anxious to please other people, and she felt that she only annoyed them by not knowing what they were talking about. But really she knew hardly anything about Dublin. She felt that she was stepping into an unknown world when she got on the train to go and work there. She hadn't asked herself why she was going. Everyone had assumed that she would go. Who would stay in a one-horse town, the end of the world, this dead-and-alive place? At school all the girls were going to get out, escape, do some real living. Some of Jo's class had gone as far as Ennis or Limerick, often to stay with cousins. A few had gone to England, where an older sister or an aunt would help them to start a new life. But only Jo was going to Dublin, and she had no relations there. She was going off on her own.

There had been a lot of jokes about her going to work in the Post Office. There'd be no trouble in getting a stamp to write a letter home; what's more, there'd be no excuse if she didn't. She could make the occasional secret free phone call, too ... which would be fine, except that her family didn't have a phone at home. Maybe she could send a ten-page telegram if she needed to say anything in a hurry. People assumed that she would soon know everything about people's private business in Dublin, in the same way as Miss Hayes knew everyone's business from the post office at home. They said that she'd find it very easy to get to know people. There was nowhere like a post office for making friends; it was the centre of everything.

Jo knew that she would be working in a small local post office, but her dreams of life in Dublin had been about the big General Post Office in the centre. She had imagined herself working there, chatting up all the customers as they came in, and knowing every single person who came to buy stamps or collect the children's allowances. She had dreamt of living somewhere nearby, in the heart of the city, maybe on the corner of O'Connell Bridge, so that she could look at the Liffey river from her bedroom.

She had never expected the miles and miles of streets where nobody knew anyone, the endless bus journeys, and setting off for work very early in the morning in case she got lost or the bus was cancelled.

'Not much time for a social life,' she wrote home. 'I'm so exhausted when I get back to the hostel that I just go to bed and fall asleep.'

Maeve Binchy, 'Flat in Ringsend', from *Dublin People* (1982)

Publin

And on a bright Sunday afternoon we stroll along the river, where one pub is called Inn on the Liffey and the next down the street is called *Out* on the Liffey. Only in Ireland, only in Ireland.

Colin Irwin, In Search of the Craic (2001)

✳ ✳ ✳

For better or worse, Dublin is famous for its pubs and clubs ... and as the home of Guinness. From those old-fashioned bars where a pint or two can oil the wheels of sociable conversation to the undignified revellers who invade the city for stag and hen nights (and the after effects of one too many), here are some extracts on the drinking side of Dublin – from Colin Irwin, Chris Binchy and William Trevor.

And so to dead dirty Dublin. Or dear, dirty, *dusty* Dublin. Yep, it looks like another 35 hotels will go up this weekend to play host to stag party revellers from Wigan, and shrieking girls wearing angel wings and devil horns. The local pubs and hotels are supposed to be operating a ban on stag and hen parties these days (Barcelona is the preferred location for pre-nuptial mayhem in the brave new text-messaging world, apparently) but a brisk peek into Temple Bar swiftly reveals that nobody seems to have told the stag and hen parties. Unless, of course, the girl in full wedding regalia with an L-plate on her back doing 'Knees-up Mother Brown' and yelling 'I'm getting married in the morning' at 300 decibels is regulation behaviour for popping out for a quiet drink in Dublin these days. I ponder this possibility as a dozen females come hurtling along Grafton St in matching black T-shirts all bearing the slogan 'BABS WEDDING MARCH, DUBLIN'. A few yards further and a bunch of lads are having noisy piggyback fights, lurching waywardly across the street as they mount repeated medieval joust-style charges that cause even the stoical Hare Krishna Orchestra to flee for cover. Only the mad-eyed bagpiper in kilt and flowing red beard standing resolutely on the corner playing at a volume to waken the dead shall not be moved. The jousters suddenly get the full force of one of his blazing hornpipes and quietly dismount to disappear towards St Stephen's Green to fill out their applications to join the Hare Krishna.

Colin Irwin, *In Search of the Craic* (2001)

✳ ✳ ✳

A couple of weeks later I went out with Patrick on a Sunday night. There was something conspiratorial about drinking on a Sunday. You could feel it in the pub, see it in the faces of those around you, all shaking from a heavy weekend, or heading off the inevitable gloom of a Monday morning with drink. We were among our own. Patrick and I only ever had one conversation, which we picked up every time we saw each other and it didn't go anywhere or do anything, it just wandered in wide slow circles as we laughed ourselves into a stupor. I should have gone home at eleven but he bought another two and then it was my round, so we had to go to Renard's to get it and once we were there it seemed a crime to leave while they were still serving.

After that we went back to his place and listened to fucking Christy Moore and drank whiskey. I remember setting the alarm on my phone for seven, so that I could go home and shower and get a suit and still get into work for half-nine, which wouldn't be too bad and then the next thing was Patrick was giving me a cup of tea and it was bright outside. He sat beside me and lit a cigarette.

'Shouldn't you be in work?' he asked.

'What time is it?'

'Ten.'

'No. Fuck no' ...

Chris Binchy, The Very Man (2003)

✳ ✳ ✳

The Excelsior Bar of Riordan's public house was a dimly lit place, with walls that had been painted pink by the late Mr Riordan in pursuit of his belief that inebriation was pleasanter if induced in an atmosphere of rosiness, which was something he had read in a trade magazine. In front of the dark uphol-stered seating that lined these walls, tables were spaced so that a customer could be alone, a little away from the other customers, in order to meditate or doze. There was matting on the floor that absorbed the sound of footsteps, and there was no television set.

Mr Riordan, having served behind his own bar for sixty-two years, had become increasingly interested in the process of inebriation. He enjoyed observing his customers becoming more like themselves; he said it was a joyful thing, and even on mornings when the back lavatory was not a pleasant place to enter Mr Riordan had not shifted his principles, the chief of which was that only in intoxication were people truly happy. He had given the Excelsior Bar its name in 1933, having been reading in a trade magazine about the cocktail bars of Manhattan, which seemed to him to be curiously and aptly titled. After his death the house had fallen into the hands of his son-in-law, Edward Trump, who had made few changes. He had kept the Excelsior Bar as a small and quiet place that few people entered, a greater number being alienated by all that Mr Riordan had hoped would attract them. It was mainly Eugene Sinnott, Morrissey, Agnes Quin, and a woman called Mrs Dargan, who enjoyed the pink haze of the Excelsior Bar these days: they welcomed a place they could call their own, with the sound of music coming lightly from the television in the public bar and the opportunity for peaceful conversation.

William Trevor, *Mrs Eckdorf at O'Neill's Hotel* (1969)

* * *

All I wanted was to be drunk anyway. I didn't want to talk or meet anyone. I wanted to be alone but I knew I couldn't stay in the house. All I would do would be think about Niamh and everything I'd done and I didn't need that. What good would it do? I needed to stop thinking. I had to get out. I went to a pub off Dame Street, a dump where you could always get a seat but they'd changed it. They'd put in a PA and they were playing dance music to a load of displaced students down the back as the same old lads held the counter. I got in among them and ordered a drink. A Scottish stag party came in, already locked, and stood behind me shouting at each other. I could see a few of the old lads looking over, bridling. The Scottish guys started jostling me, knocking off me as they ordered Guinness and vodka and Red Bull. They were spoiling for something, talking about the fuckers in Temple Bar who wouldn't let them in. It wouldn't have taken much to set them off. I got out and went to a place down the lane but there was a guy singing rebel songs to a load of scary bastards so I only had a couple there and then went over towards Parliament Street and went into a place that was packed but had a nice vibe. I bought a pint and wandered around thinking I might find someone I knew but there was nobody so I stood at the bar and moved onto large whiskeys. Staring into middle distance, stepping to one side and then the other letting people into the bar. It was too busy. I was trying to order but the barman wasn't coming anywhere near our end at all. I started talking to the guy next to me, the two of us bitching about the service. Then a girl at the far end who'd arrived way after us got served and we started flapping. She spoke to the barman and sent down two tequilas to us, which was fair enough. She lifted her glass at the far end and me and the guy downed them, clinking glasses.

'Will we go over?' I said to him.

'I would, but I'm with my missus.'

'Well I'm not,' I said.

Chris Binchy, The Very Man (2003)

✳ ✳ ✳

Author Brendan Behan was one of Dublin's most famous 'drinkers'. He treats us to a couple of amusing pub anecdotes ...

Pubs are dull enough places at any time though not so dull in Ireland as they are in England. I suppose I know most of them in Dublin and I'd rather have them than the pubs in London. I remember being in the 'Blue Lion' in Parnell Street one day and the owner said to me: 'You owe me ten shillings,' he said 'you broke a glass the last time you were here.' 'God bless us and save us,' I said, 'it must have been a very dear glass if it cost ten shillings. Tell us, was it a Waterford glass or something?' I discovered in double-quick time that it wasn't a glass that you'd drink out of he meant – it was a pane of glass and I'd stuck somebody's head through it.

It was about the Blue Lion also that I remember my grand-mother, Christina, getting into a bit of embarrassment. It's more or less at the back of what was Joyce's Night-town, near Montgomery Street, which was one of the streets in the red light district. My grandmother had me by the hand and as we were walking down the street, we met a friend of hers who said: 'Come on, Christina, and have one', meaning come in for a glass of porter. So my grandmother said all right but she didn't want to go into the 'Blue Lion' because, she says: 'All those characters go in there' – meaning whores; but her friend says: 'Ah, they won't take any notice of us.' So in they went. 'We'll go in the private part,' she says and: 'All right,' says my grandmother. So when they went into the private part all the 'characters' roll up and say: 'Ah, hello, Christina, come on in, we didn't see you these years.'

There's a pub up near Guinness's Brewery on the Liffey Quay – it must be the nearest pub to Guinness's – known as 'The Shaky Man'. [...]

I was in 'The Shaky Man' one evening when a prostitute, who combined shoplifting with prostitution, came in and discovered that a pair of nylon knickers which she had care-fully stolen from a Grafton Street shop that day, had disap-peared during one of her absences on business. There was hell to pay, but all I remember of the row was her voice roaring again and again, in tones of the bitterest indignation: 'There's no honest whores left. There's no honest whores left.'

Or you'd have some old one sitting in the snug, where ladies who were ladies could have their jorums without the rude gazes of the men, and they'd remember Johnny going off in his pill-box cap to fight Kruger, or going off to do the Kaiser in, in the war after that. [...]

Both the big Irish distilleries are not far from Guinness's – I suppose what makes both Irish whiskey and Guinness so good is the curative properties of Liffey water. Scotch whisky seems to be getting more popular than Irish now particularly in America. Its popularity there is due to the fact that Queen

Victoria drank it. She didn't like the Irish and she wanted to be Celtic so she thought that maybe the Scots weren't so mad as the Irish and she became very Scots-minded. There were other influences on her too, I expect, but they didn't stop her exporting half the population of the Highlands to Canada. Irish whiskey is made in a pot-still, which is simply a pot surrounded by Irish anthracite coal from Kilkenny. Scotch whisky is made in a patent still which was invented by an Irishman named Angus Coffey who hawked it around the Irish distillers, who wouldn't have anything to do with him. So the Scots took it over and they made whisky in a series of pipes surrounded by peat, but now presumably heated by electricity. Most Scotch whiskies are blended, and a great number of them contain Irish whiskey which is exported for that purpose. The best Scotch whiskies are what are called 'single malt' which are not blended; they are straight whiskies and are very good indeed. The other Scotch whiskies I wouldn't give to a dog. The popularity of Scotch really only dates in these countries since the First War – never mind Victoria, she only influenced America which is slavishly royalty-minded. In Trollope's novels, for instance, when they're not scoffing claret in their clubs, they're knocking back Irish whiskey. It wouldn't surprise me at all to find Mr. Macmillan, who is an admirer of Trollope, I'm told, enjoying a quiet glass of Irish now and again for his health's sake. And if you ever look at the strip-cartoon in the *Daily Mail*, Flook, you'll find the conservative landed colonels dashing into their locals for a double Irish now and again. Only the lower classes drink Scotch; it sort of marks you off to go into a London pub and ask for Irish nowadays: when they've finished looking at you, they realise slowly that you've got a very eclectic palate.

Scotch, of course, is increasingly popular in Ireland, but that's because it's a bit dearer and the fact that you drink it indicated that you've got money – enough to pay for that ball of malt anyway. Most literary men go in for it now or for the glass of wine like Yeats. What's that he drank – not that he was ever seen in a pub – 'a glass of brimming Muscadel', I think, or maybe that was somebody else.

Brendan Behan, *Brendan Behan's Island* (1962)

✳ ✳ ✳

And some more information, insights and entertainment on the subject from Pete McCarthy.

There's always a lot riding on your first pint in Dublin.

I've had a couple of hours to let the thirst incubate, and now I'm ready. The barman seems to be pouring it carefully enough, in the sense that he's walked off and is doing nothing while it settles, but he's unlikely to smooth off the head with a kitchen knife the way they used to probably because of some new nit-picking health regulation prohibiting bar staff from putting breakfast cutlery in customers' drinks. They had those ivory-coloured spatula jobs for a while, custom-designed for stout-smoothing, but I think the government must have organised an amnesty and had them all handed in and put beyond use, because you don't see them much any more. It seems a pity. Innovation has its place. But not when it comes to the serving of a pint of stout.

For years now informal research among friends, family and mad people I meet on buses and trains has suggested there are two main reasons why – despite the family links that mean more English people visit Ireland each year than any other nationality – some English people still refuse point-blank ever to cross the Irish Sea. Either they think that it's so close that it will be just the same as home; or they imagine they'll be blown up for having an English accent. I think we can safely add a third reason to that list. For many generations, certainly for longer than anyone now living can remember, people in the UK have been intimidated by the daunting reputation of the Irish pint. For many people, the prospect of visiting a country where people go out for a drink just so they can discuss the quality of the drink they are currently drinking is simply too much to bear, so they go to Corfu and have retsina instead.

The question I'm asked most frequently by people who've never visited us is, 'Is it true what they say about an Irish pint of stout?' Actually, I'm being coy here. Despite the undeniable achievements of the good people at Murphy's and Beamish, the thing people really ask is, 'Is it true what they say about Irish Guinness? Is it really that much better?' This is like being asked by a five-year-old if Father Christmas really exists. You can't let them down. In fact you could tell these people anything. That you can stand a spoon up in it, slice chunks off it, and drink twenty without getting full up or suffering from a hangover. It's so creamy it just slides down, you see, which is why it improves your singing voice, and cures tonsillitis. It's so thick you can shave with it, so dense you can lay bricks with it, and the complex bouquet and long nose means I'm getting blackcurrants, cherries, vanilla, Jerusalem artichokes, charcoal and cream, spuds and buttermilk, Shane MacGowan's trousers, peat soot, testosterone, nectar, Fungi the Dolphin ... the water's different, you see. Something to do with all those dead nuns in the Liffey. No, there's no comparison between your British and your Irish pints.

Once upon a time all this was true. [...]

The stuff that's brewed in Britain has improved. British bar staff, many of whom come from Australia, New Zealand and South Africa, have been taught how to pour. But it also seems to me – and here comes the treasonous bit – that, with occasional spoon-standing, peat-tasting, bricklaying exceptions, the stuff in your glass in Ireland is not quite what it was. Oh, it's still pretty marvellous all right. Look, I like it, I like it a lot. But no doubt about it, the gap has narrowed. [...]

I've got myself trapped in a corner of the pub now by a tour party of Belgians drinking Gaelic coffee, so I'll take a break and come back later in case anyone turns up with a grandstand seat or a reservation for the presidential suite at the Shelbourne. A hundred yards up the street is the Palace, an atmospheric old-style bar in which no one is drinking Gaelic coffee. With the hopeless inevitability of fish swept up in a drift net, tourists in Temple Bar who want to go to an authentic Irish pub are trawled up by the fake, newly designed ones that have been created just to entrap them, while places like the Palace, untouched for decades, remain exclusion zones populated almost entirely by Dubliners. There's a fierce buzz of chat and I'm the only person with no one to talk to, so I lean on the bar and read the paper, pausing occasionally to look at my wrist as if I'm expecting somebody to arrive at any moment and engage me in a conversation that'll be just as good as the ones they're all having. Unfortunately I'm not wearing a watch, so I probably look as if I'm checking whether the skin infection is getting any worse, which would explain why I'm on my own in the first place.

There's an article bemoaning the fact that the big Irish family is now a thing of the past, and that if you take children into a restaurant in the capital 'the staff look at you like you're a freak and the other diners can barely conceal their contempt.' Social attitudes tend to trickle down from Dublin, so if this is true it may be the way the rest of the country will go in a few years' time. [...]

I finish my drink and head back to MacKool's, where a few pessimists are waiting to meet me. All have the same story: they've managed to get a ticket for the match, just the one like, for themselves but not for me. Like gold dust, apparently. No matter. We make a night of it, and end up in a restaurant that seems horribly modish until the teriyaki sea bass with buckwheat noodles arrives, accompanied by a big bowl of roast spuds.

The bar of the Shelbourne Hotel makes an excellent reading room but is also a major meeting place on international match weekends, and as late morning heads reluctantly towards lunchtime it starts to fill up. My equilibrium is disturbed by a party of posh buffoons in their fifties, England fans on a corporate jolly, kitted out in leisurewear that would have been best left on the mannequins in the window of the Pringle shop. They are playing a noisy drinking game which involves whacking glasses of expensive claret down in one. I decided to adjourn to Doheny & Nesbitt, a pub just up the road with a strong literary tradition, in the sense that many writers have drunk themselves to a stand-still there over the years. When they needed to extend it they built a back bar that is an exact replica of the front one. I install myself in a corner with the intention of carrying on reading until I'm in need of solids or a lie down, whichever comes first. [...]

Seamus says he knows a nice little bar, which turns out to be a Doheny & Nesbitt. It's filled up since lunchtime, and nobody's here to read. They're three deep at the bar, and that's just on the serving side. It's unseasonably warm and the pavement outside is packed with people in shirt sleeves, some English, some Irish, all happy. It's one of those easy evenings when strangers start talking and you get invited round for Irish stew tomorrow lunchtime, and then bump into someone you once worked with and lose them in the crowd, the pints are passed over your head but nobody spills one on you, and everything seems right with the world. It's getting near closing time, which is observed in most Dublin pubs with a rigour that would horrify those brought up on Irish rural flexitime. [...]

I've been going to the Shelbourne Hotel quite a lot this week, and this morning's no exception. I may not be staying here, but I wish I was. [...]

I've a soft spot for the Shelbourne, which has a seductive aura of old-time hotel despite an updated bar and bistro. I can sit here at quarter past eleven on Saturday mornings and view the changing economic fortunes of Ireland, or at least of certain postal districts of Dublin. A woman with a mahogany-brown suntan wearing some manner of lace and leopard-skin cap just parked a BMW coupe outside the front doors and gave the keys to a flunky in a top hat with whom she was on first name terms. Two ruthless-looking sods with deep voices and Cuban cigars, who look as though they could buy, sell and get the bailiffs in to Charlie Haughey before breakfast, are discussing enormous sums of money over early morning brandy and coffee. There are also a few fragile-looking England fans nursing a range of hangover cures.

Pete McCarthy, The Road to McCarthy (2002)

✳ ✳ ✳

Perhaps the most thorough portrait of 'Publin' is to be found in this extract from Michael Cronin's Time Tracks, *where he explores the place of the Dublin pub in the lives of its citizens.*

O'Neill's. The Stags Head. The International Bar. Burke's. Peter's Pub. Neary's ... The name cards are shuffled differently for each drinker in the city, a private Monopoly board of association and recall, pubs marking out phases in existence, girlfriends, boyfriends, politics (Provos drink here, Sticks drink there), education (UCD medics there, Trinity jocks here, DCU communications students elsewhere), a new bed-sit, the first job. If directions to foreigners are often given using pubs as landmarks, the landmarks are not just public but private. You could imagine a biography that would ignore the usual chronological minimalism of 1954–1972, 1973–1993, 1994-, or the homely platitudes of "The Early Years", "Growing Awareness", "The Prime", "The Twilight years", and have a table of contents that would read Chapter One: *Delaneys*; Chapter Two: *The Buttery*; Chapter Three: *O'Neill's*; Chapter Four: *The Stag's Head*; Chapter Five: *The International*; Chapter Six: *Peter's Pub*; Chapter Seven: *Neary's*.

There are lives where there is only one chapter heading. One pub. One life. The local that is the universal, which carries you from the first public drink through the twenty-firsts, engagements, weddings and christenings to the birthdays, anniversaries and funerals. For the locals there is the imprimatur of the free pint at Christmas time but your own loyalties were too fickle or your life in the city too shifting or unstable for the ready recognition of the cocked eyebrow, the affirmative nod and the pulled pint. Instead, there was the succession of Locals, each holding a fragment of your story and there are of course the unfinished chapters, the pubs that claimed your attention but never kept it or that remain in a no-go area of the heart, cordoned off by loss.

There are bars like sitting-rooms, where you sit and stay and stare or talk. And there are other bars, which are bars of passage, where you stand and watch or talk and go. This bar is undecided. The two great doors at either end are invitations to the busy exit and entrance and standing noisily *en route* to other business is an accepted custom. The high ceiling and the turning fan and the ceaseless passage is the exotic dimension to the pub, its other life as a café-society sophisticate. But for those who remain, the doors are sealed, the narrow bar a large room where conversation deals its hand endlessly.

Pubs have their hostages. The big drinker in college who somehow mistimed his exit as he trundles from pub to pub in search of company. One minute, it seemed everybody was there roaring for more and the next they were postcards. The signatories would pile in at Christmas and mix condescension with nostalgia as they asked him was he still drinking in those same places. As students, they delighted in the social promiscuity of the pub, the unstable democracy of the barstool. This was before qualification, career and marriage led to the raising of the drawbridge and the retreat into the tower houses of privilege where they now entertain, fortified by vintage bottles and choice cheeses. For the Departed, the memory has been archived, the photos sorted, but their past is the Drinker's unchanging present.

There is the Pub Friend. You only ever see the pub friend in the pub. The conversation is always public and satirical, never personal or confessional (except in advanced and immediately regretted states of drunkenness). Jokes flourish here, newly rehearsed, topical and, as you pull away from the nightly orbit around the pub friend, you feel the humour leaking from your own memory, the off joke haphazardly remembered and repeated over and over (*Did you ever hear the one about the faith healer in Athlone ...*) to your exasperated partner and eye-rolling children (*He's not going to tell that one again*). Here is the peculiar social intimacy of the pub, the face you will see for years but never the house of the flat where pub friend lives, as if the real parlour was here on the motley tiles of a city pub and not the weekend-paper strewn front room of a bed-sit in Rathgar.

Downstairs in the International it is mid-week and the courting couples, hands clasped in front of half-emptied pint glasses of lager, hold up their childhoods for mutual inspection. The other tentative hand on the inside of the thigh is warm in the complicity of remembering. Now that the groups have dwindled to couples, the glasses are lowered more slowly and there are fewer jokes, as talk turns to How my Mother gets on my Wick or How my Oul' Fellow is always Wanging on about the Government or else it's spluttered laughs over the Terrible Times in Tramore. The tapes of early experience have a long time to run, so there will be many more of these hand-holding confessions before conversation becomes more code than revelation. Then as the years pass, there are the degrees of departure. People begin to move to more distant suburbs or faraway cities. They begin to complain about the smoke. The evolutionary regression of age, from *homo* and *femina erectus* to the seats of the established. Soon it will be wine rather than beer. The dinner party finds favour as jostling with youngsters begins to exhaust the spirit. You will of course bring your foreign visitors on a tour of the pubs but you are now as much a stranger as they. Wondering should all these people be served? Are they not under-age? Forgetting what you looked like at nineteen. Or on your holiday in the West you will sit in the late afternoon with your wife and restless children, briefly envying the monuments of ageing intellect at the bar and feeling that old, familiar languor return as evening pushes shoppers in the door. But the kids have finished the Cokes (minerals your mother called them) and scattered the crisps and any longing is disciplined by the terror of taking the wheel on dark, pockmarked roads.

On the ground level, the seats had collapsed. Sinking into them was easier than pulling yourself out of these velveteen dugouts at the end of an evening or when your bladder was threatening to burst its banks. The Depression. This is where you sat out the documentary years of Southern unemployment and Northern violence, the city a host to the tumbleweed survivors pooling resources to clasp forgetfulness in Sides or Suzy Street. Conversations rambled through the evenings to reach the same weary conclusion, that the country had once again fallen and that the only virtue of corruption was gossip. The streets outside the pub were thinned by exile, and inside the terrible truculent ghosts of the fifties would sneer at you from the bar if the evening failed to pick up. And then the World Cup spilled into this stunted world. The Romania match and we are standing on the seats. On the floor, a man from Westmeath is locked in prayer, his bowed head a still point in the sacramental silence of the penalty kicks. When Packie Bonner breaks ecstatically from the goalmouth, it is more jailbreak than victory burst and we the inmates come pouring out after him, sensing some impossible spring of change, anything to clear the brown fug of emigration and deceit from our tired lungs. In the world beyond the stately swinging doors of the pub the Guildford Four are still in prison and, along the quays, post-match revellers and marchers in the dark overcoats merge and O'Connell Street turns into a mass of Dubliners swimming in their own disbelief, riding the bumpers of Volkswagens and Fiats like drunken charioteers returning from campaigns to be remembered in the half-light of a sore morning.

The peculiar time-motion studies of the pub. This is apparent in getting down off a barstool. Like mountain climbing, it is always much more dangerous going down than going up. The drink slows time down but expands space. It now seems a long and treacherous way down from the top of this unsteady Olympus. You touch solid ground with the tentativeness of a novice ballerina. As the evening wears on, the metaphors, however, become more Spatial than spatial. The ground is now in orbit and touchdown demands timing, precision and luck. When you do land, there is the slightly self-conscious moonwalk to the Gents, the unsteady tangents and the sashaying hips as your head peers through the helmet of One Too Many at ordinary life back on earth. [...]

Tourists sometimes make their uncertain way into the International Brigade. They wear the uniform of their age. Bright-coloured, multi-zipped, Gore-Tex rain gear and walking boots with new shoelaces which always look incongruous in the most urban of pubs. They nurse a single glass of stout (an experiment) for hours and stare bemusedly at the locals as if waiting for something to happen. Nothing does. Only conversation. And more of it. Most of it incomprehensible to ears diligently schooled in the Upper Form Prefect English of continental Europe. Eventually they leave at half-past ten and wonder what all the fuss is about.

Michael Cronin, *Time Tracks* (2003)

✳ ✳ ✳

And the unmistakable voice of Samuel Beckett in an early story from More Pricks Than Kicks.

Belacqua turned left into Lombard Street, the street of the sanitary engineers, and entered a public-house. Here he was known, in the sense that his grotesque exterior had long ceased to alienate the curates and make them giggle, and to the extent that he was served with his drink without having to call for it. This did not always seem a privilege. He was tolerated, what was more, and let alone by the rough but kindly habitués of the house, recruited for the most part from among dockers, railwaymen and vague joxers on the dole. Here also art and love, scrabbling in dispute or staggering home, were barred, or, perhaps better, unknown. The aesthetes and the impotent were far away.

These circumstances combined to make of this place a very grateful refuge for Belacqua, who never omitted, when he found himself in its neighbourhood with the price of a drink about him, to pay it a visit. [...]

Sitting in this crapulent den, drinking his drink, he gradually ceased to see its furnishings with pleasure, the bottles, representing centuries of loving research, the stools, the counter, the powerful screws, the shining phalanx of the pulls of the beer-engines, all cunningly devised and elaborated to further the relations between purveyor and consumer in this domain. The bottles drawn and emptied in a twinkling, the casks responding to the slightest pressure on their joysticks, the weary proletarians at rest on arse and elbow, the cash-register that never complains, all this made up a spectacle in which Belacqua was used to take delight and chose to see a pleasant instance of machinery decently subservient to appetite. A great major symphony of supply and demand, effect and cause, fulcrate on the middle C of the counter and waxing, as it proceeded, in the charming harmonies of blasphemy and broken glass and all the aliquots of fatigue and ebriety. So that he would say that the only place where he could come to anchor and be happy was a low public-house and that all the wearisome tactics of gress and dud Beethoven would be done away with if only he could spend his life in such a place. But as they closed at ten, and as residence and good faith were viewed as incompatible, and as in any case he had not the means to consecrate his life to stasis, even in the meanest bar, he supposed he must be content to indulge this whim from time to time, and return thanks for such sporadic mercy.

Samuel Beckett, 'Ding-Dong' in *More Pricks Than Kicks* (1934)

❋ ❋ ❋

In a city where pubs and drinking are a normal part of social culture, it's inevitable that some people will start the drinking habit a little too young. Gabriel Duffy confesses all in his vivid memoir of growing up in the Dublin of the 40s and 50s.

By the time I returned to begin my final 'Sixth year', at school I was a confirmed Saturday Night Drinker and regularly joined 'the guys' in a pub called 'The Hut' in Phibsboro.

They had installed a tv and our nights began with watching 'The Valiant Years', a series of 30 minute programmes based on Churchill's war memories. – Given the supposed antago-nism of the Irish for the English, it is interesting to note that we all relished the series and identified completely with the British, standing up so doggedly to the Nazis. I guess we sensed that all this stuff about the Blitz, the RAF, El Alamain and so on, transcended mere propaganda and was based on the historical facts of a struggle that saved Ireland, as much as England, from being terminally jack-booted.

I do remember that all pub talk ceased and you could hear a silent fart, when the credits began to roll and the anthem theme music – the March from Tchaikovsky's Sixth – drowned the surrounding sounds of glassware.

Then on to talking, drinking, more talking and drinking, until we had each 'sunk' six to eight pints and staggered out at closing time to make for a nearby dance at Charleville Lawn Tennis Club.

Unlike the Carlton Hall the clientele were mainly people we knew – if sometimes only to see – or well-spoken scions of the best families in Drumcondra. We were well-known – not least to the dinner-jacketed 'bouncers' – and always got in, no trouble. The small wooden hall would be full to the rafters by the time we descended. Hot and humid as a Turkish wrestler's jock-strap, with a white-shirted Quintet on a small stage working through 'Red Sails in the Sunset' for the umpteenth time, the brylcreemed alto-sax proving that he could split a reed with the best.

Many of us were "doing a line" at the time and "the women" would already be waiting at the dance, having paid their own way in, like the good Irish girls they were (expected to be). Not only did they accept and tolerate our swaying condition, but most of them were positively pleased to see us. I suppose that they knew that a few drinks was as much a male necessity as powder and puff was to them. They were certainly very good-humoured about it.

Even when their 'man' occasionally disappeared into the Gents, to have a swig from a Baby Power (small bottle of whiskey) which one of his friends would be 'carrying'. ("Are ye carryin? Grate! See ye in the jakes in a minit.") So we topped up.

And sometimes threw up. That never happened to me as I possessed the incipient alcoholic's high tolerance for the poison. (If drink makes you sick or gives you a ferocious hang-over, count yourself lucky; you are unlikely to develop a serious drinking problem.)

I often found myself supporting a friend who'd had "one over the eight", watching him pewk his guts out against the (exterior!) slats of the dance hall wall.

Gabriel Duffy, Sham to Rock (2003)

* * *

Eric Newby is reminded that one of Dublin's great poets is rumoured to have died of drink – but then goes on to give an affectionate portrait of the traditional Dublin pub.

By now the sun was coming out and it was going to be a lovely day. Just beyond this lock, beautifully inscribed on what resembled a headstone, and miraculously unvandalized, was a poem written by Patrick Kavanagh (1905–67), son of a farmer and shoemaker in County Monaghan and himself a farmer. [...]

Just by this stone was the seat for the passer-by, one who in this instance looked more like a permanent fixture: an emaciated Gael – he would probably have described himself, modestly, as being 'on the tin soide' – fortyish, with two mid-front upper incisors missing and wispy hair. He was dressed in a thick, dark, hand-made greatcoat several sizes too large for him, with puke on the lapels and equally over-sized boots without laces, as if to emphasize, as the bound feet of Chinese ladies once did, the sedentary position of those who wear such footwear in life's race.

He was not the sort of citizen the Americans call a bum, or the British a down-and-out, but what the Dublin writer Tom Corkery used to say was 'a mouth' to his friends, 'a character' to tourists and 'a non-productive unit' to economists: non-productive, but unlike a real bum or down-and-out, certainly supported by some unfortunate woman, perhaps two unfortunate women and/or other next-of-kin.

'Have a place on Paddy's Seat,' said this non-productive unit graciously, moving sideways a perceptible bit to give me more *lebensraum* if I wanted it.

'Thank you,' I said, 'I won't actually. I'm bicycling and my wife's way on ahead; but before I go, tell me, what do you think of Kavanagh?'

'I tink of him as a thoughtful man to give me a seat here by the water, which I can use for the rest of me natural life, God willing, and as a great poet, too. Have you read "The Great Hunger", that's his best in every way, the one that begins "Clay is the word and clay is the flesh"? It's a long poem but I have most of it by heart if you would like to hear it.'

'I'm afraid it will have to be some other time,' I said. 'I've got to get on.' By now I was feeling like the Water Rat when he meets the Seagoing Rat who almost persuades him to go to sea.

'He died of the drink, they say; but he was a good age for a drinking man, sixty-two, or tree. Dere was only one man he couldn't abide, that was Brendan Behan. He was a *comic*, Paddy Kavanagh.' [...]

It is a city in which the inhabitants were, as I remembered, completely indifferent to the march of time. [...]

A city in which, at this very moment, many of them would be drinking their first pint of the day from a glass without a handle in one of what were when I was last there, its seven hundred or more pubs; pubs which, ideally for the older drinker, would have an ambiance compounded of brown-painted lincrusta and glittering glass; pubs in which the drinkers used to drink in companies or schools, each one waiting his turn to buy his round of what was called 'the gargle', which ensured that everyone had six drinks instead of three. For this was a city in which few men drank at home unless they were already drunk, or otherwise incapacitated, on the grounds that it didn't taste the same as in a bar: 'Now, Mr O'Leary sir, I tink you've had enough for a bit, sir.' I remembered singing in pubs; pubs that looked more like libraries, but with bottles not books on the shelves; theatre pubs; pubs with poetry; one pub reputed to be used only by market women and no men; another a favourite stopping-off place for mourners on their way back from Glasnevin Cemetery. Here, in The Brain Boru House, the wake still flourished and you could drink 'a ball o'malt', Irish whiskey from a wooden cask. Hickey's, on City Quay, had one of the best pints anywhere.

To me the most wonderful of all Dublin pubs was O'Meara's Irish House on the corner of Wood Quay. Its façade was topped by six round towers of the sort but not the size that soar up above Irish monastic settlements and the façade itself was embellished with coloured stucco reliefs of such heroes of Irish nationalism and Catholic emancipation as Henry Grattan (1769–1820), making his last speech to the about-to-be abolished Irish Parliament in 1800, and Daniel O'Connell (1775–1847). But despite these remembrances of things and times past in Dublin's publand, for those of a selective nature or finicky disposition it is worth heeding what Swift wrote in a letter to Charles Ford in August 1725: 'No men in Dublin go to Taverns who are worth sitting with.'

Eric Newby, *Round Ireland in Low Gear* (1987)

* * *

The traditional Dublin pub – and the stark poverty nearby. J. P. Donleavy stops us getting a too rosy or cosy view of the past.

In the inner core of Dublin city and within half a mile radius of the centre of O'Connell Street Bridge, you never at any point were more than one hundred and thirty nine and one half paces from a pint of porter or a ball of whiskey. Or your trusty bottle of stout standing in their hundreds on shelves ready for their corks to be levered out with a hand puller and a suitable pop. In the better bars were clarets and burgundies, pickled onions, sausages, boiled eggs and sandwiches of ham, cheese and roast beef. But always on the very edges of these blessings lurked the cold desperate reality of the city and its stark gloomy poverty only a stone's throw away. Begging for a penny or selling a newspaper, shoeless urchins, faces streaming phlegm, scattering across the grey glisteningly wet streets.

J. P. Donleavy, *J. P. Donleavy's Ireland* (1986)

✳ ✳ ✳

And finally, Simon Cole, on a recent visit to the city quietly observes the life in a Dublin bar where time seems to have stood still.

Leaving the high street and stepping into a great period piece pub like the Palace Bar, there's a sense of time stood still. Patrick Kavanagh, Brendan Behan and Flann O'Brien must have enjoyed the same sensation when they nursed their pints among the hacks of Fleet Street.

The tide of conversation ebbs and flows; groups come and go. Movement, yet rest. A laugh in one corner, a dispute in another. It's all here: lovers; friends; colleagues; strangers; tolerated drunks. There's stilted conversation with a visiting boss and the fizzy flirtation of the newly courting.

A television shows Man Utd v Inter Milan with the volume set low, while a fan revolves slowly far above, like a drone surveying the friendly mob. Wars happen elsewhere and economic woes become abstract. Problems at home recede as rounds arrive and the foetal familiarity of a welcoming pub keeps a bad world at bay. The only clue to any external environment is the gentle roar of a football crowd on the TV, rising and falling like a distant sea.

Old leather seats are ranged against the back walls, like a doctor's surgery. A surprising amount of light makes its way to the back, silhouetting ornaments on the semi-partition: a horse and jockey are suspended over a hedge. If they could unfreeze themselves in time and clear it, the next obstacle would be an antique hurling stick: for once a genuine antique, not ersatz ephemera.

Contrasting conversations swirl into one generic river of noise that lulls me into a pleasant lassitude. Then a raucous laugh cuts through the bar, jarring me wide awake – the crack of the craic. A gesticulating man on a mobile stands half-hidden by the partition's opaque glass. His right side casts a disproportionately large shadow against the pane, creating a bizarre Jekyll and Hyde mismatch with the exposed left half of the body.

Streams of chatter come from the islands of conversation spread across the lounge, pooling around me in a rich reservoir of dialogue. Endless variations of the same themes: X had a baby, Y passed away, Z is stressed at work. Two professors discuss the merits of a certain student, presumably a pretty protégé, and they fight over teaching rights. A tourist couple with the demeanour of generals map out their mini-break over a Lonely Planet guidebook.

All the world's a stage, but tonight I'm no player. Instead I've absconded: slipping down into the stalls to provide the audience these little performances so richly deserve. Alone in the crowd, this Quiet Man gently fades into the Palace's furniture.

Simon Cole, 'Intelligent Inebriation' (2009)

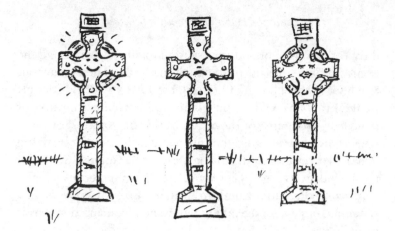

The good, the bad and the
(just a little bit) ugly

In its cocktail of beauty, excitement, visible wealth, stimulation, conflicts, poverty, shady dealings and despair, Dublin is no different from any other world city. In this section we take a head-on look at some of the contrasts that define the capital. Although the recent economic crisis has taken a toll on the phenomenon of Dublin's rapid growth in the years of the 'Celtic Tiger', the contrasts noted by Colin Irwin still hold true.

Dublin today is a very different beast from the one I first visited. Now it's one of Europe's most vibrant, thriving, cosmopolitan cities with a booming economy and is apparently in the rudest of health. The streets are jammed, the shops are full and the young people jabber constantly into their mobiles, planning the night's play in one of the myriad of night clubs and upmarket pubs. Yet you don't have to scratch far below the surface of internet cafés, stylish shops and open-topped tourist buses parading alongside the Liffey to find dear old dirty Dublin, present and correct, warts and all. And for all the excited, buzzy sense of fun and adventure tumbling over itself to shout 'PARTY! AFFLUENCE! PARTY! MODERN! EUROPEAN! PARTY!' at you in full-lunged celebration of the twenty-first century, the underclass is still painfully evident. Late at night young guys looking like ghosts huddle, shivering under blankets, away from the glare of O'Connell Street on the Ha'penny Bridge. They can't all be remnants of a rugby club weekender from Cheshire. I try to talk to one but he just stares sullenly back, seemingly too wasted to string two words together.

Colin Irwin, In Search of the Craic (2001)

✳ ✳ ✳

Chris Binchy's 2003 novel The Very Man *shows us the experience of a Dublin 'escapee' returning from the U.S.A. into the city's new-found wealth. But his jaundiced eye sees the underside of the Tiger.*

It was as if the changes had happened over night. That was exactly how it was. All the cranes and new buildings and pubs, builders in hard hats everywhere. Streets with no names. Everybody on Grafton Street and in the pubs wearing the clothes but never quite getting it right, great smells coming out of cafés but when you went in it took twenty minutes for them to get to you and when they did they could never understand you. People in shops were sloppy and rude. It was like all this money had just landed out of nowhere and nobody really knew what to do, or they knew what they should be doing, they just didn't know how and they could only make a half-assed attempt at sophistication. There was an edge in the way people dealt with each other. Everywhere you walked on the street you could hear it – fuck him, fuck it, fuck off, fucking prick, cunt, bitch. Everywhere and everybody. Phones ringing all the time and stupid inane conversations, too stupid to have face to face. Everybody smoking hard, all lighting, sucking, pulling, blowing. Skinny girls in skinny jeans with no arses hanging around with loutish young lads in shit tracksuits looking like they're only hanging around long enough to get her fags. Rubbish everywhere, piled up at the sides of the buildings and in doorways, streets lined with puke. Everybody shoving past tourists who wandered around lost and bemused. They came from Manhattan to Ireland and it was too busy for them. Traffic going nowhere. People who couldn't drive delaying people who couldn't wait. One person in every car. People beeping when you crossed the road in front of them because they were going to break the red light and now because of you they couldn't. You fucking prick. Nothing ever arrived when it was supposed to, nobody ever came when they said and if you got snotty they'd start getting up on their high horse.

'Why didn't you come?'

'I don't like your tone.'

'Yeah, well I don't like being lied to.'

'Are you calling me a liar?'

'You said you'd be here. You're not. What would you call it?'

'I think it would be better if you took your business else-where.'

What could you do? They didn't care because they had never had so much and nothing anyone could say right now would cop them on to the fact that when all this ended and the shit eventually went down, they'd go with it.

Chris Binchy, *The Very Man* (2003)

✻ ✻ ✻

Poverty is relative: Dublin no longer has the teeming tene-ments of the early twentieth century. But have today's poor retained the compensations noted by V. S. Pritchett?

In Dublin, the tenements were shocking; the women still wore the long black shawl, the children were often bare-footed. You picked up lice and fleas in the warm weather in the Dublin trams as you went to the North side to the wrecked mansions of the eighteenth century. The poor looked not simply poor, but savagely poor, though they were rich in speech and temperament.

V. S. Pritchett, *Midnight Oil* (1971)

✻ ✻ ✻

But even in a newly affluent Dublin, one could still encounter desperate beggars, as Martin, in Keith Ridgway's The Long Falling, *discovers ...*

Martin walked up O'Connell Street in the rain, distracted by the trees. He squinted, his head at an angle, his hands in his pockets, and moved slowly. The trees were in the middle of the street, on the wide island which separated the two flows of traffic. They were withered things, bare and lifeless, with barks shiny as leather. Snaking around the branches, evenly spaced one from the other, were countless dead grey light bulbs, sprouting from a green flex that dripped and cut the wood as if strangling. They looked like growths, the bulbs. Like warts or blisters. Decorations, Martin supposed, left over from Christmas. He had not noticed them before, but wondered now whether they were left there all year round. Maybe they were hidden by leaves in the spring, lost in the summer greenery that was impossible to imagine now. It didn't matter. He didn't like them. They were disgusting. He half expected them to burst open and spill a yellow mess down the trunks.

He was cold in Henry's jacket, and the scarf that Philip had left in the house the night before was stringy and damp. His haircut bothered him. They had taken too much off. He wore Henry's black cap and it was too tight and left a red mark across his forehead whenever he removed it. And when it was on he looked as though he might be bald underneath. Chemotherapy bald. He had no umbrella. He could feel the rain beginning to soak through him, dripping from the peak of the cap and down his face. He could have taken a bus but it had not been raining when he had left the house, and he had decided to walk. Halfway down Grafton Street it had started, light but insistent, a very wet kind of rain. He had hurried because of it and now he was too early and sweating.

He ducked the sharp points of passing umbrellas and wondered where he could shelter for a few minutes. He walked at the edge of the pavement, glancing at the trees, closing his eyes at the roar of buses that rushed past him, their misty wake darkening the suede of his shoes.

He was aware of a beggar up ahead, an old man in a filthy grey duffle coat with a huge, tangled beard, and skin almost black with dirt. His white eyes shone out from his face like lights. He stood with his back to the traffic and watched the scurry of people with a nodding, malicious head, thrusting his arm outwards, open palmed, and appearing to mutter. Martin changed course and headed diagonally towards the shopfronts. But the man saw him and moved to intercept. Martin adjusted direction again, moving back towards the kerb. The man smiled and followed him, limping badly. Martin cursed and came face to face with the hirsute features and the gap-toothed grin.

'Any chance of twenty pence there, sir, for a cup of tea?'

'Excuse me,' said Martin, trying to move around him. The man stepped back and sideways, getting in front of him again.

'Just a few pence please, sir, for a cap for the rain. Nice cap like yours.'

'Fuck off,' hissed Martin. He pushed past, increasing his speed and keeping his head down. He had walked only a few steps when he heard a roar behind him.

'Ya big fucker. Don't you push me. No fucking manners. You're a big man aren't ya, in her big fucking leather jacket. C'mon. C'mon.'

Martin glanced back to see him standing on his toes, his fists raised like a boxer, swaying slightly.

'C'mon, ya coward, come here and say that again.'

Martin turned and kept going, walking as fast as he could without running. There was silence for a moment and he thought that he had escaped. Then the voice came again, soiled, cracked, and he knew the man was after him. He saw people stare.

'What's wrong with ya, ya big fucker. Ya walk like a girl. C'mon.'

Martin felt the man's hand poking at his shoulder and shrugged it off fiercely and jogged a few steps, smiling an awful, embarrassed smile at those who stared. The man fell back a little but kept shouting. [...]

Martin ducked and trotted and dipped his shoulder. He reached the entrance to the Gresham Hotel and sprinted up the steps. A porter stood behind the glass, peering out into the rain, his cap pulled low over his eyes. He opened the door for Martin and stepped back.

'Rotten day,' he said. Martin nodded.

'Yeah. Rotten.' He took off Henry's cap and rubbed at his forehead and moved away from the door hurriedly, expecting to hear the loud cursing voice following behind him. He walked past reception, conscious of the squelch in his shoes, and caught sight of the bar. He glanced back to the main door. The porter stood with his back to him, his hands clasped together, his thumbs working at each other. Through the glass was the tousled grey hair of the beggar, his fist raised and shaking at the blue uniform and the peaked cap, his voice crying out something Martin could not hear. He found himself thinking of the rain falling into the man's open mouth, of how refreshing that would be, how soothing.

In the almost-empty bar he ordered a pint and sat by the fire and dried himself a little and drank.

Keith Ridgway, *The Long Falling* (1998)

✳ ✳ ✳

German novelist Heinrich Böll, visiting Ireland in the 1950s, also encounters a beggar – outside St Patrick's Cathedral … before moving on to a Catholic church in the nearby slum district and giving us a moving meditation on what he sees there.

At Swift's tomb my heart had caught a chill, so clean was St. Patrick's Cathedral, so empty of people and so full of patriotic marble figures, so deep under the cold stone did the desperate Dean seem to lie, Stella beside him: two square brass plates, burnished as if by the hand of a German housewife: the larger one for Swift, the smaller for Stella; I wished I had some this-tles, hard, big, long-stemmed, a few clover leaves, and some thornless, gentle blossoms, jasmine perhaps or honeysuckle; that would have been the right thing to offer these two, but my hands were as empty as the church, just as cold and just as clean. Regimental banners hung side by side, half-lowered: did they really smell of gunpowder? They looked as if they did, but the only smell was of mould, as in every church where for centuries no incense has been burned; I felt as though I were being bombarded with needles of ice; I fled, and it was only in the entrance that I saw there was someone in the church after all: the cleaningwoman; she was washing down the porch with lye, cleaning what was already clean enough.

In front of the cathedral stood an Irish beggar, the first I had met: beggars like this one are only to be found otherwise in southern countries but in the south the sun shines: here, north of the 53rd parallel, rags and tatters are something different from south of the 30th parallel; rain falls on poverty, and here even an incorrigible esthete could no longer regard dirt as picturesque; in the slums around St. Patrick's, squalor still huddles in many a corner, many a house, exactly as Swift must have been it in 1743.

Both the beggar's coatsleeves hung empty at his sides; these coverings for limbs he no longer possessed were dirty; epileptic twitching ran like lightning across his face, and yet his thin, dark face had a beauty that will be noted in a book other than mine. I had to light his cigarette for him and place it between his lips; I had to put money for him in his coat pocket: I almost felt as if I were furnishing a corpse with money. Darkness hung over Dublin: every shade of grey between black and white had found its own little cloud, the sky was covered with a plumage of innumerable greys: not a streak, not a scrap of Irish green; slowly, twitching, the beggar from St. Patrick's Park crossed over under this sky into the slums.

In the slums dirt sometimes lies in black flakes on the windowpanes, as if thrown there on purpose, fished up from fireplaces, from canals; but things don't happen here so easily on purpose, and not much happens by itself: drink happens here, love, prayer, and cursing. God is passionately loved and no doubt equally passionately hated.

In the dark back yards, the ones Swift's eyes saw, this dirt has been piled up in decades and centuries: the depressing sediment of time. In the windows of the second-hand shops lay a confused variety of junk, and at last I found one of the objects of my journey: the private drinking booth with the leather curtain; here the drinker locks himself in like a horse; to be alone with whiskey and pain, with belief and unbelief, he lowers himself deep bellow the surface of time, into the caisson of passivity, as long as his money lasts; till he is compelled to float up again to the surface of time, to take part somehow in the weary paddling: meaningless, helpless movements, since every vessel is destined to drift toward the dark waters of the Styx. No wonder there is no room in these pubs for women, the busy ones of this earth: here the man is alone with his whiskey, far removed from all the activities in which he has been forced to participate, activities known as family, occupation, honour, society; the whiskey is bitter, comforting, and somewhere to the west, across three thousand miles of water, and somewhere to the east, two seas to cross to get there – are those who believe in activity and progress. Yes, they exist, such people; how bitter the whiskey is, how comforting; the beefy innkeeper passes the next glass into the booth. His eyes are sober, blue: he believes in what those who make him rich do not believe in. In the woodwork of the pub, the panelled walls of the private drinking booth, lurk jokes and curses, hopes and prayers of other people; how many, I wonder?

Already the caisson – the booth – can be felt sinking deeper and deeper toward the dark bottom of time: past wrecks, past fish, but even down here there is no peace now that the deep-sea divers have invented their instruments. Float up again, then, take a deep breath, and plunge once more into activities, the kind called honour, occupation, family, society, before the caisson is pried open by the deep-sea divers. "How much?" Coins, many coins, thrown into the hard blue eyes of the innkeeper.

The sky was still feathered with manifold greys, not a sign of the countless Irish greens, as I made my way to the other church. Not much time had passed: the beggar was standing in the church doorway, and the cigarette I had placed between his lips was just being taken out of his mouth by schoolboys, the end nipped off with care so as not to lose a single crumb of tobacco, the butt placed carefully in the beggar's coat pocket, his cap removed – who, even when he has lost both arms, would enter the house of God with his cap on his head? – the door was held open for him, the empty coatsleeves slapped against the doorposts: they were wet and dirty, as if he had dragged them through the gutter, but inside no one is bothered by dirt.

St. Patrick's Cathedral had been so empty, so clean, and so beautiful; this church was full of people, full of cheap sentimental decoration, and although it wasn't exactly dirty it was messy: the way a living room looks in a family where there are a lot of children. Some people – I heard that one was a German who thus spreads the blessings of German culture throughout Ireland – must make a fortune in Ireland with plaster figures, but anger at the maker of this junk pales at the sight of those who pray in front of his products: the more highly coloured, the better; the more sentimental, the better: "as lifelike as possible" (watch out, you who are praying, for life is not "lifelike").

A dark-haired beauty, defiant-looking as an offended angel, prays before the statue of St. Magdalene; her face has a greenish pallor; her thoughts and prayers are written down in the book which I do not know. Schoolboys with hurling sticks under their arms pray at the Stations of the Cross; tiny oil lamps burn in dark corners in front of the Sacred Heart, the Little Flower, St. Anthony, St. Francis; here religion is savoured to the last drop; the beggar sits in the last row, his twitching face turned toward the space where incense clouds still hang.

New and remarkable achievements of the devotional industry are the neon halo around Mary's head and the phosphorescent cross in the stoup, glowing rosily in the twilight of the church. Will there be separate entries in the book for those who prayed in front of this trash and those who prayed in Italy in front of Fra Angelico's frescoes?

The black-haired beauty with the greenish pallor is still staring at Magdalene, the beggar's face is still twitching; his whole body is convulsed, the convulsions make the coins in his pocket tinkle softly; the boys with the hurling sticks seem to know the beggar, they seem to understand the twitching of his face, the low babble: one of them puts his hand into the beggar's pocket, and on the boy's grubby palm lie four coins: two pennies, a sixpence, and a threepenny bit. One penny and the threepenny bit remain on the boy's palm, the rest tinkles into the offering box; here lie the frontiers of mathematics, psychology and political economy, the frontiers of all the more or less exact sciences crisscross each other in the twitching of the beggar's epileptic face: a foundation too narrow for me to trust myself to it. But the cold from Swift's tomb still clings to my heart: cleanliness, emptiness, marble figures, regimental banners, and the woman who was cleaning what was clean enough; St. Patrick's Cathedral was beautiful, this church is ugly, but it is used, and I found on its benches something I found on many Irish church benches: little enamel plaques requesting a prayer: "Pray for the soul of Michael O'Neill, who died 17.1.1933 at the age of sixty. Pray for the soul of Mary Keegan, who died on May 9, 1945, at the age of eighteen"; what a pious, cunning blackmail; the dead come alive again, their date of death is linked in the mind of the one reading the plaque with his own experience that day, that month, that year. With twitching face Hitler was waiting to seize power when sixty-year-old Michael O'Neill died here; when Germany capitulated, eighteen-year-old Mary Keegan was dying. "Pray" – I read – "for Kevin Cassidy, who died 20.12.1930 at the age of thirteen," and a shock went through me like an electric current, for in December 1930 I had been thirteen myself: in a great dark apartment in south Cologne – residential apartment house, is what it would have been called in 1908 – I sat clutching my Christmas report; vacation had begun, and through a worn place in the cinnamon-coloured drapes I looked down onto the wintry street.

I saw the street coloured reddish-brown, as if smeared with unreal, stage blood: the piles of snow were red, the sky over the city was red, and the screech of the streetcar as it swerved into the loop of the terminus, even this screech I heard as red. But when I pushed my face through the slit between the drapes I saw it as it really was: the edges of the snow islands were brown, the asphalt was black, the streetcar was the colour of neglected teeth, but the grinding sound as the streetcar swerved into the loop, the grinding I heard as pale green – pale green as it shot piercingly up into the bare branches of the trees.

On that day Kevin Cassidy died in Dublin, thirteen years old, the same age as I was then: here the bier was set up, *Dies irae, dies illa* was sung from the organ loft. Kevin's frightened schoolmates filled the benches, incense, candle warmth, silver tassels on the black shroud, while I was folding up my report, getting my sled out from the closet to go tobogganing. I had a B in Latin, and Kevin's coffin was being lowered into the grave.

Later, when I had left the church and was walking along the streets, Kevin Cassidy was still beside me: I saw him alive, as old as I was, saw myself for a few moments as a thirty-seven-year old Kevin: father of three children, living in the slums around St. Patrick's; the whiskey was bitter, cool, and costly, from Swift's tomb ice needles came shooting out at him: his dark-haired wife's face had a greenish pallor, he had debts and a little house like countless others in London, thousands in Dublin, modest, two-storeyed, poor; petty bourgeois, stuffy, depressing, is what the incorrigible aesthete would call it (but watch out, aesthete: in one of these houses James Joyce was born, in another Sean O'Casey).

So close was Kevin's shadow that I ordered two whiskies when I returned to the private drinking booth, but the shadow did not raise the glass to its lips, and so I drank for Kevin Cassidy, who died 20.12.1930 at the age of thirteen – I drank for him too.

Heinrich Böll, *Irish Journal* (1957)

❖ ❖ ❖

Staying with 1950s Dublin, Nuala O'Faolain's auto-biographical Are You Somebody? *recalls her student days – some of the pleasures but also the poverty and the drinking culture.*

The boys and girls at University College Dublin, as far as I know, were prudish, and they often lived at home or in hostels run by priests and nuns, and they were prone – I was, anyway – to ambush by Catholic scruples. Honest randiness was not admitted, even by the students across Dublin at Trinity College, except by some wistful rugby types from Northern Ireland I somehow knew, who persisted in believing that Catholic girls were "easy." But even the older men at Trinity – men from Britain who had done National Service, or former servicemen from America – had to bow to the customs of quiet contraceptive-free Dublin. Drinking and talking and incessant going to the pictures were, among other things, sublimation.

There were different styles in lots of things between UCD and Trinity College. But a certain kind of person from either place – someone involved in theatre and drinking and literature – met on the shared ground of Grafton Street. "Oh, them, they're students," the middle aged would say, because middle-aged men – the ones with money, in Jammet's and the Russell and the Shelbourne; the ones with artistic reputations, in McDaid's and the Bailey and O'Neill's – were the kings of the little city. [...]

Biographers of Irish writers will be scraping the barrel very deep if they ever come to me. But I'm representative of a certain milieu. For every real writer around, there were ten merely literary-minded people like me. Perhaps "literary Dublin" needed both kinds. It was a real place, even in the 1960s. Without question, writing mattered more than money or possessions or status in any other field. But the culture was terribly dependent on drink. There was too much public anecdotal life and not enough personal lyric life. There was too much drinking. Drinking means bad breath and crusted shirtfronts and shaking hands and bottles of milk wolfed down as a meal and waking in the morning on a pile of coats with no clean knickers and being thin, being cold, being sick. And drinking is, after all, about getting drunk. Fine people all but prostituted themselves to get the money to get stupidly drunk every single night. That's what being drunk means: waking to the evidence of repeated lonely humiliations, that drive you further and further away from any thing but drink. And whatever that kind of drinking did to men, it ruined women. I can think of only a few of the women (and I'm not one of them) who hung around McDaid's who were not, sometimes, squalid. You would think that way of life had been designed to test people to their limits. Certainly it could not be survived, only abandoned.

Nuala O'Faolain, *Are you Somebody?* (1996)

* * *

Keith Ridgway captures something of Dublin's contradictory and complex nature in a passage from his novel The Parts.

The city was different at night. Entirely different. It was more than the light and the cold and that. It was more than all the obvious stuff. But he didn't really know if it was the people who were different or something in the city, in the actual air and the actual stones and the actual place. He couldn't work that one out. He listened to other people talking about Dublin as if it was a person. Dublin is friendly they'd say. Dublin is stubborn. And he knew that what they were saying was that Dublin had friendly people in it – that Dublin had stubborn people in it. And he'd heard people talk about the city itself – the buildings and the streets and the river. Dublin is dirty. Dublin is squalid. Dublin is too small. And he'd heard people talk about it as if it was the weather. As if it was the weather. Dublin is wet and windy and cold. Dublin is bitter. But there were some things that people said that he could not decipher. Dublin is cruel. Dublin eats your heart out. Dublin kills you. Dublin is great. Great fun. Great craic. Dublin rejected me. I love Dublin. Dublin is tired and winding down. Dublin is dead.

What was that about? The weather or the people or what? The stones or the river or the streets or what? Dublin does my head in someone had said to him. Really? Yeah. And when Kez investigated a little he worked out that really what was doing this guy's head in was his mother.

People were always emigrating when all they really needed was a place of their own.

He still didn't know what it was that was different at night though. Couldn't quite work out why he liked to run. So he thought of non human things. What is this atmosphere at the corner of Fownes Street? The air cut to ribbons and not a soul near. What is that high pitched cold snap that comes in at about 4 a.m. in the lane down the side of The Olympia? That is not the weather. It's more than that. That's some kind of creature made of men and the time and the cobbles. He'd seen it.

Sometimes he thought that it was only when he ran that he saw anything at all. In passing. He knew that when people said *in passing*, they meant *not seriously, not well*. But he didn't. He meant things that could only be seen when you passed them. As you passed them. Because you needed the speed. Because the speed at which you travel alters your perspective. He knew about things like this because he was a smart kid, he was a good kid. It was like those magic picture puzzles, where you had to stand back and squint before you saw the dolphin or the dragon or the crucified man. When he ran he could see the things that he missed as he walked.

Keith Ridgway, *The Parts* (2003)

* * *

The narrator of Dermot Bolger's The Journey Home *shows us the blend of good, bad and ugly that is one of the truths of Dublin: despite what is manifestly shabby in the city's poorer areas, the sense of good fellowship, humour and an enduring humanity outweigh the bad and the ugly.*

That evening was my first glimpse of Shay's Dublin. It was like an invisible world existing parallel to the official one I had known, a grey underworld of nixers and dole where people slagged Shay for actually having a job. One summer he'd worked as a messenger boy on a motor bike and knew every twisted lane and small turning. I kept intending to go home after each place we visited but then he'd suggest another and we'd be gone. There was no premeditation, the evening just drifted on its own course. I'd imagine my mother's plain cooking gradually stuck to the plate, the meat drying up, the shrivelled vegetables. Then Shay would park another pint in front of me and that would put an end to that. I began to see how Shay survived the office without bitterness or hatred. To him it was just a temporary apparition, eight hours of rest before he entered his real world.

At nine o'clock Shay insisted on buying me a Chinese meal, joking that the seagull's leg refused to stop twitching. By then I was talking as I had never talked since I sat in the old woman's caravan, living off every word he spoke, making him laugh with stories about my father's boss. But I shied away from any reference to my home, ashamed of it suddenly as I envied his freedom, his experience, his accepted adultness. Two girls sat at a nearby table. Occasionally one glanced across at him.

'What do you think?' he asked. 'Will we give it a lash? It's up to yourself.'

I got frightened of being caught out. I was not a virgin but was terrified of the direct approach. My few successes had been scored hurriedly after dances, brought to a messy climax, before bolting as though from the scene of a crime. If we approached I knew I would be tongue-tied. I hesitated and, trying to feign an experienced air, suggested they might not be the type. He grinned at them and gave a mock wave of his hand.

'I don't know,' he said, 'Cute country girls in their bedsits. They may have lost their virginity but they'll probably still have the box it came in.'

But it was obvious I was nervous and when they rose to leave he blew a kiss after them and suggested we play snooker instead.

The hall was a converted warehouse with no sign outside. The old man behind the counter was watching a black-and-white television. He greeted Shay like a son and asked him to mind the gaff while he slipped out to the pub. The walls had been whitewashed once but only vaguely remembered the event. We chose the least ragged of the vacant tables. Shay broke, then leaned on his cue to look around the semi-derelict room.

'I used to live here after I was expelled from school. Old Joe had great hopes for me but I knew I hadn't got it. The place is in tatters now but no wankers come in. I tried a few of the new ones. Deposits, video cameras, and toss-artists who think a deep screw is a mot with a BA. Fuck this, I said, I must be getting old.'

It was ten o'clock when we left. The old man still hadn't returned but occasionally men left a few quid behind the counter as they wandered out. 'Is it cool?' Shay asked. 'You sure you don't have to head home?' I lied again and followed him through the feverish weekend crowds beneath the neon lights, then down towards a warren of cobbled laneways off Thomas Street. The pub we came to looked shut, the only hint of life being a fine grain of light beneath the closed shutters. A tramp passed, stumbling towards the night shelter. He mumbled a few incomprehensible words, one hand held out as though his fingers were cupping a tiny bird. Two children sleeping rough watched us from the doorway of a boarded-up bakery. Shay tapped three times on the steel shutter and I had the sensation of being watched before it swung open. A middle-aged Monaghan man with an old-fashioned bar apron beckoned and welcomed Shay by name. The downstairs bar was thick with smoke, countrymen nursing pints, a figure with a black beard gestured drunkenly in a corner, one lifting her hand with perfect timing at regular intervals to straighten the man beside her who was tilting on his bar stool. Nobody there was under fifty, no one born in the city that was kept out by the steel door.

'Gas, isn't it?' Shay said. 'Knocknagow on a Friday evening.' He gazed in amusement, then headed downstairs to the cellar. Here the owner's son reigned, the father never coming closer than shouting down from the top step at closing time. Four women with sharp, hardened faces sat in one corner drinking shorts. The dozen people at the long table shouted assorted abuse and greetings at Shay as he grinned and waved two fingers back to them. He called for drink and introduced me to his friends. I began to suss how the locked door kept more than the industrial revolution out. The girl across from me was rolling a joint; the bloke beside Shay passing one in his hands. He took three drags and handed it on to me. The pints arrived. I dipped into the white froth, my head afloat. Two of the women in the corner rose and ascended the stairs, bored looking, stubbing their cigarettes out.

'The massaging hand never stops,' Shay said. 'Pauline there left her bag behind one night so I brought it over to her across the road in the Clean World Health Studio. She was clad in a leather outfit after skelping the arse off some businessman who was looking decidedly green in the face as if he'd got more for his forty quid than he bargained for.' [...]

I felt sick and yet had never felt better as I gazed from the window at the tumbledown lane outside. The sleeping children had gone. A man with a cardboard box and a blanket jealously guarded their spot. Far below, Dublin was moving towards the violent crescendo of its Friday night, taking to the twentieth century like an aborigine to whiskey. Studded punks pissed openly on corners. Glue sniffers stumbled into each other, coats over their arms as they tried to pick pockets. Addicts stalked rich-looking tourists. Stolen cars zigzagged through the distant grey estates where pensioners prayed anxiously behind bolted doors, listening for the smash of glass. In the new disco bars children were queuing, girls of fourteen shoving their way up for last drinks at the bar.

And here I was lost in the city, cut off in some time warp, high and warm above the crumbling streets. I think I slept and when I woke the owner was shouting time from the foot of the stairs. The singer had stopped and accepted a joint from the nearest table. The lad beside me who had been eyeing the guitar stumbled up to grab it, closed his eyes and began to sing:

> *Like a full force gale*
> *I was lifted up again,*
> *I was lifted up again,*
> *By the Lord ...*

He wore a broad black hat with a long coat and sang with his eyes closed, living out the dream of Jessie James, the outlaw riding into the Mexican pueblo, the bandit forever condemned to run. He opened his eyes again when he had sung the last refrain, handed the guitar back apologetically and moved down the stairs towards his dingy Rathmines bedsit. I thought of home suddenly, the cremated dinner, my parents waiting for the dot on the television, exchanging glances but never asking each other where I was. I felt guilty once more and yet they suddenly seemed so distant, like an old photograph I'd been carrying around for too long.

'You alive at all Hano?' Shay's voice asked. 'You don't look a well man. A tad under the weather I'd say. Listen, there's a mattress back in my flat if you want to crash there. And I'm after scoring some lovely Leb.'

'What about your wheels?'

'Leave them. Not even Dublin car thieves are that poor.'

Home, like an old ocean liner, broke loose from its moorings and sailed in my mind across the hacked-down garden, further and further though the streets with my parents revolving in their armchairs. I could see it in my mind retreating into the distance and I stood to wave unsteadily after it, grinning as I took each euphoric step down after Shay towards the takeaway drink hustled in the bar below and the adventures of crossing the city through its reeling night-time streets. [...]

In the backyard the landlord had stacked old rotten timbers of doors and window frames from the four other properties he owned along the street. In times of shortages Shay hacked away at them steadily with an axe. I'd hold a torch, shivering in the night air, and listen to the rhythmical chopping while the lights of a hundred bedsits flickered out across the black, abandoned gardens. That's what I remember most about his small flat, the glowing embers like a bird's nest as I drifted to sleep, and waking, stiff-limbed and hung-over, to the scent of wooden ash.

One night stands out from those first months when everything was so shockingly new. High up in a warren of bedsits, while far below Rathmines was awash with litter and tacky lights. At two in the morning there were still queues in the fast-food shops, music from pirate stations blaring through speakers where girls knifed open pitta bread, flickering shifts of colour carried through windows on to the street from the video screens above the counters. Traffic jammed the narrow roads where the last old ladies lived in crumbling family homes, taxis outside the flats unloading party goers who shrieked and embraced and then quarrelled about splitting the fare. A tramp was slumped on his bench where he slept each night beside the swimming baths, oblivious to the noise around him.

Earlier in the pub beside the canal I had found myself talking all evening to a girl. It had happened spontaneously, we were both drunk and at ease together, laughing in the ruck of bodies against the bar, teasing each other with the anticipation of what might come. Across from us Mick and Shay were joking with some girls from work. He caught my eye and winked in congratulation.

Dermot Bolger, *The Journey Home* (1990)

* * *

Coyne, the Dublin policeman in Hugo Hamilton's
Headbanger, sees, day in, day out, "the invisible
tragedy that lurked underneath society", the "filth
and the funny side of the city" that "had everything".
With his profound, fatherly instinct, he is dedicated
to protecting the city – and his wife – from the
"bastards" out to do harm to the innocent.

Coyne was a father figure to the city of Dublin, holding his
paternal arm around its suburbs, protecting its inhabitants like
a family. He was a member of the Garda Siochana, guardian of
peace; a cop, pig, rozzer, fuzz, bluebottle, who drove the squad
car with both hands on the steering wheel, alert and ready for
the next situation. His navy-blue Garda cap lay on the ledge
beneath the back window, along with that of his colleague,
Garda McGuinness. Now and again, the voice from headquarters broke in over the radio, drawing attention to the city's
emergencies, traffic accidents, little rust spots of criminality. It
was a bright autumn afternoon, a day on which nothing much
had happened yet, and beside him, McGuinness was going on
about golf, explaining at length how he had to let Superintendent Molloy win a game.

Molloy couldn't play golf to save his life, McGuinness was
saying. It's an act of charity. I had to turn my back and pretend
I didn't see him putting the ball back.

But Coyne was only half listening to this golf tirade because
he was more concerned with the state of the world outside,
observing every tiny detail in the street, waiting for something
suspicious to turn up. Coyne – the real policeman – a massive
database of ordinary facts and figures, licence plates, faces and
social trivia. No detail too small.

Coyne saw the woman in a motorized wheelchair moving
up the street. He saw the security van pulling up outside the
post office and one of the uniformed men getting out carrying
a steel case shackled to his arm. The reassuring emblem on the

side of the van, like a Papal insignia – two crossed keys and a slogan underneath saying: vigilant and valiant. At the traffic lights, Coyne scanned the faces at the bus stop as though they were all potential criminals. Everybody looking mysteriously down the street like a bunch of weather vanes to see the bus coming. On the pavement, the usual chewing-gum droppings stuck to the ground in their thousands; flattened discs of dirty off-white or off-pink-gum-pennies that people spat out before getting on the bus.

Garda Pat Coyne would be in a position to reconstruct every faithful detail in evidence. Your honour, the youth was seen spitting a grey substance in the direction of the oncoming bus. Your honour, the lady at the front of the queue carried an upturned sweeping brush. When the time came, Coyne was in possession of the facts.

Vigilant and valiant. Somehow, the words applied more to Coyne himself. [...]

With the afternoon sunshine sloping across the city, he turned the squad car down the street towards the sea and saw a band of water shimmering like a cool blue drink at the bottom of a glass. Even though it was autumn already, Coyne could vividly remember the summer and the people walking along with rolled-up towels, ghettoblasters on their shoulders; prams with parasols; girls who had forgotten to turn over and went crimson on one side of the face, or crimson down the backs of their legs. Now there was nobody except an old man leaning over the granite wall staring out at the ferry.

The kids were back at school, but Coyne still carried with him the rather sad image of an upturned ice-cream cone with a white pool spreading out along the pavement, and a crow with tattered charcoal wings tilting his beak to drink from some child's misfortune. To Coyne it was a symbol for all the invisible tragedy that lurked underneath society. He was there to make sure that the enemies of happiness were banished. Somebody had to deal with all the brutality and misery. And Coyne was going to kick ass, as they kept saying on TV. He was going to sort out some of these bastards. Blow them away. The Dublin Dirty Harry. He had a list of names in his head, like a top ten of local criminals. [...]

Coyne saw it all. He saw the pigeons pecking at dried vomit and discarded chips. He saw the victims, culprits – the lucky and the unlucky. Coyne could tell you more about the nature of society that anyone else. The kids sleeping rough. Boys for sale. It was difficult not to be whipped by compassion. But that was Moleshaver Molloy's golden rule to all Gardai – you couldn't allow it to get to you. Never entertain your emotions.

Coyne had witnessed everything. The amount of people he brought to Focus Point; women with their entire families on the move in the middle of the night. Whole families of junkies. Beatings, muggings, suicides. Shopkeepers held up with syringes. The distress of a woman after rape. They dragged a man in his pyjamas in a car with a young boy. Once helped to contain a riot near the British Embassy. Yobbos. Paedophiles. Alcoholics going downhill year by year. Rich kids acting the fool as though they owned the city. And the endless succession of car crimes. Road accidents.

Coyne saw the filth and the funny side of the city. In broad daylight, he once had to restrain an old traveller woman standing in the middle of a busy intersection with an oar, beating the cars and buses as they went by. A boy who had accidentally shot an arrow into his mother's neck. A burglary where the criminal called the Gardai to save him from a snake. A car parked suspiciously, only to reveal a woman's naked arse in the windscreen. And all of this had to be interpreted for the larger public audience. Each incident had to be put in official words, for the records, and for the press. Gardai at Irishtown received reports of a man interfering with himself on the canal bank. Drunk and disorderly youth, barking at the punters in Shelbourne Park. There was a lot of repetition. Lots that Coyne didn't even remember offhand. Or care to. The foreign tabloids across the water frequently had more spectacular stories, but this was Dublin. And Dublin had everything. He tried not to make a political judgement. He had his own ideas on how the society should be run, but he was only concerned with justice and fair play. Coyne's Justice. [...]

In the afternoon, he gave Carmel a lift into town to her art exhibition. The kids all piled into the back seat, separated from their parents by a massive black portfolio with its red ribbon, all wrapped up in anoraks and woollen hats, fighting among themselves behind this opaque membrane of their mother's art. Coyne couldn't see through the rear-view mirror, so he was unable to confirm the constant feeling that the car was being followed.

He pulled up in Merrion Square, where Carmel had arranged to meet Sitwell. Coyne was going to have to play this one very cool, so as not to be recognized. Quite possible too that he would simply get the urge to step out of the car and knock flying shite out of Sitwell as soon as he laid eyes on him. But there was something else to think about when they both saw the rows of paintings hanging along the railings of Merrion Square. So this was the gallery. For amateurs and enthusiasts who drew nice picture of Irish life with no rubbish in the streets, no puke and no poverty. Trinity College without the kids holding out the empty Coke cups. People who drew the faces of Joyce and Beckett five hundred times a week. Liffey paintings with severed heads of Swift and Wilde floating along the water. Halpenny bridges with pink, candy-floss skies. Where was the stature of Daniel O'Connell with the white wig of seagull shite?

Is this what you call an exhibition, he said maliciously.

Carmel and Coyne exchanged a look. He could see the moment of naked disappointment in her eyes. He was ready to say to her that she was much better then this. This is beneath you, Carmel. Your stuff is too good for here. But she misread the silent allegiance in his eyes for hostility and got out of the car, dragging her portfolio violently after her. She kissed the children goodbye and stood waiting in the cold, windy corner, within a stone's throw of the National Gallery, assailed by an inward shock of deep artistic defeat.

Coyne drove away, but he stopped again in the traffic lights, where they all looked back at her for what seemed like the last time. He was struck by an overwhelming pity. She was exposed to the wind of betrayal, on the coldest corner in Dublin, in her black coat and her blue scarf, waiting for the gobshite who had duped her into thinking he was going to offer her a future in the arts. Coyne saw Carmel the way he had once seen her waiting for him long ago when he was late for a date. He was stunned by her spontaneous anger. Her sense of independence. He secretly admired her from this distance until she saw him and all the kids staring at her and waved them away. Get lost and stop embarrassing me. Because Sitwell came sauntering along the pavement with his arms out, wearing a sheepskin coat.

Darling, he said.

But Carmel wouldn't allow herself to be kissed or welcomed. Showed resentment.

You call this an exhibition?

It's the best start you'll get, Carmel. Cheer up, for Godsake. You'll be discovered here. Merrion Square. Many a true artist has had their humble beginnings here and gone on to great things. Wait till you see.

And then he put his arm around her and led her to a small space along the railings where she was to put up her precious work. If Coyne had not already driven off, she would have asked him to take her away immediately. But then she decided to make a go of it. Hung up some of her paintings, refused to speak a word to Sitwell or any of the other artists. Frozen with fury, waiting to be discovered.

Coyne decided to take his children for a walk around town. Showed them Trinity College with its cobbled courtyard and its green railings. The railings of exclusion, he called them. Stood outside the gates holding their hands and staring at the Saturday afternoon traffic crossing College Green.

Some day there will be no traffic at all here, he told them. No cars or buses or anything. Just a big square with fountains and benches. Wait till you see.

Then he brought them to the zoo. Got them all chips and cheerful cartons of orange juice with twisted straws. He was happy to be in public places. Drove through the streets, looking at the wind pushing people along the pavements. There was always wind in Dublin, hurling everything with contempt along the street – plastic bags, cans, dead umbrellas. He saw trees beyond garden walls where all the leaves had been blown off and some of the red apples still remained.

Hugo Hamilton, *Headbanger* (1997)

✳ ✳ ✳

But the bleakest view is perhaps the long one ...

The city doesn't care. The city doesn't even notice. It's a heavy rumble by the side of the sea and the heave of the hills. It takes years to form a thought. Its blinks are generational. It takes the long view, hypermetropic, not bothered with the details, with the single dramas or the brief scenes, not bothered with the clutter of iteration. *Accumulate*, it says. *Accumulate*. Lay down your life. Add what you have. Then piss off. It's history that the city's after, not the clicks and squeals – not you, not you and your notions. Not you and your aspirations. Your grime. Locked in petty murder and the day to day. Piss off with your memoirs and your plans. Aspire elsewhere.

We are the city. We are the city, like we are the church. Like we are the neighbourhood and the street and the houses and the spirit. We name these things and live in them. Owner occupiers we are, upkeep and admittance, rules and humours. Without us there's bricks and silence and all the names are ended. We are the city. And the city doesn't care. It just squats and deep breathes. It lets people move through it. It doesn't care what you do. Do it.

Do you think that the names will survive us? Do you? Do you think that the rats and the roaches will call this place Dublin? Or that the machines will? You think the dust and the cold light will whistle out the street names and the songs? That we are making something permanent here? Well we're not. We're building a midden. And nothing much will trouble it after we're ruined. Unless a spaceship comes a digging.

Or do you think that we will always be here? In some form, recognisably ourselves, with our rancour and our porn and our opposable thumbs? In new clothes, one colour, peaceful, sorted? You think so?

No neither do I.

Keith Ridgway, *The Parts* (2003)

✻ ✻ ✻

When Michael, in Julia O'Faolain's No Country For Young Men, *returns to Dublin, the city of his youth, he is disappointed and depressed – though with a glass of whiskey inside you, things can begin to look a little better ...*

The bump of wheels on the runway set off a corresponding bounce in James Duffy's spirits. A capriole. A positive gambolling. He was alone, free and in search of a neglected aspect of his youth.

Dublin. Duv linn. Having just filled out his landing card, he remembered that his name shared a syllable with the city and that 'duv' meant black.

They taxied in. Time pleated like a fan. The city was a mnemonic. Something was said about seat-belts. This was Molly Malone's city – she of the cockles and mussels and hot-blooded fever from which none could relieve her. It was Molly Bloom's city too and the second city of Bostonian Molly Osgood whose husband had been shot by an Irish Free State firing squad and whose son lived to become the State's president. James had been boning up on the history of this island to which, in his wife's view, he had no call to have come. Crossing the Atlantic from West to East struck Therese as a regressive act. Her own people had come from Poland.

'You don't think I'd go there?' she had challenged. 'What for? To chase up old memories? Furs?' she derided. 'Vodka bottles with grass in them? Knick-knacks made from straw? Rotting dinner-jackets? It's easy to feel good where your dollars put you at an advantage.'

Her family got begging letters from cousins in Cracow and her mother sometimes sent money but Therese wouldn't.

'They're not my people,' she said. 'I want no part of them. Yours are unlikely to be better.' [...]

The humidity was tangible, a membrane through which people moved with effort. Belted into raincoats, pedestrians had a look of parcels. Cornices dripped. James bought a paper and shoved it inside his jacket to keep dry. In the nearest pub he brushed drops from his hair, ordered a whiskey – he had begun to see why people here drank – and opened the paper to see what they might be reading.

Item: a small one-engine plane had flown across the city trailing a banner inscribed with a patriotic slogan. The string of the banner had got entangled in the plane's motor causing it to crash in a rugby field. The pilot had been knocked senseless by the propeller and subsequently died. Item: a girl in South Dublin had bitten into a commercially made doughnut containing a rat's leg. 'It was very disgusting,' said Miss Maire

Breen, 'I shall never again eat anything but cakes baked at home by my mother.' Under *Positions Wanted* James noted several gentlewomen looking for posts as housekeepers. A lady desiring room and board in exchange for light duties, stated ingenuously – or not? – 'anything considered'. The Minister for Health had revealed that nearly half the hospital beds in the country were occupied by mental patients. [...]

Black-plumed horses passed the pub regularly for it was, ran the local joke, on the way to the graveyard in more ways than one. Hats came off and shutters closed to show respect. Coming back, the mourners would be in for drinks. A good funeral had several horses pulling the hearse and two to each carriage behind it. The harness was black and silver and the plumes nodding above the furry foreheads were as big as busbies on the King's hussars. Black tails matched the plumed crests and when the funeral was political it was followed by contingents of slow-stepping Cumann na mBan in their green uniform skirts. [...]

December. Rain fell like pickets, fencing people in. Fires smouldered and cooled in shaggy embers as hollow as the corpses of winter animals. Peace looked to have firmed up now that the Treaty had been signed in London. Journalists were jubilant. People cheered and laughed with relief. Some wept and others went to their churches to give thanks. Crowds of Irish Catholics had been photographed kneeling on the pavements of London, praying.

Three days later half the Dáil Cabinet repudiated the Treaty.

They did what? Which ministers? Oh. And why so?

The country was in limbo, suddenly unsure what toasts to drink in this pre-Christmas season. Debate raged in every pub, drawing room and kitchen. Peace? War? Compromise? Principle? The swish of hot pokers, plunging into mulled stout, amplified the dazed hiss of toothless pensioners who had nothing to do but wonder what the lads could be up to at all, at all? The leaders were at each others' throats. What could anyone make of that? And, the devil blast it, were we forever to be giving the world a spectacle of Irishman turning on Irishman? Heh? [...]

Michael put on his tweed coat which was long and lean: a coat of the 1930s. In his youth he had dressed eccentrically from vanity. Now, perhaps he was not even aware of being out of fashion. Arms linked, they walked with their heads down to protect their faces from the wind. Rotting leaves flicked at their ankles and they paused to watch a swan pass on the canal. She wondered whether, like her, he was deliberately putting off the moment of reaching a pub. [...]

They passed a boarded-up Georgian terrace due for reconstruction. The façade alone was to be kept: a sop to preservationists.

Michael peered between two planks. 'There used to be a sweet-shop here,' he remembered. 'I used to come here for a bar of Fry's cream chocolate whenever anyone gave me tuppence. I think it was tuppence. Two pennies. Or a Peggy's leg. It was a year or so after the war and sugar was still scarce. The old man who ran the shop kept his sweets for children who could ask for them in Irish. I was six.'

'And could you ask in Irish?'

'Yes. But I resented his high-handedness. When sweets got plentiful I boycotted his shop.' [...]

They turned into a small, wood-panelled pub where she had not been before but where Michael seemed to be known, for the bar curate greeted him and poured a small Powers unasked.

'Same for the lady?'

'Yes. The lady,' says Michael, 'is my wife.'

Is? Was?

'Good evening, Mrs O'Malley.'

The good, the bad and the (just a little bit) ugly

It was twilight outside and the faintly mauve mist to which her eyes had adjusted made the lights here look orange. Worn plush, brass, the dimmed refractions of light from glasses and coloured alcohols evoked a hundred other evenings spent in pubs like this. The place was haunted, festive, theatrical. You looked hard at the décor and saw the flaws – old vomit marks, a whiff of staleness, cigarette burns – but with the glow of the whiskey defects merged in an overall opulence.

Julia O'Faolain, *No Country For Young Men* (1980)

All in the past

It's impossible to do justice to the history of Dublin in a few short extracts. All we can do here is dip a toe into the changing stream of the city – from the time of the Protestant Ascendancy through the great struggle for and achievement of Independence, and on to a glimpse of the post-war period. We hope this will prompt the reader to go and discover more about the great events and heroes that have shaped the Dublin of today. First, Edward Rutherfurd, in his historical novel, Ireland Awakening, *describing the 18th-century period of the Protestant Ascendancy, when the city developed rapidly.*

How delightful the evening was, thought Fortunatus. Dublin was certainly a pleasant city – so long, of course, as you were a member of Ireland's ruling elite. And even if my dear brother is not, Fortunatus reflected, that is what I am. A handsome city, too. For in Dublin, at least, the Protestant Ascendancy over Ireland was expressed in bricks and mortar.

It was astonishing how the place had changed in his own lifetime. Inside the walls of the old medieval city, the narrow streets and alleys, and the landmarks like Christ Church and the old Tholsell town hall, were not much changed, except for a few repairs. But as soon as you looked beyond the walls, the change was striking.

For a start, the River Liffey was not only crossed by several stone bridges, but it was noticeably narrower. The marshes that had started just downstream from the Castle, and skirted the ancient Viking site of Hoggen Green where the precincts of Trinity College now lay, had been reclaimed and the riverflood contained within walls. Upriver on the northern bank, the Duke of Ormond had encroached on the water further when he laid out the Ormond and Arran quays, with lines of warehouses and buildings that would have graced any city in Europe. Outside the city's eastern wall, the former grassy common of St. Stephen's Green was now surrounded with fine new houses, with subsidiary streets leading down to Trinity College. The curving line of the little stream that had run from the common down to Hoggen Green and the Viking long stone, had disappeared under the roadway of one of these, a pleasant crescent called Grafton Street. On the western side of the city, not a mile from Christ Church, the huge Royal Hospital at Kilmainham had been modelled on the stately, classical Invalides of Paris; and on the northern riverbank, opposite, stood the gates to the Phoenix Park – the enormous tract that Ormond had landscaped and stocked with deer. The Phoenix Park was bigger and grander than anything London had to offer.

But what was truly striking was the appearance of the new houses.

The British might not be original in the arts, but in their adaptation of the ideas of others, they would often show genius. And during the last decades, in London, Edinburgh, and now Dublin, they had perfected a fresh method of urban construction. Taking simplified classical elements, the builders had discovered that they could endlessly repeat the same brick house, in terraces and squares, in a way that was both economic and pleasing to the eye. Elegant steps led up to handsome doors with fanlights above; outside shutters were not needed in the colder northern climes, so nothing broke the stern brick surface of the outer wall; severe, rectangular sash windows stared blankly out at the northern skies, like the shades of Roman senators. Over the doorway, like as not, there might be a modest classical pediment, for decency's sake – to omit that might have seemed like a gentleman emerging without a hat – but all other external ornament was avoided. Austere and aristocratic in style, yet domestic in scale, it satisfied lord and tradesman alike. It was, without doubt, the most successful style of terracing ever invented and would make its way across the Atlantic to cities like Boston, Philadelphia, and New York. In time, it would come to be known as Georgian.

All around St. Stephen's Green, Trinity College, and behind the quays north of the Liffey as well, these classical brick terraces and squares were spreading. As the city's wealth and population continued to grow, it seemed to Walsh that a new street sprang up every year. Dublin, after London, would soon be the most gracious European capital in the north.

Edward Rutherfurd, *Ireland Awakening* (2006)

✱ ✱ ✱

Staying with Edward Rutherford, the next extract recalls a particularly famous musical event that many may not realise took place in Dublin rather than London.

The evening sky was pink. The carriages had poured out their passengers by the precincts of Christ Church, and the fashionable world of Dublin was flowing, like a glittering stream, down to the handsome structure of the Music Hall, which now stood squarely on one side of the old medieval thoroughfare of Fishamble Street. [...]

Inside, it was a brilliant scene. The Music Hall seemed to be lit by ten thousand candles. At one end, upon a dais, sat the combined choirs of Christ Church and Saint Patrick's Cathedrals – the most powerful chorus to be found in Dublin. As the nobility and gentry came in to find their allotted places, members of every great family could be seen: Fitzgeralds and Butlers, Boyles and Ponsonbys, bishops, deans, judges, gentry, and even the greatest merchants. Seven hundred people had been issued tickets – even more than had filled the hall for the triumphant rehearsal five days before.

They were all inside when the party of the Lord Lieutenant made its entrance, coming last, as befitted the royal representative. And upon seeing the stately duke, the whole place burst into applause – not only out of respect for his office and person, but because it was he and his magnificent patronage that had brought the renowned composer to Dublin in the first place, as a result of which it was the *beau monde* of Dublin, rather than of London, who were now to hear the first performance of what was already being hailed as the composer's greatest work.

They had come to hear Handel present his new oratorio: *The Messiah*.

So magnificent and so joyous was the scene that it would have been a churlish spirit who could not forget, at least for the evening, that there was anybody starving in Ireland.

Edward Rutherfurd, *Ireland Awakening* (2006)

✳ ✳ ✳

Sean O'Casey's autobiographical work, I Knock at the Door, *gives a vivid picture of Dublin's celebrations for Queen Victoria's Jubilee, while hinting at dissenting voices not far below the surface.*

All parts of the city of Dublin where the real respectable people lived, and where the real respectable people worked, were celebrating in honour of something to do with the Majesty of

Victoria, Queen of Great Britain and Ireland and Empress of India; to show their love and manifest their loyalty to her in millions of lights and multitudes of flags, banners, bannerettes, pennons, guidons, standards, gonfalons, and diverse other symbols displayed on decorated posts linked together by lovely coloured festoons; pictures of the Queen and Members of the Royal Family, placed cunningly in suitable spots where all could see them without inconvenience or discomfort. [...]

They had tried to fight their way into the tram, for it looked as if the whole district had poured out to see the sights. Mrs Casside put Johnny in front of her, and shoved him steadily forward, crying out to the crowd that surged around her, Give a breathin' space, there, to a poor delicate child whose eyes are fit to look at things only durin' the first few weeks of the year. It'll be a sorry day for Dublin when no-one has a thought for a poor boy sufferin' the terrible handicap of ill-health.

The conductor leaned forward from the porch of the tram, stretched out a sudden hand, and pulled Johnny and his mother on, pushing them up the narrow stairs to the top, as he planked himself in front of the others, perspiring and pushing their way onto the platform.

– A man 'ud want St. Pathrick's crozier to knock a little decency into yous, he said viciously as he tried to turn the pushing into an orderly parade. [...]

The paths were packed with people, and many who couldn't find room on the paths walked along in streams beside the slow-moving tram, forging ahead like a lighted barge in the centre of a living river. Johnny saw gleaming lights and waving flags stretching out before him as far as his eyes could reach. Proud he felt, and full of delight that he could feel himself a living part of this great display given to show the Irish people's fond attachment to mighty England's Queen.

– Looka the Orange Lodge, Ma, exclaimed Johnny enthusiastically; oh, looka the Grand Orange Lodge!

From every second window floated a Royal Standard or a Union Jack. Lights gleamed behind the window blinds, coloured with the orange and blue of Nassau. In one window, with the blinds up, several radiant orangemen-faces could be seen staring down at the teeming crowds below. Right across the face of the building stretched, in gleaming gas-lights, the flaming cry of *God Save the Queen*; and above this, surrounded by a bronze laurel wreath, the steadily gleaming gas-light date of 1690. Over opposite was the stately church built for the presbyterians by Alexander Findlater, Gentleman Grocer and Wine Merchant of the city of Dublin, with its great flag flying from its spire, and its heavy railings, coloured a vivid blue with golden spear tops, shining gloriously in the gleam of the illuminations all around it. Every head in the tram leaned forward and every neck was stretched to gaze at the brilliant and wonderful sight.

– Isn't it lovely, murmured Mrs Casside, her face aglow [...]

The conductor came up the stairs with a scowl on his face, and moved along between the rows of passengers, collecting the fares. The passengers, gazing on the gleaming lights, the fluttering flags, and waving festoons, offered their fares in outstretched hands to the conductor without taking their ravished eyes from the garnished streets. He took the money from the outstretched hands, punched the tickets, and dropped them into the hands rigidly held out to receive them; the passengers never turning a head so that the vision of colour and light and jubilation wouldn't be lost, even for a moment. The conductor kept shaking his head scornfully as he went from one outstretched hand to another.

– Poor Wolfe Tone, poor Wolfe Tone, he kept murmuring, as he mouched along, poor Wolfe Tone.

Johnny watched the conductor going over to the top of the stairs after he had collected the fares. He stood there, with a hand on the stair-rail, staring at the passengers gaping at the decorations; then he sang in a low voice, half to himself and half to those who were in the tram:

Once I lay on the sod that lies over Wolfe Tone,
And thought how he perished in prison alone [...]

– Who was Wolfe Tone, Ma? Whispered Johnny, moved strangely by seeing tears trickling down the cheeks of the conductor as he sang.

– A protestant rebel who went over to France nearly a hundhred years ago, an' brought back a great fleet to help the Irish drive the English outa the counthry. But God was guarding us, and He sent a mighty storm that scattered the ships from Banthry Bay.

–What happened to poor Wolfe Tone, Ma?

– He fought on a French warship till it was captured by the British; and then he was put into prison, an' executed there by the English government.

– Why didn' the Irish save him?

– Oh, I don't know. It all happened long ago, an' everyone's forgotten all about it.

– But the conductor hasn't forgotten all about it, Ma.

Sean O'Casey, *I Knock at the Door* (1939)

* * *

Iris Murdoch's novel The Red and the Green *is set at the time of the 1916 Easter Rising. The extract, recording some of the of the preparations for this seminal event, captures the hopes, fears, and great difficulties faced by those directly involved in the struggle.*

Then they had been clumsy recruits. Now they were hard well-trained troops, real soldiers as good as their enemy and better. They had felt their power. This year on St Patrick's day they had taken the city over. They had marched straight from mass, two thousand strong, to College Green to be inspected by MacNeill. Traffic came to a standstill, police were swept aside, as they marched, disciplined and armed, to the sound of their pipe bands. Dublin stood and watched them like a breathless enchanted girl. Pat felt they could have taken Dublin that day.

Not that he had any illusions about either the difficulty or the sheer ugliness of the kind of struggle he was engaged in. He felt a detached envy of the simple open public war which he could not join. Although in a curious way he was not a man of action, he knew himself to be brave, and if he had any identity now he had the identity of a soldier. He would have liked a cleaner, straighter fight, 'a steed, a rushing steed, on the Curragh of Kildare, a hundred yards and English guards ... '. The sort of song that Cathal sang. As it was, his choice and his justification would be lonely and secret, and the killing he would do would look like murder. But that was how it had to be.

He had no illusions about the difficulties. Bernard Shaw had justly likened their struggle to an encounter between a pram and a Pickford's van. Nor was Pat at all reassured by the military strategy of his superior officers. There had been a long controversy about uniforms. Pat had been opposed to a uniformed force. He envisaged nebulous mobile irregular columns which could strike and disappear. He had studied the methods of the Boers who, with a much larger army, had preferred guerrilla tactics. In the face of heavy artillery, mobility seemed an obvious essential. But the military mind in the Volunteers and even in the I.C.A., seemed old-fashioned in cast. There was much talk of *ésprit de corps*, and other even wilder talk of status under International Law. It was imagined that the green puttees, the slouch hats and the Sam Brownes would bestow on their wearers the status of belligerents, and entitle then to the privileges of the International Code in battle and as prisoners. Whereas Pat knew perfectly well that if they failed they would be treated as murderers and traitors. [...]

Pat was giddy with impatience. It was still only Thursday morning. Sunday rose up in front of him like a black cliff.

The mountain must open to admit him, how he knew not. He could foresee nothing except that he would be fighting. This time next week he would have been fighting. Perhaps would be dead. His first startled fear was diffused now into an aching desire for action, and his body was weary of the interim. In the two days since he had been told he had grimly lived the reality of it into himself. To the mystery of Sunday he was dedicated and resigned, become in every cell of his being a taut extension of that violent future. When it came he would enter upon it coldly. It was only the waiting which was an agony and a fever. He could hardly sleep at night but lay telling himself vividly and lucidly how much he needed sleep. His flesh twitched and ached with expectation.

There was much to do each day. He had attended a staff conference at Liberty Hall about the dovetailing of plans between the Citizen Army and the Volunteers, and had been impressed, as always, by the efficiency of Connolly's men. He had visited a quarry at Brittas where some gelignite was hidden which was to be rushed into Dublin on Sunday morning. He had checked over all the ammunition allotted to his own company, which was hidden, often in small quantities, in various places throughout the city, and made arrangements for it to be moved at short notice. He had made a point of seeing individually all the men under his command, and, without revealing anything, satisfying himself that they were equipped and ready.

Pat was one of the most junior officers to have been told of the plan. The great majority of the Volunteers, including some officers, knew nothing except that 'very important manœuvres' were to take place on Sunday and that 'the absence of any Volunteer would be treated as a serious breach of discipline'. Of course the men had been told, from long ago, that they must be prepared for anything on any occasion when they marched out in arms. But they had marched out in arms so often and returned afterwards to their tea. There was a ferment in Dublin all the same, which it was to be hoped was not attracting the attention of the Castle. Visiting Lawlor's gun shop in Fownes Street, Pat had found it almost emptied of stock. Streams of people had been in to buy bandoliers and water bottles and even sheath knives; and it was said that you could not get hold of a bayonet from one end of Dublin to the other. Perhaps the men were simply 'stocking up', for the 'important manœuvres'. Or perhaps the news was gradually leaking out to the rank and file. If so, this was dangerous. It was still only Thursday.

To most of us at most times past history seems like a brightly lit and faintly clamorous procession, while the present is a dark rumbling corridor off which, in hidden shafts and private rooms, our personal stories are enacted. Elsewhere in that obscure continuum, and out of quite other stuff, history is manufactured. Rarely are we able to be the intelligent spectators of an historical event, more rarely still its actors. At such times the darkness lightens and the space contracts until we apprehend the rhythm of our daily actions as the rhythm of a much larger scheme which has included us within its composition. Pat felt for the first time this nearness of history, this almost physical sense of a connection with it, when he learnt that on the previous day at a secret meeting Patrick Pearse had been appointed President of the Irish Republic.

At the same meeting James Connolly had been appointed commandant general of the Dublin district and MacDonagh commandant of the Dublin brigade. Final decisions had also been taken about what points of the city should be occupied. There was argument about where the military headquarters should be. Connolly had favoured the ready-made fortress of the Bank of Ireland. But eventually the choice fell upon the General Post Office in Sackville Street. The fate of Dublin castle was then debated. Pearse had been for attacking the Castle, but Connolly had opposed this. The 'castle' in fact consisted of a straggle of buildings which would be hard to defend, and there was also a Red Cross hospital inside it. A full attack on the Castle seemed to present too many problems, and it was resolved instead to isolate it by occupying the City Hall and the offices of the *Evening Mail* opposite the gates.

Pat, who had thought long and soberly about the shortage of arms, had food now for further gloomy reflection as he reviewed the gratuitous folly of his leaders. It was surely essential that Dublin Castle should be attacked and preferably burnt. It was the Bastille of the regime, the symbol of its brutality. The Post Office was an insane choice as headquarters: a building hemmed in by others and quite unsuitable for a prolonged defence. In any case, the whole scheme of establishing fixed strong points inside the city was ill-considered. Faced with an enemy who possessed and would use artillery, some degree of mobility was essential. Mobile troops could also make more use of the good will of the civilian population. A number of flying columns, able to retire rapidly out of the city if necessary, would do the enemy more damage, and baffle and scare him far more than a number of isolated strongholds, however bravely defended. There were two thousand five hundred British troops in the city itself and more at the Curragh. The joint forces of the I.C.A. and the Volunteers might reach twelve hundred or fifteen hundred at a good turn-out. Mobile forces could seem more numerous than they were. Static forces could be studied and counted. But revolutionary leaders can be just as childish and old-fashioned and romantic as the most reactionary of regular soldiers. There was even a plan to occupy Stephen's Green and dig trenches there, although it was agreed that there were not enough men to take the Shelbourne Hotel; and this particular 'strong point' could be dealt with in a matter of minutes by a Lewis gun on top of the Shelbourne.

Pat reflected coolly on the folly of it all, the shortage of arms, the absence of sensible plans, the lack of elementary medical supplies and medical skill. He thought that he could accept death now, for himself and others, a death for Ireland. But driving his imagination on to savour the worst that was possible he pictured himself, unaided and horribly wounded, unable to stop from moaning and crying out, lying in the back of some wrecked blood-splattered room, while his comrades knelt at the window returning the enemy fire. At that time he would be empty of destiny. History would exist no more. Even Ireland would exist no more. There would be just a half-crushed animal screaming to be allowed to live: screaming perhaps to be allowed to die. He wanted now to be beyond prayer, to ask nothing more for himself as if he had already ceased to be. But he could not help clasping to him, as an amulet, the hope that if he were to die he might die quickly.

Yet in spite of all these reasons for a steady pessimism Pat could not, at the same time, at the back of his blackest arguments, help feeling a most tremendous glow of hope. He had heard Pearse say that the armed rising was to be thought of simply as a sacrifice of blood, after which Ireland would be spiritually reborn.

Iris Murdoch, *The Red and the Green* (1965)

* * *

In Frank Delaney's Ireland, *an old man recounts his memories of 1916, passing on 'history' to the younger audience for whom it is just a distant story. He sits on a kitchen chair in the middle of the stage, wearing a raincoat and hat and lighting his pipe ...*

I'm to talk to you, this anniversary year, about the insurrection of nineteen sixteen. The Irish Rebellion, the Easter Rising, the Poets' Rebellion – people have given it many names. Let me be clear immediately as to how I think of it: it was the final movement that gave Irish people back most of their country from the English. On a personal level, it made me look at people and their capacity for bravery in a way I have never since forgotten to do. [...]

The building that housed the Easter Rising was the General Post Office in Dublin and it must be the largest building ever constructed in the world, to judge from the number of people who claim to have been in it on the famous Easter Monday, the twenty-fourth of April, nineteen sixteen. I was twenty-seven-and-a-half years old when I entered its carved portals.

Let me begin by describing the morning, the way the world felt. It was mild, the weather was what we'd call 'soft', people were still in an airy mood after Easter Sunday.

I had been in a good billet outside Dublin in the village of Chapelizod on the river Liffey. After five hospitable nights, I found myself on the Monday morning walking in the tranquillity of the Phoenix Park. More than a few carriages clopped by on their way through the park, heading off to be in plenty of time for the first race at Fairyhouse, which, as you know, is about twenty miles outside Dublin. Some of the carriages were lovely, elegant brough.ams and painted side-cars, and I stood to watch them drive by, with the spokes of their wheels flashing. The ladies in them wore bonnets and looked grand. [...]

The odd thing was, and I can capture this feeling now: something in my heart had begun to stir. I don't know what it was; I could call it excitement but it was more than that. Was it elation, a sense of triumph or something dark? Yes and no to all of those things. It was a strange feeling: it hurt me, it worried me, and made me happy at the same time. I might have been as near to tears as to laughing.

At the next bridge I stopped to admire the view; the sky was clear, except for a lovely wisp of cloud like the tail of a white mare. In my reverie, I thought I heard something very definite approaching, something considerable, but I could see nothing. Remember, banks, shops and offices were to stay closed that day, a public holiday. A woman walked by: she looked thoughtful, she was wearing black and she was probably going to half-past-eleven Mass somewhere in a church along the quays.

The kind morning air seemed to grow clearer. Then I heard it again – from behind me, steady and in a rhythm. I still couldn't see anything and the noise puzzled me. I walked to the far side of the bridge – and round a corner they came. I shall never forget it.

A troop of armed men marched along that quayside towards me, about eighty of them, a people's army you'd call them, mostly in civilian clothes. Country boys, I thought immediately. They had complexions ruddy from fields, not pale from offices; they lacked the general smoothness to which a city rubs its dwellers. A few, not more than nine or ten, wore a green uniform with a slouch hat – that is to say, a hat with one side of the brim standing up at right angles.

Who were these men, these boys? I think of them now as Irish tribesmen, with names such as Dolan, MacEnroe, Cusack, Egan, O'Donnell, Keogh, Brady, Daly, Lahiffe, Curran, MacMahon, O'Loughlin – any and all of the names in Ireland's long genealogy, names from before the time of St Patrick, names you have all known and heard, the music of our daily lives.

They had faces like priests and they had faces like pikers – by which I mean they looked like everybody else and nobody else; simple faces, anxious or excited or resigned faces, some with little evident experience of life, some with eager attitudes, some afraid, some apprehensive, some grim.

Almost all carried guns, mostly bolt-action rifles; I saw one submachine gun and a number of double-barrelled shotguns, more suited to shooting wildfowl. Most had Sam Browne belts or some other harness for carrying ammunition. But no matter how briskly they marched, how hard they tried, they looked anything but military; two lads in the middle of the ranks had no weapons but, oh, how they swung their marching arms.

Yet they, like all the troop, had something about them. Was it determination? Or had they embraced the idea of blood sacrifice? I doubt it. These were lads who, in part, were caught up in the romance of a patriotic idea. It has happened across the world over and over again. I will say that what I think I saw in their faces was a genuine and modest nobility. Maybe they truly so loved their country they would have done anything for it and that patriotic light was a fire inside them. Or is that memory again? Memory is the best tailor in the world.

I was immediately engaged with what I saw, with no idea of whether this was some isolated, crackpot, stupidly brave troop of rebels, or whether an insurrection was taking place. There had been talk of it for months – that, one day, men from each of the thirty-two counties of Ireland would march on Dublin and throw out the British. Somehow it didn't matter to me if these men were the only ones rebelling: their bearing, the expressions on their faces, a mixture of strength and tranquillity, captured my spirit.

They marched right in front of my face: I stood two feet or so above them, owing to the height of the bridge. A number glanced up at me – nothing in their look other than serene friendliness. Those not in uniform were dressed mostly in working-men's clothes – rough jackets, many in dungarees, corduroy trousers, mostly boots, those big strong working boots with broad thick soles that I myself like.

The officer who led them – I saw him many more times that day and the next, and you will hear more of him – was a tall young man with a powerful presence: he had a rangy build, no flesh on him, a head of tawny hair and a moody face. His sandy colouring suited the green uniform and he had polished his brown shoes and gaiters to a bright shine. Somehow I expected him to have a sword but he didn't: he had a revolver at his waist, in a holster whose flap had lost its button. It's strange the details you remember from such a moment.

I watched them out of sight – they disappeared into a side street and I wondered where they were going. Then I decided to follow them and began to run. A man standing in a doorway grabbed my arm to halt me, so hard that I almost fell.

'What'n the hell are youse thinking of?' he said.

He had a cigarette and wore blue braces over a working shirt.

'What are they? Where are they going?'

'Leave 'em alone,' he said. 'Buncha clowns. Uniforms! Guns! Jesus!' He hadn't let go of my arm. 'Leave 'em go. They're going to jeopardize the whole bloody day.'

'Are they rebels?'

'They're jackasses. Have youse a light on you?'

'No.'

'What kind of a man goes out without a box of matches?'

He let go of my arm and off I went after the troop. After a few minutes of quick walking, I saw them again in the distance, on the wide boulevard then called Sackville Street. As I hurried to catch up, some members of the Dublin Metropolitan Police, who had evidently not been alarmed by the marchers, watched me, too, but did nothing and said nothing. At the next bridge I stopped and asked a lady what was happening; she and the people near her said gruff, unpleasant things.

'Oh, a bunch of loonatics has gone into the General Post Office with guns and they've locked the doors. And that crowd' – indicating my marchers – 'they're going in there too.'

A man near her pointed vaguely. 'And there's more down at Liberty Hall. But the military'll rout them out soon enough.'

'Disturbing us all,' said someone else. 'D'ja ever hear anything like it?'

Then a peculiar thing happened: such few police as stood about went away. A man called after them, 'Where are youse going?' and a policeman shouted back, 'We're leaving it to the soldiers.'

I hurried on and caught up with my band of marching men, who by now were hearing shouts of abuse from the passers-by: 'Ah, would youse go home outta tha'!' and, 'Leave us alone, would'ja?'

211

In short, Dublin had little encouragement for these rebels. A woman in a shawl threw a cabbage at the back of one of the armed men but it didn't hit him: it fell in the street and she retrieved it.

'I'm not one to waste my dinner on the likes of them,' she said. Those around her laughed and approved.

By now I was abreast of the troop and we had reached the post office; it was past noon. The marchers halted. Performed what seemed like a fairly correct military manoeuvre, turned left and into the building.

As I made to follow them, a man stopped me and said, 'If I was youse I wouldn't go into the GPO.'

'Why?' I said.

'There's a bad crowd gone in there, guns 'n' all. They went in about twenty minutes ago. And you know who they went in with? That fella, that bloody rabble-rouser, Connolly.'

'But–' I began to say, and he cut me off, very angry.

'Ah, that's it, that's it! That's what the fault of the country is today. We don't know when we're well off. Most of us are happy to be subjects of the King but there's always some smart few donkeys who think they're better than that.'

I tried to speak again but he went on berating me. 'Go ahead! Go on! On your own head be it!'

Bear in mind that I had never seen this man in my life and I never expected to see him again.

'Well?' said he. 'Are youse going in there? You're not to, d'you hear? You're just not to.'

He made my mind up for me. A life on the road, however lonely it may be at times, gives you certain gifts of independence and I couldn't see that it was any of his business what I did. But that's Dublin for you, someone always on hand to tell you what they think you should be doing. I walked away from him and straight to the GPO.

The door was locked tight and I went along under that fine portico to the second door – but it was also locked. I could hear much commotion inside but nobody would answer my knocking so I decided to wait for a while and see if a door would open. Quite a few people were now gathering under the grand columns, wondering what was going on.

Well, I had to wait for about half an hour. In those days, I carried no watch: I took my time from the sun in the morning and the moon at night. But there was a clock across the street on a jeweller's shop and when it said a quarter to one, a door opened and a group of men came out of the post office. Some wore the uniforms I had already seen and some wore their own clothes. A slightly built, pale man led them; he had a crossed eye and a gentle face.

'Who's that?' I asked a man near me and he said, 'He's a fellow called Patrick Pearse. He's a bit of a poet, like.'

All of you here tonight know who I mean; no doubt you learned his poems in school.

> The beauty of the world hath made me sad,
> This beauty that will pass;
> Sometimes my heart hath shaken with great joy
> To see a leaping squirrel in a tree
> Or a red lady-bird upon a stalk.

That was his last poem, and you'll understand why it always mattered a lot to me: its name is 'The Wayfarer'.

I edged closer to see and hear what was happening. This man Pearse stood there until his small group had assembled around him. Mr Pearse had a piece of paper in his hand, and after looking around to see that his comrades were listening, he began to read aloud. The ordinary people around and about, who had been inclined to jeer, fell silent.

'Irishmen and Irishwomen, in the name of God and of the dead generations from which she receives her old tradition of nationhood, Ireland, through us, summons her children to her flag and strikes for her freedom.'

Every schoolchild in this country has long since heard those words. Without any fear that I'm exaggerating. I can tell you now that when I heard them I knew I'd never forget it. This was momentous and I, whose lot had been dusty roads and rainy fields, I knew I was privileged to be there. It was the Proclamation of the Irish Republic and Mr Pearse was the first president. He was an idealist, an educated man. In his writings and speeches, he had tried to fight England intellectually as the Founding Fathers of America had done, but he, too, had been forced to take up arms. Now he had written the Proclamation, which was signed by him and six others.

Someone gave a kind of cheer when he had finished and the men with Mr Pearse reached across and shook his hand – very solemnly and respectfully, I thought. One man, with a moustache, wearing a green uniform, said to him, 'Pearse, thanks be to God that we lived to see this day.'

Frank Delaney, *Ireland* (2004)

✽ ✽ ✽

The 1916 Easter Rising was, of course, brutally put down. Kathleen Clarke's husband, Tom, was among those executed by the British. She herself was heavily involved in the struggle, and in her memoirs she gives a moving and courageous account of the events – including her farewell to Tom on the eve of his execution. In 1939, Kathleen Clarke became the first woman Lord Mayor of Dublin.

My mind was in too great a tension to sleep. I could think of nothing but my husband and brother. Were they blackened corpses in the smouldering city, or prisoners in the hands of our enemy, perhaps being tortured?

A knock on the door again startled us. This time it was the Sergeant. He entered and said, 'Which of you is Mrs Tom Clarke?'

I said I was, and he handed me a paper which read:

Detention Barracks, Kilmainham
Dear Madam,

I have to inform you that your husband is a prisoner here and wishes to see you. I am sending a motor car to bring you here.

I am, Madam, Your obedient servant,

W S Lennon, Major, Commandant.

Mrs T J Clarke, 10 Richmond Avenue, Dublin.

This had been sent to my home, now changed to 31 Richmond Avenue, and the maid had told the messenger that I was in Dublin Castle, a prisoner.

I had lit a candle when the sergeant came in, and after reading the message I put on my costume. While I was doing this, Miss Perolz asked what was in the paper the Sergeant had given me, and I told her. 'I wonder what that means' she said. 'It means death,' I told her. 'Oh God no, surely not that!' she exclaimed. 'Surely,' I said, 'you do not think the British are so good and kind as to send for me to say goodbye to my husband if they were sending him any shorter journey than to the next world.' 'God, you are a stone,' she exclaimed. I felt like one. It seemed to me as if it were not I that was acting, but someone looking on. It was a queer feeling; my actions were more or less automatic. The predominating idea in my mind was to keep a brave front to the enemy, and not let them see me broken, no matter how I suffered.

I said goodbye to them all, and joined the Sergeant who was waiting outside. He had two soldiers with him. They had rifles with fixed bayonets. He handed me over to them. The order to march was given, and off we went into the open. It was pitch dark, and I did not know where we were going. The only thing I had to guide me was the tramp of the soldiers each side of me.

The ground was level for some time, then we turned left and it became uphill. We went under what seemed to be an arch, then turned right and into a building which I afterwards found out was in the Upper Castle Yard. I was told to wait there until someone came, I thought they said the Provost Marshal. He came and looked me over, and gave an order for me to be driven to Kilmainham Jail. I was then put into an open car, with the same soldiers, and a third one who was driving. Snipers were still busy; we were stopped every now and then by British military, permits examined, torches flashed in our faces. Our journey to Kilmainham seemed endless; I began to wonder if we would ever get there.

When we did arrive there, it presented a scene of gloom and decay. It had been abandoned as a prison for many years. A damp smell pervaded the whole place, and the only light was candles in jamjars. [...]

After a short delay, I was taken up a stone staircase and along a narrow passage with doors on both sides. In the gloom it was hard to make out what kind of passage it was. The soldier who conducted me inserted a big key in the lock, and the door opened. There was Tom lying on the floor. He jumped up when he saw me. I rushed to him, saying, 'Why did you surrender? The last thing you said was no surrender.' I could not stop myself saying it when I saw the way he was treated; I thought any death would be preferable. He was very gentle with me, and said, 'I know, Katty, and I meant it. Had it rested with me there would have been no surrender. On a vote, I was outvoted. I had hoped to go down in the retreat from the GPO, but it was not to be. Perhaps it's all for the best.' [...]

He said, 'I suppose you know I am to be shot in the morning. I am glad I am getting a soldier's death.' I said, 'I know, although so far on-one has told me; it has been left to you to do so.' He faced death with a clear and happy conscience, and knowing him to be one of the purest souls I had no fear. Then he told

216

me my brother Ned would also be shot. 'Surely not Ned, he is so young,' I said. 'Yes,' he said. 'He is very young, but from the British point of view he has earned death. Tell John that he has every reason to be proud of Ned. He has proved himself a fine soldier and a hero.' Continuing, Tom said that all our men had been heroes, that he felt very proud of them, but that many would be shot. He knew McDonagh and Pearse were to be shot with him that morning, and Ceannt, Plunkett, MacDermott, Connolly and many others would go too. [...]

All through our interview, I was conscious of the exalted, very exalted state of mind he was in. Looking into the future he saw suffering, but at the end freedom. He said, 'My comrades and I believe we have struck the first successful blow for freedom, and so sure as we are going out this morning, so sure will freedom come as a direct result of our action. It will not come today or tomorrow, and between this and freedom Ireland will go through Hell, but she will never lie down again until she has attained full freedom. With this belief, we die happy. I am happy and satisfied at what we have accomplished.'

Kathleen Clarke, *Revolutionary Woman* (1991)

✳ ✳ ✳

As seen in Kathleen Clarke's memoir of the Easter Rising, women have played a major part in the shaping of modern Ireland. The following letter, from Orna Ross's Lovers' Hollow, *is based on actual events during the Civil War of the early 1920s.*

North Dublin Union, May 21st 1923

Dear Peg,

You'll have noticed the change of address above. So much has happened since I last wrote, I hardly know where to start.

I have to say that we felt not altogether unfortunate to be in Kilmainham prison for Easter weekend, as you can imagine.

The seventh anniversary of the 1916 Rising felt like a good day to take again our Oath of Allegiance to the Republic and to be in the place where those brave men were executed. Now, two weeks later, what a contrast! It began when we were told that we were to be moved from Kilmainham to North Dublin Union, a former workhouse, and we were none too keen on this idea, as Kilmainham with its noble association suited us far better. Also Mrs O'Callaghan and Miss MacSwiney were still on their hunger strike (nineteen days by then) and we were very anxious about them.

At about three o'clock on the Monday word came that we were to be moved to the Union that night. A meeting of the prisoners was immediately summoned and it was unanimous: it was unthinkable that we would leave the hunger strikers alone in the empty jail, at the mercy of such cruel tricks as were played on Miss Costello (remember what I told you in my last letter – it got worse after that if you can believe it). So we sent our decision to the governor: no prisoner would consent to leave until the hunger strikers were released.

Next thing, the news came that stretcher bearers had come in. We had a moment of joyous triumph followed quickly by the shock of dismay: Mrs O'Callaghan was released but not Miss MacSwiney. This was appalling news. We knew that Miss MacSwiney was no less dangerously ill than Mrs O'Callaghan. They had been on hunger strike the same number of days, arrested in similar circumstances. It suggested malice against Miss MacSwiney that, for all we knew, might intend her death. So we were more determined than ever: we would not be moved until that poor suffering woman was released.

Our best strategic position seemed to be the top gallery, as it is caged in with iron bars running around the horseshoe-shaped building, with an iron bridge joining its opposite sides. So we took our places and waited. Our officers gave our instructions: we were to resist but not attack; we were not to come to one another's rescue; no missiles to be thrown, above all, for the sake of the patient in her cell, no one was to cry out. Then we knelt and said the rosary. We had fastened the doors of our cells and the great well-like place was in darkness, except for one lit window beside a gateway, behind which figures of soldiers and wardresses hurried to and fro. We waited and sang some of Miss MacSwiney's favourite songs.

Suddenly the gate opened and the men rushed in, across the compound and up the stairs. The attack was violent but unorganized. Brigid O'Mullane and Rita Farrelly, the first seized, were crushed and bruised between men dragging them down and men pressing up the stairs. Our Commandant, Mrs Gordon, was next. It was hard not to go to her rescue as she clung to the iron bars, the men beating her hands with their clenched fists again and again. When that failed to make her loose her hold, they struck her twice in the chest, then one took her head and beat it against the iron bars. I think she was unconscious after that. I saw her dragged by the soldiers down the stairs.

The men became determined, they had many methods. Some twisted the girls' arms, some bent back their thumbs. Some were kicked by a particular CID man who was fond of using his feet. One was disabled by a blow on the ankle with a revolver. Annie McKeown, one of the smallest and youngest, was pulled downstairs and kicked (perhaps accidentally) in the head. One girl had her finger bitten, Lena O'Doherty had been struck on the mouth, one man had thrust a finger down Moira Broderick's throat. Lily Dunn and May O'Toole, who have been ill, fainted. They do not know where they were struck.

My own turn came. After I had been dragged from the railings, a great hand closed on my face, blinding and stifling me, and thrust me back down to the ground, among trampling feet. After that I remember being carried by two or three men and flung down in the surgery to be searched. Mrs Wilson and Mrs

Gordon were there, their faces bleeding. One of the women searchers was screaming at them like a drunkard on a Saturday night; she struck Mrs Gordon in the face. They removed watches, fountain pens and brooches, kicking Peg Flanagan and beating Kathleen O'Farrell on the head with her shoe. The orders not to hit back were well obeyed.

The wardresses were bringing us cups of water and they were crying and some of the soldiers too looked wretched. But the prison doctor – and a few other soldiers – looked on, smiling, smoking cigarettes. The doctor seemed to have come along for the entertainment, he did nothing to help any of the injured girls.

After another long struggle, we were thrown into the lorries, one by one, and driven away. The whole thing took five hours.

Peg, you have to let the world know of this disgrace. I don't know whether word has reached the newspapers or not, we're so much more isolated in this place than we were in Kilmainham. Please also tell the world that Republican women are housed in a place that is filthy and freezing, with no privacy or facilities for washing or bathing. The sentries can (and do) look into our wards on the ground floor. We've asked to have the lower window panes frosted or painted but no, so we have to hang clothes over them to get in or out of bed. We're experiencing every kind of discomfort: hunger, cold and dirt. And, though only a few yards from one of the populous districts of Dublin, cut off from everything.

We have had no news since of Miss MacSwiney. And we hear rumour of peace moves outside but never see a paper. Please fill me in on everything you know when you write. And tell Cat I haven't heard from her this long time and she's not to forget me. Nora too. Not a single word from her in months. The person who gives you this letter will tell you how to get mail through to me untampered.

Please also tell your mammy and daddy I was asking for them and that I keep Barney in my prayers. I was thinking of you and the family at Easter time.

Write soon, won't you?

Your friend

Molly

Orna Ross, *Lovers' Hollow* (2006)

✳ ✳ ✳

Ireland's neutrality during the Second World War was an understandable result of the bitterness of the earlier struggle to break free from British domination. But neutrality did not entirely protect the population from the food rationing that was the war-time norm in Britain. And even after the war, 'going without' was the norm rather than the exception. Gabriel Duffy remembers the food of those times.

In Ireland, the war brought a certain amount of food rationing, with a scarcity of fresh fruit from the tropics in particular. I must have been four when I saw my first orange and I clearly remember the first time I handled that real novelty – a banana. (Tales of dockers being fatally bitten by tarantulas in the bunches.) Kelloggs' corn flakes and wheat flakes only reappeared about 1948.

As my father liked a drink and a game of cards we were often obliged to buy our own food "on tick" (credit). I was sent "to get the messages" (groceries), as a kind of decoy, when the tab was overdue. I was never refused, presumably because "a polisman's credit" was good indemnity in itself. If only they knew my rake of a da ...

Occasionally, to spread the debt, I was despatched for victuals to Miss Dawe of the Dee creamery – a hunched old 'huckster' in sack-cloth and sashes, with a hairy wart on her chin; she frightened me to death. (In my youth Dublin was full of such shops, run by childless balding old women with facial protuberances; generally united by total devotion to The Church and with pictures of the (haemorrhaging) Sacred Heart and (fra angelical) Blessed Virgin well-displayed about their dismal premises, competing with age-yellowed adverts for detergents. – No washing machines then; all was hand-wash, with Persil or Rinso.)

Rashers, eggs, sausages and fried tomato for Sunday breakfast indicated better times, as did roast beef for "dinner" – lunch in England.

Fish was Friday – a Fast Day when meat was forbidden by the stern Church. Fish 'n' chips from a "chipper" (chip-shop) was the nearest we got to junk-food Valhalla; no Wimpey, Burger King or MacDonald's then.

Cakes were rare treats – cream-buns ("from the Monument" Creamery) a benison. Figrolls were the biscuit. ... One day a year for pancakes, another (halloween) for the "barn brack" – a big currant cake which always contained "a gold ring" for one lucky child in their slice.

Halloween also meant "apples and nuts" and you and your pals went door-to-door begging for them, in Halloween Masks so no one knew you. Or so you thought. They'd know the voice. But they'd pay up, laughing. Easter meant those enormous (hollow) chocolate eggs, after six weeks of Lenten frugality.

Sweets were precious, although you could buy a stick of liquorice, a handful of jelly babies or "nancy balls" (aniseed balls) for a penny. It was "like Christmas" to be given a golden Crunchie, a Kit Kat, a cylinder of Smarties, a tube of Rolo, an Aero Bar, or a slab of Cadbury's Milk Chocolate. All of these Anglo-Irish confections remain name unchanged (except for price) today. Branding is forever in the deathless sweet trade apparently.

Christmas itself meant open boxes of chocolates on the sideboard, cake galore, Thwaites Lemonade and American Cream Soda till it came out your ears. Even ice-cream – normally only available in hot weather. Hunks of fruity Christmas Pudding in yellow clusters of Bird's Custard. Who needed roast spuds and turkey?

The spud itself was, in Ireland, as rice to a Chinaman. Old people told us how lucky we were to have plenty of spuds, reminded us that The Potato Famine of the last century "halved the population by starvation and emigration". Spuds were also Murphys and anyone of the surname drew the former as a nickname. Spud Murphys abounded.

Old people were always respected and listened to then; most families would die rather than abandon their sires to an old people's 'home'.

That is one bit of tradition we might have done well to retain.

Gabriel Duffy, *Sham to Rock:*
Growing up in forties and fifties Dublin (2003)

✳ ✳ ✳

By the late forties, things appear to have been getting better. Certainly students, like the then young J. P. Donleavy, could enjoy the delights of Dublin café life.

My first college invitation was to go and have a cup of coffee. Thus one embarked upon this sacred rite in Dublin. To be indulged either by morning, noon, afternoon or all three. Each café with its adherents. In my case it became Bewley's Oriental Café in Grafton Street which involved turning left out the front gates, past the Provost's House and traversing the city's cultural spine of Grafton Street. Paved with its wooden blocks aswarm with bicycles and off which variously extended Suffolk, Duke, Ann, Harry and Lemon Streets. Although there were cafés in these side street nooks and crannies, the élite coffee scented emporiums were all on the socially desired thoroughfare of Grafton Street. Where early morning gossip could be meteorically spread between the cheerful chattering of briefly pausing pedestrians. And where the wives of bank managers with light hearted things to think and do could flaunt their better than thou high heeled utter respectability.

Starting at the bottom of Grafton Street on the left, in a grey stone nco Georgian building, was Mitchell's. Definitely for the lady of society who had been at a play the evening before, and carrying a catalogue from an exhibition of painting, had just been to a fitting for a frock. Then further up, the glass table tops of Bewley's, its butter balls piled high on plates, its stacks of fragrant fresh buns, its creamy glasses of Jersey milk and its roasted coffee smells perfuming the street. This sacredly oriental interior was especially favoured by mothers whose sons had become priests. And by young ladies who were thinking of becoming nuns. Occasionally the tranquility would be broken by a hungover poet rustling his paper who would sit examining the day's racing from the courses while nursing in his celibacy his agonising impure thoughts. Tucked away on the other crimson banquettes were solitary men of the minor merchant class who secretly read recently banned novels and were experts at crossword puzzles. But I had repaired for my first Dublin coffee to Switzer's, down iron balustraded stairs to the warm and cosy basement of this, for Dublin, large department store. There, frequented by hockey playing lady students from Trinity and tweedy Anglo Irish matrons from the country, one luxuriated in the optimism pleasantly floating on the din of these animated voices.

J. P. Donleavy, *J. P. Donleavy's Ireland* (1986)

✳ ✳ ✳

People from all over the world with distant (or not so distant) roots in Ireland love to go back to see 'where they've come from'. And many choose to make a visit coincide with St Patrick's Day and to join in the fun of the great parade that has become a regular feature of Dublin life. So we take a final look at the city in full celebration, drawing together its colourful past into the development of 'new traditions' in the twenty-first century. Journalist Enda Mullen pays tribute to some rollicking Irish fun in that great, contradictory, poetic, enchanting, puzzling, welcoming, great-writer-spawning city we call Dublin.

The Irish capital was alive and kicking this March as visitors and locals thronged the streets for what is now a serious rival to the largest St Patrick's Day parade in the world.

Over 600,000 people lined the streets of Dublin and more the length and breadth of the country for the St Patrick's Day Parade which falls in the middle of the five day St Patrick's Festival. The parade itself is one of the most visible celebrations of Irishness. The theme for this year's parade was 'Legendary' and participants took to the task of creating floats along that theme with great gusto. Silly hats, shamrock, Aran jumpers and plenty of green were worn. Carroll's Irish Gift Stores surely made their biggest profits of the year! Children (and adults) sprayed their hair green and wore face paint in the colours of the Irish flag or expertly painted shamrocks on their cheeks. Tricolours hung from most windows and poles.

The parade started at Parnell Square, working its way down to O'Connell Street over O'Connell Bridge, up Westmorland Street, and right up Dame Street past the Central Bank where it ended. On O'Connell Street opposite the GPO a tier of seats were in place for politicians and dignitaries to view the parade as it passed. The rest of us took our places along the route from the early hours to ensure a good vantage point.

Micheál Ó Muircheartaigh was parade marshal and guest of honour. The famous broadcaster, commentator and author led the parade seated in the back of a convertible.

The displays of creativity were inspirational. Entrants from all parts of the country and all across the globe made fabulous efforts. Giant monsters towered above the crowds. Creatures from myth and legend strolled over O'Connell Bridge.

More traditional fare was also on display. Irish pipe bands, representatives from An Garda Síochána, the Irish Army and much loved Irish Wolf Hounds participated.

Multicultural Ireland made its presence felt in a big way this year. Recent census reports show that about 10% of the population of Ireland are now born outside of the country. What has taken years to happen for other countries has happened in a relatively short period of time in Ireland.

The Irish Sikh Council gave an impressive display of swordsmanship, traditional dance and music. The first St Patrick's Day parades took place in America so as always there was a large American contingent in the parade. Representatives from New York, who boast the biggest parade in the world, were prominent, alongside dozens of marching bands from schools, colleges and universities from across the United States. One unfortunate marching band arrived in Dublin but found that their instruments had not arrived with them. They decided to just walk in the parade anyway. It is that eagerness for participation that sums up the St Patrick's Day spirit.

Visitors from most countries in the world must surely have been present on the 17th of March. Numerous sideshows were in place around Dublin for one of the busiest tourist days of the Irish calendar.

The 'Luminarium' was in place in George's Dock – the 'Luminarium' being a giant maze aimed at adults and children alike. George's Dock is now frequently used for unusual attractions. An exotic food fair was also a big crowd puller at the RDS.

Seachtain Na Gaelige runs the week up to St Patrick's Day promoting the Irish language to visitors and Irish people alike.

The annual Skyfest, which promised to be one of the biggest fireworks displays in Ireland, was due to be held on Sunday 18th but was cancelled due to bad weather. High winds and a one metre swell on the Liffey made conditions unsafe.

Minor disappointments aside, the St Patrick's Festival was a thoroughly enjoyable few days. New policies were in place this year to reduce underage and public drinking. Off-licences around the city were closed until 4pm. This made the day more family friendly and certainly reduced the amount of public drunkenness, vomit etc that has blighted previous years.

The atmosphere in Dublin was jovial and friendly as everyone was Irish for a day. Streets were as jam-packed as the pubs. Dublin is always worth visiting but never so much so as when celebrating its Catholic heritage, culture, history and a little bit of over the top Oirishness!

Enda Mullen, 'St Patrick's Day Dublin', *The Harp* (2007)

Selective Index

*after name indicates a writer whose work is excerpted in this book

Acknowledgements

Oxygen Books would like to thank the many people who have supported *city-pick DUBLIN* with their enthusiasm, professional help, ideas for texts to include, and generosity. In particular we would like to mention the invaluable contributions of Orna Ross, Mikka Haugaard, Eduardo Reyes, Jane Alger, Claire Higgins and Sarah Bannan.

Samuel Beckett, *More Pricks Than Kicks*, first published in Great Britain by Chatto and Windus, 1934; further editions published by Calder and Boyars, 1966, 1967, 1970, 1973 and by Calder Publications Ltd, 1993. Copyright The Samuel Beckett Estate. Reprinted by permission of Faber and Faber Ltd and the Samuel Beckett Estate.

Brendan Behan, *Brendan Behan's Island*, Published by Hutchinson & Co Ltd., 1962; Hutchinson Paperback, 1984. Copyright © Brendan Behan 1962. Reprinted by permission of The Random House Group Ltd.

Chris Binchy, *People Like Us*, published by Macmillan, 2004. Pan Books edition, 2005. Copyright © Chris Binchy, 2004. Reprinted by permission of Pan Macmillan, London.

Chris Binchy, *The Very Man*, published by Macmillan, 2003. Pan Books edition, 2004. Copyright © Chris Binchy 2003. Reprinted by permission of Pan Macmillan, London.

Maeve Binchy, *Dublin People,*. Reproduced by permission of Oxford University Press and the Christine Green Agency from *Oxford Bookworms Library Level 6: Dublin People* by Maeve Binchy. Original edition © Maeve Binchy 1982. This simplified edition © Oxford University Press 2008.

Maeve Binchy, *Evening Class*, published by Orion, 1996. paperback edition by Orion, 1997. Copyright © 1996 Maeve Binchy. Reprinted by kind permission of Orion Books Ltd.

Eavan Boland, *Object Lessons: The Life of the Woman and the Poet in Our Time*, published by Carcanet Press Ltd., 1995. Copyright © Eavan Boland 1995, 2006. Reprinted by permission of Carcanet Press Ltd.

Dermot Bolger, *The Journey Home*, published by Viking, 1990. Published by Penguin Books, 1991. Copyright © Dermot Bolger, 1990. Reprinted by permission of Penguin Books.

Heinrich Böll, *Irish Journal*, originally published in German as *Irisches Tagenbuch*, copyright © Keipenheuer & Witsch, Cologne-Berlin, 1957. Translation © 1967 by Leila Vennewitz. Northwestern University Press edition, 1994. The Marlboro Press/Northwestern edition, 1998. Reprinted by permission of Keipenheuer & Witsch, Cologne-Berlin.

Elizabeth Bowen, *Collected Impressions*, published by Longmans Green, 1950. Copyright © 1950 by Elizabeth Bowen. Reprinted by permission of Curtis Brown Ltd, London, on behalf of The Estate of Elizabeth Bowen.

Elizabeth Bowen, *The Shelbourne*, published by George Harrap & Co Ltd., 1951. Copyright © 1951 by Elizabeth Bowen. Reprinted by permission of Curtis Brown Ltd, London, on behalf of The Estate of Elizabeth Bowen.

Meghan Butler, 'Travels with my Father' (2008), dublintravelwriting.wordpress.com, reprinted by kind permission of Dustin Morrow on behalf of the author.

Kathleen Clarke, *Kathleen Clarke: Revolutionary Woman*, Published by The O'Brien Press Ltd., 1991. Copyright © The Estate if Dr Emmet Clarke.Reprinted by permission of The O'Brien Press Ltd, Dublin.

Simon Cole, 'Intelligent Inebriation' (2009), reprinted by permission of the author.

Mary Colum, *Life and the Dream*, published by Macmillan, 1928.

Michael Cronin, *Time Tracks*, published by New Island Books, Dublin, 2003. Copyright © Michael Cronin 2003. Reprinted by permission of New Island Books.

Acknowledgements

Ita Daly, *A Singular Attraction*, published by Jonathan Cape, 1987. Black Swan edition, 1988. Copyright © Ita Daly 1988, reprinted by kind permission of Christine Green Author's Agent, on behalf of the author.

Frank Delaney, *Ireland*, first published by Time Warner Books. Copyright © 2004 Frank Delaney. Reprinted by permission of HarperCollins Publishers Ltd.

Frank Delaney, *James Joyce's Odyssey* published by Granada Publishing Ltd, 1983. Copyright © Frank Delaney 1981. Reprinted by permission of HarperCollins Publishers Ltd.

Eilís Ní Dhuibhne, *Blood and Water*, copyright © Eilís Ní Dhuibhne, reprinted by permission of Cork University Press, Youngline Industrial Estate, Pouladuff Road, Togher, Cork, Ireland.

J. P. Donleavy, *J. P. Donleavy's Ireland*, first published by Michael Joseph in association with the Rainbird Publishing Group 1986. Published by Penguin Books 1988. Copyright © J. P. Donleavy 1986. Reprinted by kind permission of the author.

Emma Donoghue, *Hood*, first published by Hamish Hamilton 1995. Published by Penguin Books 1996. Copyright © Emma Donoghue 1995. Reprinted by permission of Caroline Davidson Literary Agency.

Roddy Doyle, *The Deportees*, published by Jonathan Cape, 2007. Copyright © Roddy Doyle 2007. Reprinted by permission of The Random House Group Ltd.

Gabriel Duffy, *Sham to Rock* Aengus Books, 2003. By kind permission of Megan Duffy.

Anne Enright, 'The Brat', in *The Portable Virgin*, published by Secker & Warburg 1991. Vintage edition 1998. Copyright © Anne Enright 1991. Reprinted by permission of The Random House Group Ltd.

Caitlin Gerrity, 'The Travelling Identity', (2008) dublintravelwriting.wordpress.com, by kind permission of Dustin Morrow on behalf of the author.

Hugo Hamilton, *Headbanger*, published by Secker & Warburg 1997. Copyright © 1997 by Hugo Hamilton. Reprinted by permission of The Random House Group Ltd.

Hugo Hamilton, *The Speckled People*, published by Fourth Estate 2003. Copyright © Hugo Hamilton 2003. Reprinted by permission of HarperCollins Publishers Ltd.

Mark Harkin, interview with Senator David Norris, 'James Joyce's *Ulysses*: why the fuss?', first appeared in www.threemonkeysonline.com . Reproduced by permission of Andrew Lawless at Three Monkeys Online.

Neil Hegarty, *Waking up in Dublin*, published by Sanctuary Publishing Ltd. Copyright © Neil Hegarty 2004. Reprinted by permission of the author and of Helen Donlon, Music Sales Ltd..

Denis Ireland, *From the Irish Shore*, published by Rich and Cowan, 1936.

Colin Irwin, *In Search of the Craic*, published by André Deutsch Ltd 2003. Paperback edition 2004. Copyright © Colin Irwin 2003. Reprinted by permission of Carlton Books Ltd.

Brian Lalor, *The Laugh of Lost Men*, published by Mainstream Publishing, 1997. Copyright © Brian Lalor 1997. Reprinted by kind permission of the author.

Nell McCafferty, 'Next to Godliness', in *Goodnight Sisters*, copyright © Nell McCafferty. Reproduced by permission of Cork University Press, Youngline Industrial Estate, Pouladuff Road, Togher, Cork, Ireland.

Pete McCarthy, *The Road to McCarthy*, published by Hodder and Stoughton, 2002. Copyright © Pete McCarthy 2002. Reproduced by permission of Hodder and Stoughton Ltd.

Evan McHugh, *Pint-Sized Ireland*, first published by Thomas C. Lothian Pty Ltd in 2001. 2005 edition published by Summersdale Publishers Ltd. Copyright © Evan McHugh 2001. Reprinted by kind permission of the author.

Pat Mullan, 'Tribunal', from *Dublin Noir*, first published in 2006 by Brandon, an imprint of Mount Eagle Publications. Copyright © the authors, 2006. Reprinted by kind permission of Brandon Books.

Enda Mullen, 'St Patrick's Day Dublin', first published by The Harp News, 7 April 2009 (www.theharpnews.com). Reprinted by permission of the author.

Iris Murdoch, *The Red and the Green*, first published by Chatto and Windus 1965. Copyright © Iris Murdoch 1965. Reprinted by permission of The Random House Group Ltd.

Eric Newby, *Round Ireland in Low Gear*, first published by William Collins Ltd 1987. Picador edition published by Pan Books Ltd., 1988. Copyright © 1987 Eric Newby. Reprinted by kind permission of HarperCollins Publishers Ltd.

Andrew Nugent, *Second Burial*, first published in 2007 by the Headline Publishing Group. Copyright © 2007 Andrew Nugent. Reproduced by permission of Headline Publishing Group Limited.

Flann O'Brien, *The Dalkey Archive*, first published by MacGibbon & Kee Ltd 1964. Grafton Edition 1986. Copyright © Brian O'Nolan 1964. Reprinted by kind permission of HarperCollins Publishers Ltd.

Sean O'Casey, *I Knock at the Door*, first published 1939. *Pictures in the Hallway*, first published 1942. First combined edition of the autobiographies (*I Knock at the Door*, *Pictures in the Hallway* and *Drums Under the Windows*) published by Macmillan and Company Ltd in 1963. Pan Books edition 1980. Reprinted by permission of the Estate of Sean O'Casey, through Macnaughton Lord Representation.

Joseph O'Connor, *The Secret Life of the Irish Male*, first published by New Island Books, 1994. Copyright © 1994 by Joseph O'Connor. Reprinted by permission of New Island Books.

Mary O'Donnell, 'Little Africa' in *Storm Over Belfast*, published by New Island Books, 2008. Copyright © Mary O'Donnell 2008. Reprinted by permission of New Island Books.

Mary O'Donnell, *The Light-Makers*, published by Poolbeg Press Ltd., 1992. Copyright © Mary O'Donnell 1992. Reprinted by permission of the author.

Julia O'Faolain, *No Country for Young Men*, published by Allen Lane and Penguin Books 1980. Copyright © Julia O'Faolain, 1980. Reprinted by permission of Penguin Books.

Nuala O'Faolain, *Are You Somebody?* Published by New Island Books. Copyright © 1996 by Nuala O'Faolain. Reprinted by permission of New Island Books.

Nuala O'Faolain, *Almost There*, published by Michael Joseph, 2003. Penguin edition 2004. Copyright © Nuala O'Faolain, 2003. Reprinted by permission of Penguin Books.

Sean O'Reilly, *The Swing of Things*, published by Faber and Faber Ltd, 2004. Copyright © Sean O'Reilly, 2004. Reprinted by permission of Faber and Faber Ltd.

Lloyd Praeger Robert, *A Populous Solitude*, published by Methuen, 1941.

V. S. Pritchett, *Midnight Oil*, published by Chatto & Windus, 1971. Copyright © V. S. Pritchett, 1971. Reprinted by permission of PFD (www.pfd.co.uk) on behalf of the estate of V. S. Pritchett.

Deirdre Purcell, *Follow me Down To Dublin*, published by Hodder Headline Ireland, 2007. Copyright © Deirdre Purcell 2007. Reprinted by permission of Hodder Headline Ireland, a division of Hachette Livre.

Keith Ridgway, *Standard Time*, published by Faber and Faber, 2001. Copyright © Keith Ridgway, 2001. Reprinted by permission of Faber and Faber Ltd, and Rogers, Coleridge and White on behalf of the author.

Keith Ridgway, *The Long Falling*, published by Faber and Faber, 1998. Copyright © Keith Ridgway, 1998. Reprinted by permission of Faber and Faber Ltd.

Keith Ridgway, *The Parts*, published by Faber and Faber, 2003. Copyright © Keith Ridgway, 2003. Reprinted by permission of Faber and Faber Ltd.

Orna Ross, *A Dance in Time*, published by Penguin, 2008. Copyright © Orna Ross, 2008. Reprinted by permission of Penguin Books.

Orna Ross, *Lovers' Hollow*, published by Penguin, 2006. Copyright © Orna Ross, 2006. Reprinted by permission of Penguin Books.

Edward Rutherfurd, *Ireland Awakening*, published by Century, 2006. Copyright © 2006 by Edward Rutherfurd. Reprinted by permission of The Random House Group Ltd.

Honor Tracy, *Mind You, I've Said Nothing!*, published by Methuen, 1953. Penguin edition, 1961. Copyright © Honor Tracy 1953.

William Trevor, *Mrs Eckdorf at O'Neill's Hotel*, published by Bodley Head, 1969. Penguin edition 1973. Reprinted by permission of Johnson and Alcock, on behalf of the author.

Every effort has been made to trace and contact copyright holders before publication. If notified, the publisher will rectify any errors or omissions at the earliest opportunity.

Praise for *city-lit PARIS*

'An essential guidebook ... It maps the Paris of the imagination beautifully'

Kate Muir, author of *Left Bank*

'It's terrific ... all the best writing on this complex city in one place'
Professor Andrew Hussey, author of *Paris: The Secret History*

'A great and eclectic set of writings ... an original book on Paris'
Sylvia Whitman, Shakespeare & Co, Paris

'Whether you're a newcomer to Paris or a die-hard aficionado, this gem of a book will make you think of the city in a completely new way'

Living France

'The ideal book for people who don't want to leave their minds at the airport'

Celia Brayfield, author of *Deep France*

'The *city-lit PARIS* guide is essential reading for anyone remotely interested in Paris, or planning a visit'
Mike Gerrard, best-selling travel guide writer

'This innovative guide takes us from Marcel Proust on that perfect erotic moment to Gertrude Stein on the origins of the croissant to Agnès Catherine Poirier on the lure of the Paris café'

Paris Voice

£8.99 ISBN 978-0-9559700-0-9

Praise for *city-lit* LONDON

'This treasure trove of a book ... a unique way to explore the ever-changing landscape of a city, through the voices of those that know it intimately'

Rachel Lichtenstein, author of *On Brick Lane*

'For those visitors to London who seek to do more than bag Big Ben and Buckingham Palace, this is the ideal guide, a collection of writings that expose not only the city's secret places but its very soul ... I can't imagine a more perfect travelling companion than this wonderful anthology'

Clare Clark, author of *The Great Stink*

'Brings London to life past and present in a way no conventional guide book could ever achieve'

Tarquin Hall, author of *Salaam Brick Lane*

'The latest offering in this impressive little series concentrates on the spirit of London as seen through the eyes of an eclectic selection of writers. Part of the joy of this collection is that the writers span several centuries, which means that multiple faces of London are revealed. It's an exciting selection, with unexpected gems from novelists, travel writers, journalists and bloggers. Keith Waterhouse, for example, writes with gentle pathos about the double life of a transvestite in Soho; Vita Sackville-West wryly observes a coronation in Westminster Abbey; Virginia Woolf promenades down Oxford Street; and Dostoyevsky strolls down the Haymarket'

Clover Stroud, *The Sunday Telegraph*

'For some time now, small publisher Oxygen has been producing the excellent city-lit series, which uses descriptions of a city penned by writers, both living and dead to illuminate the metropolis in question. The most recent is London, compiled by Heather Reyes. This includes Jan Morris arriving at Heathrow, Monica Ali on Brick Lane, Virginia Woolf shopping in Oxford Street, Barbara Cartland at a West End Ball, Dostoyevsky strolling down Haymarket and Will Self inside the head of a cab driver'

Giles Foden, *Condé Nast Traveller*

'We can't declare it with absolute certainty, but it's a fair bet that Dame Barbara Cartland and Diamond Geezer have never before snuggled up between the same covers. *City-lit: LONDON* places these strange bedfellows alongside Will Self, Virginia Woolf, Alan Bennett and sixty others in a frenzied orgy of London writing. You'll love it'

Londonist

'The second volume in this enticing new series includes extracts from the work of 60 wonderfully diverse writers, including Will Self, Monica Ali, Alan Bennett, Dostoyevsky, and yes, Barbara Cartland (writing about a West End ball)'

Editor's Pick, *The Bookseller*

£8.99 ISBN: 978–0–9559700–5–4

Praise for *city-lit BERLIN*

'A gem ... an elegant, enjoyable and essential book'

Rosie Goldsmith

'This wonderful anthology explores what it is really like to be a Berliner by bringing together extracts about the city from a range of genres, including some specially translated. This was the city of Einstein, Brecht, George Grosz, and Marlene Dietrich. It was 'the New York of the old world', a melting pot of new ideas and lifestyles ... This collection is timely: on 9 November 20 years ago, Berliners tore down the hated wall'

The Guardian

'City-Lit Berlin gathers more than a hundred extracts from writers on aspects of Berlin's conflicted heritage ... the editors have trawled widely to try to capture the modern city's rule-bound yet permissive tone, as well as its persistent state of cultural and architectural renewal. The result is an eclectic pillow-book ... a stimulating intellectual tour of the idea of the city that would complement any guidebook's more practical orientation'

Financial Times

'A new kind of literary travel guide where the reader can find snatches of literature relevant to Berlin'

BBC Radio 4 *Excess Baggage*

'A fascinating cornucopia of Berlin writing by authors such as John Simpson, Ian McEwan and Anna Funder; artists such as David Bowie and Marlene Dietrich, and writers such as Jeffrey Eugenides, Philip Kerr and Thomas Pynchon. The beauty of this clever series is the breadth and reach of it contributors, be they artists, musicians, musos or writers - in turn, each lays claim to the city.

Many were inspired by the Wall coming down, the inventive vibe, or simply the cheap rents – all took ease in the bohemian exuberance the city offered up. This collection of writing gives a flavour to a city that has long nurtured its artists, giving them space to create, whether for one week or a lifetime'.

Real Travel Magazine

'Although there are plenty of old favourites such as Christopher Isherwood, Alfred Döblin and Len Deighton, the emphasis of the book is on unexpected vantage points and new, less familiar voices. So there is no dutiful trot through the city's history "from earliest times to the present day", but instead themed sections which try to get under the skin of the city.'

George Miller, *Podularity*

'Another in this sterling series of city-writings compilations, this one follows the pattern of short excerpts gathered into chapters ... The simplest one is also the most gripping: it's called 'The past is another country', but don't let that put you off. Its well-chosen pieces take you through Berlin's history from the early 19th Century to today, and make for an almost perfect, and very moving, slice through history ... Further interest is added by co-editor Katy Derbyshire's translations of bits from works not otherwise available in English. This manages to be not just a fine and fascinating introduction to the literature, but to rise above its expected status as a dipping thing to become a mighty fine cover-to-cover read in itself'

Jeff Cotton, *Fictional Cities*

'A welcome contrast to the many formulaic travel guides in print and online, City-Lit Berlin reveals the city as seen through the eyes of 60 writers of all description – from novelists such as Christopher Isherwood and Ian McEwan to local bloggers like Simon Cole, reporters (Kate Adie), historians (Peter Gay) and untranslated German writers, including Inka Parei, whose novel Die Schateenboxerin (The Shadow-Boxing Woman) captures the volatility of Berlin in the Nineties, just a few years after the Wall collapsed. We keep David Bowie company as he cycles around the city, and contemplate Marlene Dietrich's grave in a volume that has greatly enriched the field of travel books.'

Ralph Fields, *Nash Magazine*

Coming soon – *city-pick AMSTERDAM, city-pick VENICE, city-pick MUMBAI, city-pick ST. PETERSBURG* ... and many more.

www.oxygenbooks.co.uk